What "They" Say . . .

"For centuries, the Psalms have bee~~~~~~~~~~~ ~ ~~~~~~~~
worship, witness, and soul care. In this volume, Imes invites readers
to engage this life-giving book alongside their fathers and mothers
in the faith, an important antidote to the modern temptation to
look only at the latest 'hot takes' and interpretive trends—what C. S.
Lewis called 'chronological snobbery.' The nuggets of wisdom here
should direct readers to engage the world of early Christian theology
further, where they will find faithful friends and wise guides on the
road of discipleship."

~ Stephen T. Pardue, PhD,
Associate Professor of Theology,
International Graduate School of Leadership (Philippines),
Asia Graduate School of Theology (Philippines)

"It is a delight to recommend the Sacred Roots Spiritual Classics series
and this wonderful prayer companion by Carmen Imes! This book will
help you to re-hear the Psalms as you pray through them with the
saints of old. It is a book to carry around with your Bible, to savor slowly
with your morning coffee, as you learn from great Christian thinkers as
well-known as Augustine and as little-known as Gertrude. It will touch
your prayer life and calm your soul."

~ Donald M. Fairbairn, Jr., PhD,
Robert E. Cooley Professor of Early Christianity,
Gordon-Conwell Theological Seminary

"What a delight to read the Psalms in the company of the righteous!
In **Praying the Psalms with Augustine and Friends**, Carmen Imes
invites us to put our roots down deeply into each of the 150 psalms,
accompanied by old friends including Athanasius, Augustine, Luther
and Calvin, and new friends such as Valerian of Cimiez, Dhuoda,
Gertrude the Great, and Mary Sidney Herbert. The pithy and apt extracts
from these scholars give extra insights for our daily meditation.
I am looking forward to using this book!"

~ Jill Firth, PhD,
Lecturer in Old Testament and Hebrew,
Ridley College (Melbourne)

Praying the Psalms with Augustine and Friends

© 2021. The Urban Ministry Institute. All Rights Reserved.

ISBN: 978-1-955424-02-8

Published jointly in 2021 by TUMI Press and Samuel Morris Publications

TUMI Press is a division of World Impact, Inc.

> TUMI Press
> The Urban Ministry Institute
> 3701 E. 13th Street, Suite 100
> Wichita, KS 67208

Equipping Leaders. Empowering Movements.

Samuel Morris Publications:

> Samuel Morris Publications
> Sacred Roots Project at Taylor University
> 236 W. Reade Avenue
> Upland, IN 46989

Samuel Morris Publications publishes texts in service to the evangelical church's life together and its ongoing pursuit of a deeper conformity to Jesus Christ (Galatians 4:19).

SACRED ROOTS SPIRITUAL CLASSICS

"Toward Ten Thousand Tozers"

Praying the Psalms
with Augustine and Friends

SACRED ROOTS SPIRITUAL CLASSICS 1

Dr. Carmen Joy Imes

Table of Contents

*For Mike Rowe and Maggie Wallem Rowe,
our pastors who walked with us through our darkest valley
and prayed the Psalms with and for us.
Your supportive friendship was tangible evidence
that the goodness and love of God had not let us go
(Psalm 23:6).*

Acknowledgments

I am grateful to Hank Voss for the opportunity to contribute the first volume in the Sacred Roots series. This project has stretched me and given me a greater appreciation for Christian Classics. Hank, your vision to make these writings more accessible to our generation is truly inspiring. I've enjoyed the collaboration with you and so many others. All of us involved are grateful for the generous support of the Lilly Foundation.

I would not have agreed to write this book without the enthusiasm of my daughter, Eliana, who spent dozens of hours wrangling these texts into digital documents and then dozens more reworking selections to make them easier to read. Eliana, you have a gift for writing and I am grateful for your good work on this project. Without the cheerful staff at the libraries of Regent College, Prairie College, and Taylor University, and Isaiah Swain, who scanned selections from a huge stack of books, this project would have been impossible.

Friends at Prairie College agreed to "test out" this devotional. Thanks to their help, it is much more readable. Danny Imes, Marji Krahn, Pamela Fraser, April Schlieck, Lydia Nelson, James Enns, Susan Esau and Don Bookless all helped by reading sections and providing valuable feedback. Donna Preater, Sneha Reddy, Karen Hagens, and Shannon Warnock deserve special mention for carefully reading the entire manuscript. Sneha and Shannon also developed the discussion questions and helped with psalm headings. Abigail Guthrie developed the first drawing of my dream about the project, which became the prototype of the one included in the Introduction. Easton Imes (age 11!) helped with formatting. And a big thank you to Douglas Lewis for his help decoding the old English poetry of Philip Sidney and Mary Sidney Herbert.

It is not yet possible to personally thank those whose diligent study and devoted prayer produced what we read on these pages. In the new creation, I hope to meet each man and woman whose voices we have heard here and offer my gratitude. May their wisdom and godliness be reflected in our transformed lives.

This book is dedicated to Mike and Maggie Rowe, our pastors who walked with us through our darkest valley and prayed the Psalms with and for us. Your supportive friendship was tangible evidence that the goodness and love of God had not let us go (Psalm 23:6).

Soli deo gloria! To God alone be the glory.

Introduction

Why the Psalms?

Have you ever needed the Psalms? I mean *really* needed them?

I cannot say that I ever needed the Psalms until recent years. I always loved the Bible, even as a child, but I do not remember really connecting with the Psalms until I was well into adulthood. Out of nowhere, I experienced a debilitating interpersonal conflict at work that quickly escalated from tense to vicious. My attempts to reconcile only added fuel to the fire. Eventually, my colleague filed false accusations against me, initiating three grueling months of investigation, during which I was charged by administrators to say nothing to anyone. Set against the extensive evidence fabricated by my colleague, my simple, honest testimony was not believed. I was found guilty. In the midst of this traumatic sense of helplessness, I discovered the Psalms. I could not defend myself. No one else could defend me because they were not allowed to know about the investigation. The consequences of a

negative outcome would be devastating to my career.
I was desperate for God to intervene.

> *Arise, LORD! Lift up your hand, O God.*
> *Do not forget the helpless.*
> *Why does the wicked man revile God?*
> *Why does he say to himself, 'He won't call me to account'?*
> *But you, God, see the trouble of the afflicted;*
> *you consider their grief and take it in hand.*
> *The victims commit themselves to you . . .*
> *Break the arm of the wicked man;*
> *call the evildoer to account for his wickedness*
> *that would not otherwise be found out.*
>
> ~ Ps 10:12–15

The Psalms invited me to pour out my heart to God during
those dark days. They gave me language for prayer when I
was struck speechless. I discovered I was not alone—others
had been falsely accused, back-stabbed by friends, pursued
by enemies. These prayers assured me that God saw my grief.
No one could stop me from appealing to him for justice.

> *In you, LORD, I have taken refuge;*
> *let me never be put to shame;*
> *deliver me in your righteousness.*
> *Turn your ear to me,*
> *come quickly to my rescue;*
> *be my rock of refuge,*
> *a strong fortress to save me.*
> *Since you are my rock and my fortress,*
> *for the sake of your name lead and guide me.*
> *Keep me free from the trap that is set for me,*
> *for you are my refuge.*
> <u>*Into your hands I commit my spirit;*</u>
> *deliver me, LORD, my faithful God.*
>
> ~ Ps 31:1–5

Perhaps you recognized verse five as Jesus' prayer on the cross? Jesus and the New Testament authors quote the Psalms more than any other Old Testament book—a striking 41% of Old Testament quotations in the New Testament are from the Psalms, and Jesus alludes to the Psalms more than fifty times![1] When we pray the Psalms, we are joining a long line of faithful men and women—stretching thousands of years, all the way back from Moses to David and then Jesus—who have sought God's help. I discovered this beloved community as the Psalms taught me to pray. They helped me cultivate a deeper trust in God and nurtured my hope during a dark time.

At the close of that devastating year, I met with one of my mentors, someone with whom I had not been able to speak throughout the investigation. Without a single word of explanation from me, he looked me in the eye and said with great compassion, "Carmen, this year must have been hell for you." In that moment, I knew that God had answered my prayers for vindication. Though I had been unable to protect my own reputation, God had been at work behind the scenes. I was seen. I answered my mentor,

Yes and no. Yes, this has been the most painful experience of my life. But if hell is the absence of God, then I can't describe this year as hell, because I have never felt the presence of God more tangibly.

I attribute the peace of God's presence that I experienced to the Psalms. Cut off from human support, the Psalms became my lifeline. They connected me to the God who was deeply concerned for my well-being, shared my

---

1   Bruce K. Waltke and James M. Houston, The Psalms as Christian Worship: A Historical Commentary (Grand Rapids: Eerdmans, 2010), 110.

desire for justice, and had full authority to act on my behalf. I was never alone.

I do not know your story, but it is a safe bet that you have been through trying circumstances, too. People you love have suffered. You have needed divine intervention. And if they have not already, the Psalms can become your lifeline, too. The alternative is precarious. When we neglect the Psalms, our prayers become flat and repetitive—there is much more to prayer than *good health, the ability to pay bills, a good job interview*, and *finding food for our families*. God invites us to bring our whole selves before him—the good, the bad, and the ugly—our joys and sorrows, our desperation and gratitude. When we fail to practice this kind of prayer, we cease to be the kind of community where those who suffer can find a home. Let me offer an example:

My friend Charlene has been married fourteen years. She and her husband have watched as one after another of their friends' bellies have bulged with new life. Their arms have ached to hold a child of their own, but after years of prayer and good diet and doctor visits and tests, her womb is still empty. As with all grief, theirs has ebbed and flowed. During one particularly intense season, where the loss felt especially acute, Charlene showed up at her women's group at church. They were talking about prayer. Charlene could not hold it in any more. She exploded:

> I don't understand why God isn't answering our prayers. What are we doing wrong? We've tried everything! We've been serving him our entire marriage and yet he withholds from us the one thing we want most. How could God do this to us?!

The room fell awkwardly silent. The ladies around the circle looked at the floor, or sideways at each other. They had never seen Charlene so broken and they did not know how to fix her. This was not the plan. It did not fit the curriculum. Charlene left that day feeling profoundly alone and decided not to return.

What a missed opportunity! If these women had known the Psalms, Charlene's honest expression of pain would have resonated with Psalm 88, the darkest psalm:

> *I am overwhelmed with troubles*
> *and my life draws near to death.*
> *I am counted among those who go down to the pit;*
> *I am like one without strength.*
>
> ~ Ps 88:3–4

Charlene's friends would have realized that praying with brutal honesty connects us deeply with God and guards against despair. They would have understood that such prayer is not only tolerated, but invited. After all, prayers like this one are part of sacred Scripture!

When we pray the Psalms, we enlarge our capacity for healthy Christian community. When we pray the Psalms, we exercise our faith muscles. When we pray the Psalms, we make room for healing. This book invites us to sit and learn from men and women of ancient times who have suffered unimaginable grief, for they have discovered the riches of the Psalms for connecting with God during that sorrow. These believers have so much to teach us! What are we waiting for?

Why Me?

You already know one story of why the Psalms mean so much to me. But honestly, I did not feel qualified to write this book. I am an Old Testament scholar, not a historian.

I am far more comfortable talking about what a psalm means than in navigating hundreds of years of church history to discover how others have read and prayed it. I know so little about the life and times of most of the people you will meet in this book. I met many of them for the first time as I was working on this project.

When I was asked to write this book, I planned to say no. Two things changed my mind. First, my teenage daughter begged me to say yes. Eliana is a philosophy major in the Honors Program at George Fox University. She loves reading ancient texts, and she wanted to help. The chance to work on a mother-daughter project was enticing. Second, I had a dream (literally). It was not the typical process-random-parts-of-my-day-with-a-strange-combination-of-people-from-my-entire-life kind of dream. It seemed significant. As I awoke the next morning the interpretation took shape. *It felt like a message from God straight to me.*

The dream was a single image, a painting. It looked like a Greek Orthodox icon (which is outside of my own church experience). A man was standing on a bridge in the center of the painting, reaching into the "nave" of a church with his left hand to grasp a yellow pear, and extending his right hand to a group of people huddled outside. As I awoke, I somehow knew that the pear represented the Psalms. I was not entirely sure what a "nave" was (though I knew it was some part of cathedral architecture), so I looked it up. The "nave" is the sanctuary of the church where worshipers gather. As I reflected on this dream, it began to make sense.

A drawing of my dream

The vision of the Sacred Roots Project is to make Christian spiritual classics available and accessible to everybody. If you are hungry for more knowledge of God and thirsty for mentoring from faithful and fruitful Christians, then we have you in mind. After all, the Psalms are for the whole church, but especially for those afflicted—for those resilient men and women for whom every day presents a new challenge. The Psalms have been the mainstay of the Church's worship for thousands of years, but our generation has nearly lost them. We lack the habit of praying the Psalms, either individually or together. It is from the ancient Church that we need to recover the practice of praying the Psalms. That is why the man in my dream was reaching into the church. He was recovering the fruit of faithful Christian worship in order to make it available for us today.

I know very little about art history, but I have a great little book called *Signs and Symbols in Christian Art*.[2] It explains that in Christian art, a pear usually represents Christ. This is significant. Ancient readers of the Psalms saw Christ as the primary voice in the Psalms. True, they were written hundreds of years before the birth of Jesus. However, because God took on human flesh and joined us in the suffering of this world, Jesus could pray the Psalms along with us. He entered into our joys and sorrows, finding in the Psalms the language of prayer. If they were essential to Jesus' faith, they are essential to ours as well. In these ancient prayers Christ identifies with our struggles and expresses dependence upon the Father. It is appropriate, then, to see Jesus as the center of the painting in my dream. By praying the Psalms, Christ demonstrates the life of faith, inviting us to pray with him.

So I said yes to this project, and I have learned so much along the way. In the pages that follow, you will find a brief mediation on each psalm from believers in Jesus who lived long ago. These ancient voices will give us a sense of the sacred roots of our faith. Our primary teacher will be an African man named Augustine.

Why Augustine?

Augustine is one of history's most influential Christian leaders. Among many other writings, he produced a commentary on the Psalms. His work is the fruit of thirty years of reflection and preaching on the Psalms in a North African context. His work was not done for scholars, but in and for the church. Augustine wrote as a pastor.

---

2   George Ferguson, *Signs and Symbols in Christian Art* (New York: Oxford University Press, 1954), 36.

He believed that the words of the Psalms could become the prayers of his own congregation, and that in praying the Psalms believers would be healed of their own heart-sickness. From Augustine's perspective, the Psalms provide a context in which the church can interpret its own suffering.[3] Though he lived more than 1,500 years ago, his writings continue to shape the church. His observations about human life and faith are strikingly relevant today.

The book you are holding does not offer a full cross-section of Augustine's interpretation of the Psalms. Instead, I have selected some of his richest pastoral insights. Augustine is not the only ancient writer you will meet on these pages. I have chosen two dozen other voices for this project as well—men and women who lived between the AD 200s and the 1500s and were also passionate about the Psalms.

We will listen in on what some of Augustine's peers in the 4th and 5th centuries have to say: John Chrysostom and Basil the Great, Ambrose and Athanasius. We will eavesdrop on instruction from a 9th century noblewoman named Dhouda to her warrior son on how to read the Psalms. From the 13th century we will meet the very logical Thomas Aquinas, who thinks in outlines, and the effusive Gertrude the Great, who relishes the sweetness of God's love as she prays the Psalms. You will also meet writers from the 16th century: John Calvin, the level-headed interpreter of the Protestant Reformation, and Katharina Schütz Zell, whose pastoral sensibility brings the Psalms to life for those who suffer. A full list of contributors and a timeline of when they lived are included in the appendices.

---

3   Michael C. McCarthy, "An Ecclesiology of Groaning: Augustine, the Psalms, and the Making of Church," *Theological Studies* 66 (2005) 23-48.

My hope is that these selections will inspire you to pray the Psalms personally and with your faith community, joining generations of faithful believers who have turned their faces to God.

How to Use this Book

Every generation of the church has had many faithful believers who used the Psalms as a daily guide to prayer—praying one or more psalms every day. By reading three psalms a day (and their corresponding devotional entries), you will make it through the entire book in eight weeks. You might consider a rhythm of a psalm at breakfast, lunch, and dinner on weekdays or a psalm when you wake up, mid-afternoon, and at bedtime. That rhythm will give you one "free" spot a week to take off or to re-read a selection that meant a lot to you. If that is too fast for you, slow it down. You can read one psalm a day and make it through the book twice in one year. Remember: the goal is to cultivate a daily habit of prayer using the Psalms as a guide, not just to get through this book. Hopefully these devotional selections will give you a sense of community as you pray the Psalms. If you are part of a small group working through the Psalms or would appreciate prompts for personal journaling, you can find discussion questions at the end of each week's section.

Also note: these meditations are designed to be read alongside the book of Psalms, not to replace it. Most of them focus on a few key verses or phrases in the psalm (printed in italics). Some of them reflect more broadly on life with God. Others paraphrase the psalm in their own words or re-write it as English poetry. When possible, I have updated the language and used the NIV as the base text for commentary.

If using this book for personal devotions, I suggest the following order:

1. Read the psalm from your Bible.

2. Read the devotional insight from this book.

3. Re-read the psalm.

4. Respond in prayer, either silently, out loud, or in writing.

However you choose to use this book, I would love to hear how it goes!

Eight-Week Reading Plan

If you are using this book as part of an eight-week study of the Psalms, here is how I suggest you break up the reading of the Psalms.

Week 1 – Read Introduction and Psalms 1–17

Week 2 – Psalms 18–38

Week 3 – Psalms 39–59

Week 4 – Psalms 60–80

Week 5 – Psalms 81–101

Week 6 – Psalms 102–119:32 (count every two "stanzas" of Psalm 119 as one psalm)

Week 7 – Psalms 119:33–130

Week 8 – Psalms 131–150

Thank you for joining us as we learn to pray the Psalms with Augustine and his friends. The end of our introduction is also the beginning of our prayer. We commence with a prayer from Augustine.

> *We turn to the Lord God, the Father Almighty, and with pure hearts offer to him, as far as we are able, great and true thanks, with all our hearts praying for his exceeding kindness, that of his good pleasure he would be willing to hear our prayers, that by his power he would drive out the enemy from our deeds and thoughts, that he would increase our faith, guide our understanding, give us spiritual thoughts, and lead us to enjoy him, through Jesus Christ his Son our Lord, who lives and reigns with him, in the unity of the Holy Spirit, one God, for ever and ever. Amen.*

The Text

BIBLICAL STUDIES

Chapter 1

Psalms 1–17

Psalm 1 with Athanasius – Delighting in God's Law

How different are the righteous and faithful servants of the Lord [from the wicked]! They meditate on the words of the Lord when they sit in their houses, when they lie down, when they rise up, and when they walk by the way (Deut 6:7). They have a good hope because of the promise of the Spirit: *Blessed is the one who does not walk in step with the wicked or stand in the way that sinners take or sit in the company of mockers, but whose delight is in the law of the LORD, and who meditates on his law day and night* (Ps 1:1–2).

Being grounded in faith, rejoicing in hope, zealous in spirit, they boldly say, "My mouth will speak words of wisdom; the meditation of my heart will give you understanding" (Ps 49:3). And they add, "I meditate on all your works and consider what your hands have done" (Ps 143:5). And further, "On my bed I remember you; I think of you through the watches of the night" (Ps 63:6).

Then, advancing in boldness, they say, "May . . . this meditation of my heart be pleasing in your sight" (Ps 19:14). And what is the reward of such a person? The psalmist adds immediately, "LORD, my Rock and my Redeemer" (Ps 19:14). For those who examine themselves in this way and bring the desires of their hearts into agreement with the Lord, nothing truly bad can happen. Indeed, their hearts are strengthened by confidence in the Lord, as it is written, "Those who trust in the LORD shall be as Mount Zion: those who live in Jerusalem shall never be moved" (Ps 125:1, LXX).

Psalm 2 with John Calvin – Submitting to God's Anointed

Many plotted against David, trying to prevent his kingship. Their hostile attempts might have made him give up hope of ever becoming king. No doubt he often struggled with difficult temptations. But, since his conscience was clear— he had not acted out of personal ambition, but had been made king by divine appointment. Therefore he was able to condemn rebellious kings and their armies.

We can draw encouragement from this passage in two ways: First, whenever the world rages, attempting to disrupt Christ's kingdom, we can see that things are playing out just as God announced through David, so that these circumstances need not surprise or trouble us. Of itself the kingdom of Christ would be peaceable, and from it true peace flows out to the world. However, due to human wickedness and hostility, God's kingdom never advances without pushback. The second encouragement is that when the ungodly fight against God's anointed, while depending on their vast numbers, their riches, and their means of defense, we may safely laugh at them. They are attacking God in heaven—a war they can never win.

You will break them with the rod of iron (v. 7). It may seem strange that, while other parts of Scripture celebrate the mercy and gentleness of our Lord, he is described here as full of terror. But this severe and dreadful sovereignty serves no other purpose than to strike alarm into his enemies. This wrath is not inconsistent with the kindness with which Christ tenderly cherishes his own people.

He who shows himself a loving shepherd to his gentle sheep must treat wild beasts with severity, either to convert them from their cruelty or to restrain it. Christ was sent by the Father to cheer the poor and the wretched with the news of salvation, to set the prisoners free, to heal the sick, to bring the sorrowful and afflicted out of the darkness of death into the light of life (Isa 61:1). But for those who provoke his wrath by their ingratitude, Christ takes on a new character—to beat down their stubbornness. If it appears that God does not punish the wicked, we must simply wait patiently for the last day, when he will utterly destroy them. In the meantime, let us rest satisfied that he rules in the midst of his enemies.

Be warned, you rulers of the earth (v. 10). David proceeds to urge unbelievers to repent before it is too late, before they discover by experience that these divine threats are not empty. And he addresses by name kings and rulers, who are not very easily brought to submission. If David does not spare kings, who seem exempt from ordinary laws, how much more does his exhortation apply to common people, so that all, from the highest to the lowest, may humble themselves before God. The beginning of true wisdom is when we lay aside our pride, and submit ourselves to the authority of Christ.

Psalm 3 with Augustine –
God, Our Shield and Deliverer

LORD, how many are my foes! How many rise up against me! (v. 1) They wish to exterminate the Christian name. *Many are saying of me, "God will not deliver him"* (v. 2). For they would not imagine that they could destroy the Church, branching out so very far and wide, unless they believed that God did not care. *But you, LORD, are a shield around me* (v. 3). Let the people of God also say, *I will not fear though tens of thousands assail me on every side* (v. 6), of the ungodly who surround me to extinguish the Christian name everywhere, if they could. But how can they be feared, when the fervency of love is inflamed by the blood of Christian martyrs as fire is inflamed by oil? *Arise, LORD! Deliver me, my God! Strike all my enemies on the jaw; break the teeth of the wicked* (v. 7).

Each one of us may also say, when a multitude of vices and lusts draws us toward sin in spite of our resistance, *LORD, how many are my foes! How many rise up against me!* (v. 1) And, since despair of recovery generally creeps in through the accumulation of vices, as though these same vices were mocking the soul, or even as though the Devil and his angels through their poisonous suggestions were at work to make us despair, it is said with great truth, *But you, LORD, are a shield around me* (v. 3).

I will not fear though tens of thousands assail me on every side (v. 6). Besides those enemies which the Church universally has carried and carries, each of us also has temptations, by which, when surrounded, we may say, *Arise, LORD! Deliver me, my God!* (v. 7); that is, make me rise again. *Strike all my enemies on the jaw.* It is well within God's determined purpose to pray this against the Devil and his angels, who rage not only against the whole body of Christ, but also against each one in particular. *Break the teeth of the wicked* (v. 7). Each person has those who revile him, he also has the primary authors of vice, the Devil and his angels, who strive to cut him off from the body of Christ. But *from the LORD comes deliverance* (v. 8).

Psalm 4 with John Calvin – Hoping in God's Promises

After David in the beginning of the psalm has prayed to God to help him, he immediately turns his discussion to his enemies, and relying on the promise of God, triumphs over them as a conqueror. Therefore, he teaches us by his example that as often as we are weighed down by adversity or involved in very great distress, we should meditate upon the promises of God. By these the hope of salvation is offered to us, so that defending ourselves by this shield, we may break through all the temptations which attack us. By his praying, David testified that when utterly deprived of all earthly aid, hope remained for him in God. Content with God's favor alone, David protests that he sets no value on objects that others fervently desire. The faithful, forming a low estimate of present good things, rest in God alone. Therefore, David suggests that all those who wish to enjoy prosperity but do not seek God's favor are fools. By neglecting to do this, they are carried about by the various false opinions which circulate. He also rebukes another vice, namely, that of ignorant people who give themselves wholly to the ease and comforts of the flesh and content themselves with the enjoyment of these alone, without thinking of anything higher. So also it comes to pass that as long as they are supplied with whatever they desire, they are indifferent toward God as if they had no need of him. David testifies that although he may lack all other good things, the fatherly love of God is sufficient to compensate for the loss of them all. This, therefore, is the point: Most people

> ### John Calvin on Psalm 4
>
> *"David testifies that although he may lack all other good things, the fatherly love of God is sufficient to compensate for the loss of them all."*

greedily seek after present pleasures and advantages; but I maintain that perfect happiness is only to be found in the favor of God.

This passage teaches us that those who do not, with full resolution, rest wholly in God and find satisfaction in him are miserable, even though they may have an overflowing abundance of all earthly things; while, on the other hand, the faithful, although they are tossed amidst many troubles, are truly happy when there is no other ground for it but this: that God's fatherly face shines upon them, which turns darkness into light.

Psalm 5 with Augustine – Seeing God

Hear my cry for help, my King and my God, for to you I pray. In the morning, LORD, you hear my voice (vv. 2–3). The psalmist understands why he does not see, because the night is not yet past, that is, the darkness which our sins deserve. Therefore, he says, *for to you I pray*; that is, because you to whom I pray are so mighty, *in the morning, LORD, you hear my voice*. You cannot be seen, he says, by those from whose eyes the night of sins is not yet lifted: when the night of my error is past, and the darkness gone, which by my sins I have brought upon myself, then *You will hear my voice*. We must not cling to earthly things, if we want to be able to truly see God, who is seen by a clean heart.

As for the wicked, their eyes (that is, their minds) are beaten back by the light of truth, because of the darkness of their sins; which they practice habitually so that they are not able to maintain the brightness of right understanding. Therefore even they who see sometimes, that is, who understand the truth, are yet still unrighteous. They are held back by love of those things that turn them away from the truth. They carry their night with them, not only the habit, but even the love, of sinning. But if this night passes away, if they shall stop sinning, and this love of sin be put to flight, the morning dawns, so that they not only understand, but also cling to the truth. *With you, evil people are not welcome. The arrogant cannot stand in your presence. You hate all who do wrong* (vv. 4–5). *But I, by your great love, can come into your house* (v. 7).

Psalm 6 with Gregory of Nyssa – Repenting

Surely when we consider the precision of the coming judgment, when even the most insignificant of our sins of omission will be subjected to investigation, we will be frightened by such a dreadful idea, uncertain where the process of judgment, in our case, will lead. . . . For this reason, speaking as if he were already suffering, the psalmist represents the voices of those in distress, to whom what is being done to punish the unrighteous seems to convey anger and wrath. He is saying, in effect: I do not wait for the correction of my hidden faults to take place in me, through the dreadful punishments that proceed from that anger. Instead, by my confession, I choose to experience beforehand the sorrow of his wrath. Those who are punished against their will experience pain that reveals the hidden aspects of lawlessness. Those who repent of their own free choice welcome punishment through repentance and expose the sin hidden in the deepest parts of themselves. . . . However, the psalmist shows in verse 9 the good hope of repair that also arises from repentance. For immediately—almost in the same breath—he speaks of God's reaction to repentance. Coming to an awareness of God's pleasure in it, he proclaims his gratitude aloud and rejoices in the gift, saying, *The LORD has heard my cry for mercy; the LORD accepts my prayer* (v. 9).

Psalm 7 with John Chrysostom – Praying to Be Heard

[David prays as he is pursued by Cush, a Benjamite.]

They will tear me apart like a lion and rip me to pieces with no one to rescue me (v. 2). To be sure, he had built an army, and had a large number with him; so why does he say, *with no one to rescue me?* Because he considers not even the whole world as help if he does not enjoy influence from on high, nor does he think of it as solitude if he is alone, as long as he shares in help from him. Hence he also said, "No king is saved by the size of his army; no warrior escapes by his great strength" (Ps 33:16).

LORD my God, if I have done this and there is guilt on my hands (v. 3). This must be our concern, not simply to pray but to pray in such a way as to be heard. It is not enough that prayer affects what is intended, unless we direct it to God. For the Pharisee prayed and achieved nothing (cf. Luke 18:10–14), and again the Jews prayed but God turned away from them in their prayer (cf. Isa 1:15); they did not pray as they should have prayed. That is why we were invited to pray the prayer most likely to be heard. He suggested this in Psalm 6 as well, begging to be heard not unconditionally but with the condition that he made an effort of his own. Now, what effort was that? This: "All night long I flood my bed with weeping and drench my couch with tears." This: "I am worn out from my groaning." This: "Away from me, all you who do evil" (Ps 6:5–8). All these win God over: lament, tears, groans, parting company from the wicked, living in fear and trembling of judgement.

Psalm 8 with John Chrysostom – God's Care for Humans

What is mankind that you are mindful of them, human beings that you care for them? (v. 4). After speaking of creation in the first few verses of Psalm 8, the psalmist inserts a reference to God's care for human beings. Even those former statements, after all, were made about the human race, though they also have to do with God's providence. All of creation, you see, is for humans. Taking full account of such marvelous care and wonderful providence on God's part, and the arrangements he put in place for the salvation of the human race, he is struck with complete wonder and amazement as to why he considered us worthy of attention. Consider, after all, that all the visible things were for our sake. For us the design implemented from the time of Adam and Eve up to his coming; for us paradise, commandments, punishments, miracles, retribution, kindnesses after the Law; for us the Son of God became human. What could anyone say of the future we are intended to enjoy? So all those things are going through his mind: To be thought worthy of such wonderful privileges, what must the human being be? I mean, if you consider what was done and is being done for our sake, and what we will enjoy afterwards, you will be struck with awe, and then you will see clearly how humans are objects of such attention on God's part.

Psalm 9 with John Chrysostom – Trusting in God

Those who know your name trust in you (v. 10). In other words, those who know you, your support and assistance, trust in you as sufficient anchor, sufficient assistance, secure tower, the one who not only promises relief from problems but does not permit us to be alarmed by present problems. You see, people who are rid of human concerns and dependent on hope from above not only secure for themselves the speediest freedom from problems but are not even alarmed and disturbed by the problems themselves, helped as they are by that undying hope. Greater, in fact, than the sway based on fear is the security based on trust in God. The one is human, the other divine and invincible. If, however, he does not relieve the problems at once, this too proves to be for your testing. You see, though he is quite capable of not allowing troubles to happen to you, he does allow them to make you stronger. Though quite capable of giving you relief from the beginning, he delays and postpones to increase your stamina, exercise your hope and make your trust in him more zealous. His habit is not to allow you to suffer hardship to the point of growing weary, nor enjoy relief to the point of giving up.

He does not ignore the cries of the afflicted (v. 12). Note once again the esteem in which the afflicted are held. Now, he is referring not simply to the needy but to those poor in spirit, as Christ says (Matt 5:3). These most of all are heard when they pray, you see, the humble and contrite of heart. Everywhere you will find humility to be the basis of prayer. The Lord, you see, is near to the contrite of heart.

John Chrysostom on Psalm 9

"It is especially after being freed from troubles that we need grace to cope with good times more easily."

David prays constantly. Though freed from troubles and made secure, he does not stop praying again, *Have mercy* (v. 13), and begs him for future benefits. You see, we always stand in need of God's providence, but especially at a time of freedom from troubles. Without troubles, we face a more difficult battle—against indifference and numbness. It is then that the devil comes panting more aggressively. And so it is especially after being freed from troubles that we need grace to cope with good times more easily. Hence the need to be cautious is most urgent at the time when we are free of troubles. For this reason you will often find success productive of greater troubles than failure. That is why the psalmist says elsewhere, "It was good for me to be afflicted so that I might learn your decrees" (Ps 119:71).

Psalm 10 with John Chrysostom –
The Foolishness of Sin

The wicked says to himself, "Nothing will ever shake me."
He swears, "No one will ever do me harm" (v. 6). Do you
see the foolishness? Do you see the destruction gradually
increasing? The wicked are applauded in their sins,
commended in their wrongdoing. This is the first pitfall,
enough to trip up those who do not expect it. Hence it
is necessary to welcome those who rebuke and correct us
rather than those who applaud and flatter us to the point
of destruction. We need to mourn deeply for sinners, not
applaud them. Do you see the perversity of evil, that it
not only escapes accusation but even results in celebration?
From their own foolishness they increased the wickedness
of the praises, they forgot the fear of God and his
judgements, forgetting their own nature as well. Those
who forget the judgements of God, after all, lose self-
awareness. *His mouth is full of lies and threats, trouble and*
evil are under his tongue. He lies in wait near the villages;
from ambush he murders the innocent. . . . He lies in wait to
catch the helpless (vv. 7–9). What could be more pitiful
than this, what could be more desperate, to feel the need
to steal the possessions of the poor? So then shall we
consider these people rich? Do you see their moral
bankruptcy and cruelty? Moral bankruptcy, because they
lust after the goods of the poor; cruelty, because far from
being moved by their predicament they make it worse
when they should be helping. Justice does not follow close
on their heels, since God in his long-suffering summons
them to repentance; but when they profit nothing from
the long-suffering, then he punishes them. Those who are
wronged, you see, came to no harm; rather, they emerged
better and more visible from their hardship. God for his

part displayed his own long-suffering by showing restraint and patient endurance, but along with long-suffering his power and resourcefulness as well, because when they outdo themselves, that is the time God defeats them. Having persisted in their stubbornness, they pay the ultimate penalty. Coming to their senses is no trivial experience for those who are well off.

Psalm 11 with Philip Sidney – God's Day of Reckoning

Since I do trust Jehovah[1] still,
Your fearful words why do you spill?[2]
That like a bird to some strong hill
I now should fall[3] a flying.

Behold the evil have bent their bow,
And set their arrows in a row,
To give unwares[4] a mortal blow
To hearts that hate all lying.

But that in building they begun,
With ground-plot's[5] fall, shall be undone:
For what, alas, have just[6] men done?
In them no cause is growing.

God in his holy temple is:
The throne of heav'n is only his:
Naught[7] his all-seeing sight can miss;
His eyelids peise[8] our going.

---

1   Jehovah – the LORD

2   Spill – waste

3   Fall – start, begin, commence

4   Unwares – the unsuspecting

5   Ground-plot's – foundations

6   Just – righteous

7   Naught – nothing

8   Peise – take note of

The Lord does search the just man's reynes,[9]
But hates, abhors, the wicked brains;
On them storms, brimstone, coals he rains:
That is their share assigned.

But so of happy other side
His lovely face on them does bide,[10]
In race of life their feet to guide
Who be to God inclined.

---

9   Reynes – kidneys – inmost feelings
10 Bide – linger

Psalm 12 with Valerian – Guard My Mouth

Hear the prophet's voice: "Set a guard over my mouth, LORD" (Ps 141:3). This is a profitable guard for our mouth: not to let our heart easily turn its attention to any words which would disturb the pursuit of peace, or which the immoral acts of some person bring it to utter. No one has regretted keeping silent amid confused speech. For, as we see, the acts which spring from words often result in crime, and those who are quick to dislike others undermine friendships. If a person is either boastful or mean in their speech, how can they fail to be disliked? However, we are not mentioning all this to bring anyone to keep their voice always confined inside a closed mouth, and have perpetual silence shut the sound of their tongue behind silent lips. Just as it is unpleasant to have the wicked talk too much, so it is harmful to have the good always keep silent. Therefore, when need arises, let us speak out the words of justice. Let ours be a speech well flavored. Therefore, let us speak, but with fear and trembling, aware that we must give an account for every word (Matt 12:36). Thus we will ensure that nothing immoral springs from our hearts, nothing blasphemous flies from our lips, nothing harmful remains in our thought. The Prophet condemns not only what offends the ears, but also the attitude which some people cherish in their minds. *They flatter with their lips but harbor deception in their hearts* (v. 2).

Unspoken thoughts, too, then, should be listed among the faults of a disrespectful tongue. Whatever you speak in your heart you are confessing to the Lord, because God is the Searcher of hearts. Since you cannot hide your thoughts from him, can your shouting remain hidden from him or excused? Reflect on this.

In all zeal, therefore, dearly beloved, let us keep our mouths controlled by a proper filter. May our tongue utter nothing unpleasant, may no immoral speech of ours devise anything harmful, anything deceitful. May our hearts contain nothing sly, harsh, or idle. For the Lord has said that an account must be given even of idle words (Matt 12:36). Although a person may fortify their life by faith, rule it by wisdom, and arrange it with purity and sobriety, there is nothing pleasing in them if their tongue alone of all the parts of their body speaks offense.

Psalm 13 with Theodoret of Cyrus – Handling Discouragement

How long must I wrestle with my thoughts and day after day have sorrow in my heart? (v. 2). I am constantly worn out night and day, turning over my thoughts again and again, at one time hoping to enjoy your loving-kindness, at another wondering if my mind will hold, at another surrendering my firm hope. How long will my enemy be lifted up? It is appropriate to apply this prayer to ourselves when under attack from the devil, and to call on divine help unceasingly: David was distressed to see his enemies more powerful than he.

Look on me and answer, LORD my God, give light to my eyes, or I will I sleep in death (v. 3). By night I am overwhelmed by my problems, in the grip of discouragement like a kind of sleep. But if the light of your assistance shines, it will disperse the darkness of trouble and put an end to the sleep of discouragement. If, on the other hand, you delay your help, I am afraid the sleep will turn into death, as the distress becomes stronger than my resolve.

My heart will rejoice in your salvation (v. 5). Now I have hope in your mercy, and enjoying salvation I shall be rid of my downheartedness and make music with complete satisfaction. He added this, in fact: *I will sing the LORD's praise, for he has been good to me* (v. 6).

Psalm 14 with John Calvin – The Folly of the Wicked

It is painful to see wickedness triumph in the Church—the good and the simple unjustly afflicted, while the wicked cruelly domineer according to their pleasure. We need encouragement from David's example, so that, in the midst of the great distress of the Church, we may comfort ourselves with this assurance that God will finally deliver her. In Psalm 14, David does not bring against his enemies the charge of common foolishness, but rather condemns the folly and wild boldness of those the world considers famous for their wisdom. We commonly see that those who are thought wise by themselves and others employ their cunning by laying traps, and use their intelligence to despise and mock God. It is therefore important for us to know that however much the world applauds these characters who indulge in wickedness, the Holy Spirit condemns them as fools; for there is no stupidity more offensive than forgetfulness of God. These men indulge themselves in their lusts so boldly and so outrageously that they pay no regard to righteousness or equity; in short, they wildly rush into every kind of wickedness. Obviously they have shaken off all religion, and extinguished, as far as they can, all remembrance of God from their minds. When the ungodly allow themselves to follow their own inclinations so stubbornly, without any sense of shame, it is evidence that they have cast off all fear of God.

> **John Calvin on Psalm 14**
>
> *"There is no better resolution we can make than the resolution to depend on God and to rest in his salvation, and on the assistance he has promised us."*

Whenever unbelievers see the children of God overwhelmed with calamities, they mock them for their groundless confidence, as it appears to them to be, and with sarcasm laugh at the assured hope with which they rely upon God. David, therefore, defies and mocks the wicked's disrespect, and threatens that their mockery of the poor and the miserable who depend on God's protection will be the cause of their destruction. At the same time, he teaches us that there is no better resolution we can make than the resolution to depend on God and to rest in his salvation, and on the assistance he has promised us. Although we may be surrounded with calamities, this is the highest wisdom.

Psalm 15 with John Calvin – Living as Servants of God

LORD, who may dwell in your sacred tent? . . . The one whose walk is blameless (v. 2). There is an implied contrast between the empty boasting of those who are only the people of God in name and the sure and genuine evidence of true godliness which David applauds. He describes the approved servants of God as distinguished by their righteous fruits. In the first place, he requires blamelessness; in other words, that people should always act with singleness of heart, and without trickery. Secondly, he requires *righteousness*; that they should determine to do good to their neighbors, hurt no one, and abstain from all wrong. Thirdly, he requires truth in their speech, so that they may speak nothing falsely or deceitfully. *To speak . . . from the heart* (v. 2) denotes agreement and harmony between the heart and tongue, so that the speech is a vivid representation of the hidden feeling.

After having briefly listed the virtues with which all believers should be characterized, David now lists certain vices from which they should be free. In the first place, he tells them they must not be *slanderers*; secondly, that they must restrain themselves from doing anything *wrong* or harmful to their neighbors; and, thirdly, that they must not participate in the *slur* of false reports that damage another's reputation (v. 3). Slander is the first point of injustice by which our neighbors are injured. If a good name is a treasure more precious than all the riches of the world (Prov 22:1), no greater injury can be inflicted upon others than to wound their reputation. The Holy Spirit condemns all false and wicked accusations. In the clause which immediately follows, the doctrine that the children of God ought to be far removed from all injustice is stated more generally: *who does no wrong to a neighbor*. By the word *neighbor*, the psalmist means not only those with whom we enjoy friendship, but all people, to whom we are bound by the ties of humanity and a common nature. When people make a promise to each other, there is nothing more common than for them to make excuses and back out when keeping their word becomes inconvenient. That is why we generally see so much unfaithfulness, because people do not require themselves to keep their promises, unless it will promote their own personal interests. Therefore, David condemning this fickleness, requires God's people to exhibit the greatest steadfastness in the fulfillment of their promises.

Psalm 16 with Augustine –
The Lord as Our Inheritance

Those who run after other gods will suffer more and more (v. 4), not for their destruction, but so they will long for the Physician. *I will not pour out libations of blood to such gods or take up their names on my lips.* But by a spiritual change what they have been will be forgotten. They will no longer be called sinners, or enemies, or even mortals, but rather righteous, and my brothers and sisters, and children of God who are at peace.

LORD, you alone are my portion and my cup (v. 5). For together with me they will possess this inheritance: the Lord himself. Let others choose for themselves portions, earthly and temporal, to enjoy; the portion of believers is the Lord eternal. Let others drink of deadly pleasures, the portion of my cup is the Lord.

I keep my eyes always on the LORD (v. 8). Even among things that pass away, I keep my eyes on him who lives forever, anticipating that to him I will return after passing through temporary things. *With him at my right hand, I will not be shaken.* For he shows me favor, so that I may remain with him.

You make known to me the path of life; You will fill me with joy in your presence (v. 11). You will fill us with joy, so we will seek nothing further, when we see you face to face.

Psalm 17 with Augustine – Testing the Heart of One Who Prays

Hear me, LORD, my plea is just; listen to my cry. Hear my prayer—it does not rise from deceitful lips. Let my vindication come from you (vv. 1–2). From the knowledge of you, let me judge truth. That is, may I not judge by anything except that which I learn from you.

You examine me at night and test me (v. 3). For my heart has been tested and found genuine by the experience of tribulation. *You will find that I have planned no evil.* This testing is not only at night, but is also called fire, in that it burns. By these I was examined and found righteous.

My mouth has not transgressed, though people tried to bribe me (vv. 3–4). That nothing may come out of my mouth, but that which relates to your glory and praise, not to human works, which they do against your will. *I have kept myself from the ways of the violent, through what your lips have commanded* (v. 4), because of the words of your peace.

I call on you, God, for you will answer me (v. 6). With a free and strong effort have I directed my prayers to you: so that I might have this power. You have heard me even when praying weakly. *Rise up, LORD, confront them, bring them down* (v. 13). Arise, Lord, you who they think is asleep, and regardless of people's sins, let them be blinded by their own malice, that vengeance may prevent their act, so that they are cast down. *By your hand save me from such people, LORD* (v. 14). Deliver my soul by restoring me after the serious injuries the ungodly have inflicted on me.

Discussion Questions

 Some Christian denominations regularly pray and sing the Psalms. Others rarely do. What role (if any) do the Psalms play in your church?

 After this first week of reading ancient Christian writers, what stands out to you? How have their ideas challenged your interpretation of the Psalms? In what ways would you want to challenge these writers?

 Re-read Psalm 5. Can you think of a time when you knew what was right, but still gave into your sinful desires?

 In Psalm 12, Valerian reflects on the power of speech. How can we tell when it is wise to speak up and when we should remain silent?

 In his reflection on Psalm 4, Calvin speaks about resting "in God alone." What daily or weekly practices cultivate this kind of rest?

Chapter 2

Psalms 18–38

Psalm 18 with Augustine – God, My Rock and Refuge

I love you, LORD, my strength (v. 1). You make me strong. *The LORD is my rock, my fortress, and my deliverer* (v. 2). Lord, you have sustained me, because I sought refuge in you, and I sought refuge, because you delivered me. *My shield and the horn of my salvation, my stronghold.* My defender, because I have not leaned on myself, lifting up the horn of pride against you; but have found you to be a horn indeed, that is, the sure height of salvation.

He has rescued me from my powerful enemy (v. 17), who afflicted and attempted to overturn me. And from my foes, who were too strong for me, as long as I was under those who do not know God. *They confronted me in the day of my disaster* (v. 18). They have first injured me, while I endure a mortal and tiresome body. *But the LORD was my support.*

He brought me out into a spacious place (v. 19). And since I was enduring physical distress, he brought me forth into the spiritual breadth of faith. *He rescued me, because he delighted in me.* Before I desired him, he delivered me from my most powerful enemies, and from those who hated me. *The LORD has dealt with me according to my righteousness* (v. 20). Though he first showed mercy before I had good will. *I pursued my enemies and overtook them* (v. 37). I will pursue my fleshly desires in order to master them, rather than be seized by them, so they may be consumed. *I did not turn back till they were destroyed.* And from this purpose I will not rest until those who create confusion around me fail.

Psalm 19 with Augustine – Proper Fear of the LORD

The fear of the LORD is pure, enduring forever (v. 9). *The fear of the LORD*, not that distressing fear under the law, dreading the withdrawal of temporal things, by the love of which the soul commits unfaithfulness; but that holy fear with which the Church, the more passionately she loves her Spouse, the more carefully does she take care not to offend him. Therefore, perfect love does not cast out this fear (1 John 4:18), but it endures forever.

The decrees of the LORD are firm, and all of them are righteous. His judgments are justified in truth unchangeably. For neither in his threats nor his promises does God deceive anyone, nor can any take his punishment from the ungodly, or from the godly his reward. *They are more precious than gold* (v. 10). The judgments of God are more desirable than the empty glitz of this world, as the latter leads to fear and hatred of God and his truth. But if anybody is gold or precious stone, they may not be consumed by fire, but received into God's treasury. They desire the judgments and will of God more than their own. They are sweeter than honey, than honey from the honeycomb. To the godly, the judgments of God are sweetest of all.

Keep your servant also from willful sins (v. 13). From the lusts which hide in me, cleanse me, Lord. Let me not be led astray by others. For one who is cleansed from their own faults is not prey to the faults of others. Preserve your servant rather than the proud person from the lusts of others and one who seeks to master them. *May they not rule over me. Then I will be blameless* (v. 13). If neither my own secret sins, nor those of others, gain dominion over me, then I will be undefiled.

Psalm 20 with John Calvin – Confidence in God

This psalm contains a prayer on behalf of the King of Israel, that God would aid him in danger; and on behalf of his kingdom, that God would safely maintain and cause it to prosper: for in David the safety and well-being of the whole community centered. To this is added a promise that God will preside over the kingdom he founded and effectively watch over it to preserve it securely.

Now this I know (v. 6). Here the faithful gratefully declare that they have experienced the goodness of God in the preservation of the king. God showed his faithfulness by his power to maintain the kingdom of David. God is the guardian of the kingdom he himself founded. For David is called Messiah, or anointed, that the faithful might be persuaded that he was a lawful and sacred king, whom God had chosen by anointing. Faithful people attribute David's deliverance from great dangers to the grace of God.

Some trust in chariots (v. 7). It seems natural to almost all people to be more courageous and confident the more riches, power, and military forces they possess. The people of God here protest that they do not place their hope in their military forces, but only in the aid of God. As the Holy Spirit here sets God's assistance in opposition to human strength, it ought to be noticed that whenever our minds are occupied by human confidence, they fall at the same time into forgetfulness of God. It is impossible for those who expect victory by confiding in their own strength to have their eyes turned towards God. The inspired writer, therefore, uses the word *remember* to show that when the saints approach God they must throw off everything which would hinder them from placing an exclusive trust in him. This remembrance of God serves two important purposes to the faithful. First, however much power and resources they may possess, it prevents their confidence in these empty things, so that they do not expect any success except from the pure grace of God. Second, even if they are deprived of help, it strengthens and encourages them to call upon God both with confidence and constancy.

Psalm 21 with Aquinas – The Penalty of Rebellion

[Beginning in verse 10], the psalmist determines the enemy's penalty, first with respect to the evils inflicted upon them, and secondly the goods taken from them, at *Eliminate their fruit*. He sets down a three-fold order of penalties . . . First, there will be fire burning the surface of the earth: "In his going round, he will set (his enemies) on fire" (Ps 96). And so he says *Burn them as though in a fiery oven*, . . . oppressed as it were by fire on all sides . . . Or *as though in an oven*, that is it contains the fire in itself, and by this is understood the interior fire of perverse desire and anger which the evil suffer. . . .

Second, an examination of the judgement is determined, during which he will reproach the sins of the impious,[1] and will reveal the sentence of damnation, either vocally or mentally. And *thus the Lord in his anger will throw them into confusion*, that is he will incite the disturbance of sorrow concerning the evils inflicted and the goods taken away.

Third, they are enveloped by fire: and so, *the fire will consume them*: "The fire will consume them, which is not kindled" (Job 20), that is by human breath, but rather is kindled by divine power. . . .

At this point the removal of goods is determined. Of the goods which men enjoy in this world, some consist in the fruits which they long for in this life, and others in those which they desire to leave behind them: and they lose them both. And so, with respect to the first, he says *Eliminate their fruit from the earth*, for which fruit they have been seeking . . . With respect to the second he says *and their offspring, will pass away, from the sons of men*, namely from the society of the holy.

---

1 Impious – ungodly

Psalm 22 with Cassiodorus – The Wealth of the Poor

He has not despised or scorned the suffering of the afflicted one (v. 24), as people who boast of their distinction in this world often do; they are insulting toward the poor, despising beggars, assessing a person's cause by the quality of their clothing, so that if they are well dressed they are considered truthful, but if their clothing is shabby, they are regarded as a complete liar. But it is totally different in the eyes of God, who does not judge by clothing, and who does not honor wealth. He hears and aids the prayers of the faithful poor. The needy person is precious to him, provided that he is wealthy in holiness.

> **Cassiordorus on Psalm 22**
>
> *"The rich accumulate treasures on earth, the poor grow rich with heavenly abundance."*

The poor will eat and be satisfied (v. 26). These are the vows which the psalmist spoke of earlier. Realise that by poor he meant those who rejected the attractions of this world with the richest contempt; not the wealthy, stuffed with this world's happiness, but the poor, those hungry for God's kingdom. So he added: *will . . . be satisfied*; only those possessed by such hunger could be filled. *Those who seek the LORD will praise him— may your hearts live forever!* He stood by his previous words, for when the poor have been filled, they will praise the Lord. The poor praise the Lord, the rich exalt themselves. The rich accumulate treasures on earth, the poor grow rich with heavenly abundance. Their resources differ, but their mentalities are totally at odds. In short, the rich get their wealth from the world, the poor from God. How very different are the vows which they have fulfilled! The poor possess what they can never lose; the rich hold what not only the dead but even the living often lose.

Psalm 23 with Gertrude the Great – Cherishing God as Shepherd

The LORD is my shepherd, I lack nothing (v. 1)

Antiphon:[1] Hear me, I will teach you the fear of the Lord!

Prayer: Ah Jesus, good shepherd, make me hear and acknowledge your voice apart from everything that keeps me from you. Lift me up in your arms. Make me, your sheep newly delivered in your Spirit, rest against your breast. There teach me how I may fear you. There show me how I may cherish you. There, instruct me how I may follow you. Amen.

Then, as if you were somewhat refreshed by praising your God, your king, who is in the sanctuary, rise up now with heart wide open to delight in God, your lover, throwing into him all the love of your heart so that here he may nourish you with the blessing of his gentleness and there may lead you to the blessing of his plenitude[2] of fruition[3] forever. And [say] this with these words:

God, my God, because you are mine I lack nothing. And because I am yours, I will glory in you, God, my savior, for eternity. In all my sadness, you prepare for me in you the banquets of homage.[4] And where is my soul's well-being if not in you, O God of my life? If the memory of your praise is so dulcet[5] in this misery, what will it be like, my God, when in the splendor of your divinity your

---

1   Antiphon – musical recitation

2   Plenitude – abundance

3   Fruition – fruit

4   Homage – honor

5   Dulcet – sweet

glory appears? If the small drops of this foretaste of you are so refreshing, what will it be like, O God of my salvation, when you absorb my spirit in you?

He makes me lie down in green pastures (v. 2)

Oh how rich will be the pastures of the intimacy of your mellifluous[6] face when, admitted to the pastures of your gentleness here, (in, alas, an hour rare and for a moment brief) my soul, having melted, may thus pass over into you. Oh, what will be the refreshment in the presence of your divine countenance[7] when [even] here, at the waters of internal refreshment, you so merrily and so pleasantly nourish . . . my spirit and soul. God, my God, when you turn my soul to you, you do not allow me either to think or to sense anything but you, and you take me away from myself into you so that nothing can be of concern to me because you hide me from myself in you.

And then, what joy there will be, what exultation, what jubilation when you open to me the comeliness[8] of your divinity and my soul sees you face to face? Surely, then, there is nothing I would more willingly do than be at leisure and see your glory, God.

---

6 Mellifluous – soothing

7 Countenance – face

8 Comeliness – beauty

Psalm 24 with Gertrude the Great – The Generation That Seeks God

The earth is the LORD's, and everything in it (v. 1)

Psalm: To the Lord belongs the earth.

Antiphon:[1] *This is the generation of those who seek the Lord, who seek the face of the God of Jacob* (v. 6).

Prayer: Make me, dulcet[2] Jesus, to be listed and numbered in the generation of those who know you, God of Israel; among the generation of those who seek your face, God of Jacob; in the generation of those who cherish you, God of hosts. Ah! That I, an innocent woman, with [clean] hands and a clean heart, may accept your blessing and mercy, God, my savior.

---

1   Antiphon – musical recitation

2   Dulcet – sweet

Psalm 25 with Augustine – Walking the Narrow Road

I trust in you; do not let me be put to shame (v. 2). O my God, from trusting in myself I was brought even to this fleshly weakness; and I who on abandoning God wanted to be equal to God, fearing death from the smallest insect, was in ridicule ashamed for my pride; now, therefore, *in you I trust, I shall not be ashamed.*

Nor let my enemies triumph over me (v. 2), who by ensnaring me with serpent-like and secret suggestions, and prompting me with "Well done, well done," have brought me down to this. *For no one who hopes in you will ever be put to shame* (v. 3).

Let them be confounded who do vain things unrighteously, in order to acquire things that pass away. *Show me your ways, LORD, teach me your paths* (v. 4): not those which are broad and lead many to destruction (Matt 7:13); but your paths, narrow, and known to few, *teach me. Guide me in your truth* (v. 5), avoiding error. *And teach me*, for by myself I know nothing but falsehood. *For you are God my savior, and my hope is in you all day long* (v. 5). For banished by you from Paradise, and having taken my journey into a far country, I cannot return by myself, unless you meet the wanderer. My return awaits your mercy.

Good and upright is the LORD (v. 8). The Lord is gracious, since even sinners and the ungodly he pitied by forgiving all that is past. But the Lord is upright too; after the mercy of undeserved grace, he requires from us good works appropriate for the final judgment. *Therefore he instructs sinners in his ways.* For he first expressed mercy to bring them into the way. *He guides the humble in what is right* (v. 9), and will not condemn in the judgment those who follow his will rather than prefer their own. *And teaches them his way*, not to those who desire to run ahead, as if they were better able to rule themselves, but to those who do not respond proudly when the easy yoke and the light burden is laid upon them. *All the ways of the LORD are loving and faithful* (v. 10). He has exhibited love in forgiving sins, and faithfulness in judging rewards.

Psalm 26 with Augustine – God's Purifying Fire

Vindicate me, LORD, for I have led a blameless life (v. 1). Judge me, Lord, so that, after the mercy which you first showed me, I have some reward for my innocence. *I have trusted in the LORD and have not faltered. Test me, LORD, and try me* (vv. 1–2). If any of my secret sins are hidden from me, try me, Lord, making me known, not to you who sees everything, but to myself, and to others. *Examine my heart and my mind.* Purify my thoughts and desires as if with fire. *For I have always been mindful of your unfailing love* (v. 3). So that I will not be consumed by that fire, my eyes are not on my merits, but on your mercy, by which you have brought me on to such a life.

> **Augustine on Psalm 26**
>
> *"If any of my secret sins are hidden from me, try me, Lord, making me known, not to you who sees everything, but to myself, and to others."*

I do not sit with the deceitful (v. 4). I have not chosen to give my heart to those who try to provide what is impossible, although they may be blessed with earthly things. Nor do I associate with hypocrites. And since this is the cause of all wickedness, therefore I will not hide my conscience with those who work wickedly. *I abhor the assembly of evildoers* (v. 5). But to arrive at this council of pride, congregations of evildoers are formed, which I have hated. *And refuse to sit with the wicked* (v. 5), that is, I will not join or consent with them. *Do not take away my soul along with sinners* (v. 9). My soul has loved the beauty of your house.

My feet stand on level ground (v. 12). My love has not withdrawn from your righteousness. *In the great congregation*

I will praise the LORD. I will not hide your blessing, LORD, from those you have called; for next to my love for you I join the love for my neighbor.

Psalm 27 with Augustine –
Seeking the Most Precious of All

The LORD is my light and my salvation—whom shall I fear?
(v. 1). The Lord will give me both knowledge of himself,
and salvation. Who shall take me from him? *The LORD is
the stronghold of my life—of whom shall I be afraid?* The
Lord will repel all the assaults and snares of my enemy.
I will not be afraid of anyone.

*One thing I ask from the LORD, this only do I seek: that I may
dwell in the house of the LORD all the days of my life* (v. 4).
That as long as I am in this life, nothing may exclude me
from those who hold the unity and the truth of the Lord's
faith throughout the world. *To gaze on the beauty of the
LORD*, so that the delightful vision may appear to me that
I may enjoy face to face.

My heart says of you, "Seek his face!" (v. 8) For I have not
exposed my thoughts to people; but in secret, where only
you can hear. My heart has said to you: I have not asked
anything from you, except the reward of your presence. *Your
face, LORD, I will seek* (v. 8). I will persist in this search,
not for anything common, but your presence, Lord, that
I may love you freely, since I find nothing more precious.

Do not hide your face from me (v. 9), so I may find what
I seek. *Do not turn your servant away in anger*, if, while
seeking you, I fall in with something else. For what is
more grievous than this punishment to one who loves
and seeks the truth of your presence? *You have been my
Helper.* How shall I find help, if you do not help me? *Do
not reject me or forsake me, God my Savior.* Do not scorn
a mortal daring to seek the Eternal; for you, God, heal
the wound of my sin.

Psalm 28 with Theodoret of Cyrus – Calling for Justice

To you, LORD, I call; you are my Rock, do not turn a deaf ear to me. For if you remain silent, I will be like those who go down to the pit (v. 1). The psalm was spoken by David when he was pursued by Saul and was betrayed by false friends who tried to reveal his location to Saul, like Doeg (cf. 1 Sam 22:9) and the Ziphites (cf. 1 Sam 23:19–20) and many others. This psalm is suited to everyone encountering distress of this kind. Like David, it is possible for the person intent on persevering both to petition God and to secure his providence. *Do not drag me away with the wicked, with those who do evil, who speak cordially with their neighbors but harbor malice in their hearts* (v. 3). The prayer of David is to be uninvolved with those who practice deceit. He calls those who say one thing but mean another despicable.

This is surely the reason he also wishes that they reap the consequences of their exploits, saying, *Repay them for their deeds and for their evil work; repay them for what their hands have done and bring back on them what they deserve* (v. 4). Let no one think, however, that the righteous person is cursing his enemies. The words are not a mark of cursing but of a just verdict. *Bring back on them what they deserve*, he says, meaning, May their own schemes turn on them, which they plot against one another. This is also said in the seventh psalm, "The trouble they cause recoils on them; their violence comes down on their own heads" (Ps 7:16). Then he teaches the reason for the retribution: *Because they have no regard for the deeds of the LORD and what his hands have done* (v. 5). Now, they committed these things, he is saying, because they had no wish to learn either the divine word or work.

Psalm 29 with John Calvin – The Existence of God

The voice of the LORD is over the waters; the God of glory thunders (v. 3). David now rehearses the wonders of nature. It is fitting to celebrate the power of God as well as his goodness in his works. Since there is nothing in the ordinary course of nature, throughout heaven and earth, which does not invite us to the contemplation of God, he might have mentioned, as in Psalm 19:1, the sun and the stars or the earth with its riches; but he selects only those works of God which prove not only that the world was at first created by him, and is governed by his power, but which also awaken the sleepy, and drag them to adore him humbly in spite of themselves.

Experience, too, tells us that those who are most daring in their contempt of God are most afraid of thunder, storms, and such violent commotions. With great wisdom, therefore, does the prophet invite our attention to these instances which strike the rude and clueless with some sense of the existence of a God, and rouse them to action, however sluggish and inattentive they are. He does not say: the sun rises from day to day, and sheds abroad its life-giving beams, nor that the rain gently descends to fertilize the earth with its moisture. Instead, he speaks of thunder, violent storms, and things that strike human hearts with dread by their violence. God, it is true, speaks in all his creatures, but here the prophet mentions those sounds which rouse us from our drowsiness, or rather our numbness, by the loudness of their noise. We have said, that this language is chiefly directed to those who with stubborn recklessness, cast away from them all thought of God. The very examples he uses sufficiently declare that David's intention was to subdue by fear the stubbornness which does not willingly yield otherwise. Three times he repeats that God's voice is heard in great and violent storms, and in the next verse he adds that it is full of power and majesty.

Psalm 30 with Augustine – Giver of Eternal Joy

I will exalt you, LORD, for you have lifted me out of the depths (v. 1). I will praise your high Majesty. You *did not let my enemies gloat over me*, those who have so often tried to oppress me with various persecutions throughout the world.

LORD, my God, I called to you for help, and you healed me (v. 2). Lord, my God, I have cried to you, and I no longer carry around a body weakened and sick by mortality. *You, LORD, brought me up from the realm of the dead; you spared me from going down to the pit* (v. 3). You have saved me from deep darkness, and the lowest swamp of corruptible flesh. *When you hid your face, I was dismayed* (v. 7), for you have sometimes turned away your face from the sinner, and I became troubled, when you held back from me your illuminating knowledge. But now *you turned my wailing into dancing; you removed my sackcloth and clothed me with joy* (v. 11). You have torn off the veil of my sins, the sadness of my mortality; and have wrapped me with the first robe, with eternal joy.

Psalm 31 with Augustine – Desperate for God

Be merciful to me, LORD, for I am in distress (v. 9). How can these persecutors be so cruel, striking such dread into me? For I am no longer scared of death, but of torments and tortures. *My life is consumed by anguish* (v. 10). For my life is to praise you, but it is consumed by pain when the enemy says: Let them be tortured until they deny Him. *And my years by groaning.* The time that I pass in this world is not taken from me by death, but persists, and is spent groaning. *My strength fails because of my affliction.* I lack physical health, and racking pains come on me. I desire to die, but death delays in coming, and this unfulfilled desire weakens my confidence. *I am . . . an object of dread to my closest friends* (v. 11). And my dreadful hardship struck fear into them. *Those who see me on the street flee from me.* Because they do not understand my inward and invisible hope, they flee from me to things outward and visible. *I am forgotten as though I were dead; I have become like broken pottery* (v. 12). I have seemed to be lost to the Lord's service, living in this world, and gaining nothing, when all were afraid to associate with me.

Let your face shine on your servant (v. 16). Make it known to people who do not think that I belong to you that your face is watching me, and that I serve you.

How abundant are the good things that you have stored up for those who fear you (v. 19). Even those whom you correct, you love much: but if they go on carelessly, you hide from them the sweetness of your love, for whom it is profitable to fear you. But you perfected this sweetness for those who hope in you. For you do not withhold from them what they look for perseveringly until the end.

Psalm 32 with John Calvin – Reconciliation with God

David, having largely and painfully experienced what a miserable thing it is to feel God's sorrow over our sin, here teaches us that happiness consists only in the free forgiveness of sins, for nothing can be more terrible than to have God for our enemy; nor can he be gracious to us in any other way than by forgiving our sins.

Blessed is the one whose transgressions are forgiven (v. 1). Almost the whole world, turning their thoughts from God's judgment, brings upon themselves a deadly forgetfulness, and intoxicates themselves with deceitful pleasures. David, as if he had been struck with the fear of God's wrath, awakens others by declaring distinctly and loudly that the only people who are blessed are those to whom God is reconciled. The two reasons for which the psalmist insists so much on the subject of forgiveness are these: that he may, on the one hand, raise up those who are asleep, inspire the careless with thoughtfulness, and awaken the dull; and that he may, on the other hand, calm fearful and anxious minds with an assured and steady confidence.

The more greatly that anyone excels in holiness, the farther they feel from perfect righteousness, and the more clearly they perceive that they can trust in nothing but the mercy of God alone. Therefore, it appears that those who think the pardon of sin is necessary only when someone first becomes a Christian are badly mistaken. As believers are involved daily in many faults, it does not help them that they have once entered the way of righteousness, unless the same grace which brought them into it accompanies them to the last step of their life. Psalm 32 teaches that whenever sinners present themselves at the throne of mercy with true confession, they will find reconciliation with God awaiting them.

Psalm 33 with Basil the Great –
The Immeasurable Wisdom of God's Love and Justice

Sing joyfully to the LORD, you righteous; it is fitting for the upright to praise him (v. 1), not when the interests of your home are flourishing, not when you are in good health of body, not when your fields are filled with all sorts of fruits, but when you have the Lord—such immeasurable beauty, goodness, wisdom. Let the joy that is in him be enough for you. *The LORD loves righteousness and justice; the earth is full of his unfailing love* (v. 5).

> **Basil the Great on Psalm 33**
>
> *"Let the joy that is in him be enough for you."*

It is as if love is God's co-worker, standing before the royal throne of his judgment, and thus he leads each one to justice. "If you, LORD, kept a record of sins, Lord, who could stand?" (Ps 130:3) Neither is love without justice, nor justice without love. He loves mercy, therefore, before judgment, and after mercy he comes to justice. However, these qualities are joined to each other, love and justice, because without justice, love alone produces arrogance, and judgment alone causes despair. The Judge wishes to have mercy on you and to share his own compassion, but on condition that he finds you humble after sin, repentant, lamenting your evil deeds, announcing publicly without shame sins committed secretly, begging the brethren to labor with you in making things right. In short, if he sees that you are worthy of pity, he provides his mercy for you willingly. But, if he sees your heart unrepentant, your mind proud, your disbelief of the future life, and your fearlessness of the judgment, then he desires judgment for you, just as a reasonable and kind doctor tries at first with hot compresses to reduce a tumor, but, when he sees that the mass is rigid and refuses to soften, casting away the gentle method of treatment, he prefers from then on to use a knife. Therefore, God loves mercy in the case of those repenting, but he also loves judgment in the case of the unyielding. *And on those whose hope is in his unfailing love* (v. 18). The humility of those who serve the Lord indicates how they hope in his mercy. He who does not trust in his own good deeds nor expects to be justified by his works has, as his only hope of salvation, the mercies of God.

Psalm 34 with Augustine –
Seeking the Lord Above All Else

I will extol the LORD at all times (v. 1). When shall you *extol the Lord*? When He blesses you? When your worldly possessions abound? When you have abundant wealth; when your physical health remains sound; when all your children grow up, no one dies prematurely, and happiness reigns in your house, then will you bless the Lord? No, but *at all times.*

I sought the LORD, and he answered me (v. 4). Have you not been heard? Then you must not have sought the Lord himself. Notice, he did not say, I asked the Lord for gold, and he heard me; I asked the Lord for long life, and he heard me; I asked the Lord for this or that, and he heard me. It is one thing to seek anything from the Lord, another to seek the Lord himself. *The lions may grow weak and hungry, but those who seek the LORD lack no good thing* (v. 10). You see that many wicked rich men grow old, and come to the end of life amid great abundance and riches. You see their funeral celebrated lavishly—the man himself brought rich even to the grave, having been laid in an ivory coffin, his family weeping—and you say to yourself, I know that man's crimes! Has the Scripture deceived me by speaking falsely? When was this man in need? When did he suffer hunger? But as for me, daily I rise up to go to Church, daily I kneel, daily I seek the Lord, and have nothing good. This man did not seek the Lord, and he died in the midst of all these good things! However, when you are filled with spiritual riches, can you be poor? And are you poor when the chamber of your heart is filled with such jewelry of virtues, justice, truth, charity, faith, endurance? Unveil your riches, if you have them, and compare them with the riches of the rich. "Blessed are those who hunger and thirst for righteousness, for they will be filled" (Matt 5:6).

Someone says, *The righteous cry out, and the LORD hears them; he delivers them from all their troubles* (v. 17), but I have cried, and he did not deliver me! Either I am not righteous, or I do not do the things he commands, or he does not see me. Fear not. Only do what he commands, and if he does not deliver you physically, he will deliver you spiritually. *The righteous person may have many troubles* (v. 19): Does he say, "Therefore let Christians be righteous, and let them hear my word, so they may suffer no hardship?" He does not promise this. Rather, if they are unrighteous they have fewer troubles, if righteous they have many. But after few hardships, or none, the unrighteous will come to eternal hardship, but the righteous will come to everlasting peace, where they will never suffer any harm.

Psalm 35 with Augustine – Retribution and Reward

Contend, LORD, with those who contend with me; fight against those who fight against me. . . . Brandish spear and javelin against those who pursue me (vv. 1, 3). Who persecutes you? By chance your neighbor, or someone you have offended, or someone you have wronged, or who would take what is yours, or someone whose sin you rebuke, or someone who is jealous of you. These enemies are indeed against us, and they persecute us: but other enemies we fight invisibly, who the Apostle warns us about, saying, "Our struggle is not against flesh and blood," that is, against humans; not against those we can see, but against those we can not see; "against the rulers, against the authorities, against the powers of this dark world" (Eph 6:12).

> **Augustine on Psalm 35**
>
> *"Seek him, who made all things, and in him and from him you will have all things which he made."*

But what can be done? *Since they hid their net for me without cause* (v. 7). I have done nothing against them, I have hurt them not at all. *May the net they hid entangle them* (v. 8). There is nothing more just than a magnificent retribution! They have hidden a trap for me; let a trap come upon them. They are deceived when they want to deceive. Mischief will come to them, where they made mischief. This then for the wicked that would hurt me.

Then my soul will rejoice in the LORD and delight in his salvation (v. 9), not seeking other riches, not seeking earthly pleasure, but loving freely the true Spouse. For what better thing than God will be given to me? When God says to you, ask what you want, what will you ask? Empty your mind, stretch forward as far as possible, and enlarge your desire. It is not anyone other than Almighty God who said, "ask what you will," yet nothing will you find more precious than the One who made all things. Seek him, who made all things, and in him and from him you will have all things which he made. All things are precious, because all are beautiful, but what is more beautiful than he? They are strong, but what is stronger than he? And nothing would he rather give you than himself.

Psalm 36 with Augustine –
A Sincere Search-and-Destroy Mission for Sin

The wicked have determined to sin: *there is no fear of God before their eyes* (v. 1). David speaks not of one person, but of a race of ungodly people who fight against themselves, by not understanding so they may live well; not because they cannot, but because they will not. So it is when people love their own sins and hate God's Commandments. For the Word of God is your enemy if you are a friend to your ungodliness; but if you are an enemy to your ungodliness, the Word of God is your friend, as well as the enemy of your ungodliness. *In their own eyes they flatter themselves too much to detect or hate their sin* (v. 2). They work hard not to find their own sin. For there are people who try to seek out their sin, and fear to find it; because if they find it, it is said to them, "Depart from it." Thus they seek it, but fear finding it; for they seek it deceitfully. For if they had worked sincerely rather than deceitfully, they would now have found it out and hated it; now they have found it out, but they defend it. Therefore, they worked deceitfully when they looked for it.

As for the righteous, *they feast on the abundance of your house* (v. 8). People drowning themselves in drunkenness receive wine without measure, but lose their senses. When the righteous have received the indescribable joy of being in God's presence, they have lost the human soul, replacing it with the deep satisfaction of the fullness of God's House. *You give them drink from your river of delights.* What is that pleasure? A torrent quenching thirst. Let the one who thirsts now have hope. "Blessed are those who hunger and thirst for righteousness, for they will be filled" (Matt 5:6).

Psalm 37 with Augustine –
The Apparent Success of the Wicked

Christians, you are disturbed when you see people with bad lives prospering, and surrounded with abundance of things. You see them sound in health, distinguished with honors, their family unvisited by misfortune, the happiness of their relatives, their influence, their life uninterrupted by any sad event, their external resources most affluent. Your heart says that there is no divine judgment, that all things happen at random. For if God regarded human affairs, would his iniquity flourish, and my innocence suffer? *Do not fret because of those who are evil or be envious of those who do wrong; for like the grass they will soon wither, like green plants they will soon die away* (vv. 1–2). That which to you seems long, is soon in the sight of God. Conform yourself to God; and it will be soon to you. That which he here calls grass occupies only the surface of the ground; it has no depth of root. In the winter it is green; but when the summer sun begins to scorch, it will wither away. For now it is winter. Your glory does not yet appear. But if your love has deep roots, like trees during winter, then when the frost passes away, the summer (that is, the day of judgment) will come and the green grass will wither away. Then the glory of the trees will appear.

What should you do then? *Trust in the LORD* (v. 3). For they too trust, but not in the Lord. Their hope is short-lived, frail, fleeting. *Trust in the LORD and do good.* Do not do that evil which you see in those men, who are prosperous in wickedness. . . . And you will *enjoy safe pasture.* What are the riches of that land? Her riches are her Lord! Her riches are her God! It is said to him, "LORD, you alone are my portion and my cup" (Ps 16:5).

God is our possession, and we are at the same time God's possession. *Commit your way to the LORD; trust in him, and he will do this* (v. 5). Mention to him what you suffer, mention to him what you desire. *For the salvation of the righteous comes from the LORD; he is their stronghold in time of trouble. The LORD helps them and delivers them; he delivers them from the wicked and saves them, because they take refuge in him* (vv. 39–40).

Psalm 38 with Augustine – God, the Righteous Judge

LORD, I wait for you; you will answer, Lord my God (v. 15). He warns you about what to do if trials come. For if you seek to defend yourself, perhaps your defense is not heard by any one. Then you struggle, as if you had lost your cause, because you have none to defend or to bear testimony in your favor. Maintain your innocence within, where no one can pervert your cause. Perhaps false witnesses have prevailed against you before humans. Will it prevail before God, where your cause must be pleaded? When God is Judge, there will be no other witness than your own conscience. In the presence of a just Judge, and of your own conscience, fear nothing but your own cause. If you have not a bad cause, you will have no accuser to dread, no false witness to disprove, nor truthful witness to find. Bring into court a good conscience, so you may say, *LORD, I wait for you; you will answer, Lord my God.*

And my pain is ever with me (v. 17). What sorrow is that? Perhaps a sorrow for my punishment. And, in good truth, let me say to you, people mourn for their punishments, not for the causes they are punished for. But see here the reason for the psalmist's sorrow! It is not a sorrow arising from punishment. For punishment is a remedy against sins. Do not be free from anxiety when you have confessed your sin, as if you can always confess your sin and commit it again. Declare your iniquity in such a manner as to be *troubled* by your sin. What is meant by *I am troubled by my sin?* (v. 18) If you were to say, "I am troubled by my wound," you mean "I will try to have it healed." For to be troubled by one's sin, means to be ever struggling, ever exerting yourself, earnestly and zealously, to heal your wound.

Discussion Questions

In a world where needs are rampant, Psalm 23:1 makes a bold statement: "The LORD is my shepherd, I lack nothing." What in your life seems to contradict this? What evidence is there that this is true?

Have you ever felt that God has abandoned you in your hardship? What do you think of Augustine's claim (on Psalm 34) that those who have not been heard "must not have sought the Lord himself"?

John Calvin's reflection on Psalm 20 warns about putting our confidence in anything but God. Has your or someone else's failure ever exposed your false confidence? What did it show you about the state of your heart?

In Psalm 31, the psalmist struggles desperately. What gives him the strength to go on? How can you find this strength when you are struggling?

What has it been like for you to develop new rhythms of praying the Psalms? Has it made a difference in your life already? If not, keep at it! Change takes time.

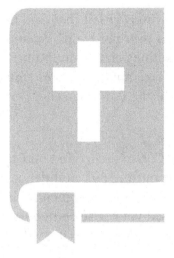

BIBLICAL STUDIES

Chapter 3

Psalms 39–59

Psalm 39 with Ambrose – Keeping Silent

I will watch my ways and keep my tongue from sin. I will put a muzzle on my mouth while in the presence of the wicked (v. 1). Have no doubt about it, when people annoy and torment you for doing the right thing, those people are the servants of the most wicked sinner of all. They are slaves of the author of every evil deed. David saw this with prophetic eyes and recognized the face of the evil one. So he kept quiet. He had no wish whatever to do the will of him who ruins one's peace of mind. He simply said nothing. He closed his doors in silence; patience lay before him, and silence kept a sleepless vigil. No enemy could creep in, and from his closed lips came no ambivalent speech, no careless talk. Far mightier is the patient person who can govern himself than the valiant one who captures fortresses. The righteous person is his own eternal guard.

Ambrose on Psalm 39

"The reports of other people cannot nail any sin to a conscience that knows itself to be innocent."

So I remained utterly silent, not even saying anything good (v. 2). If you know there is sin, be silent. Do not add to your guilt by denying it. If you are not aware of sin, be silent. You are secure in your innocence. The reports of other people cannot nail any sin to a conscience that knows itself to be innocent. *Save me from all my transgressions* (v. 8). It is not merely one mistake that he is confessing, for he prays to be forgiven for all his sins. He knows that without God's forgiveness no one can be saved. For we were born in sin.

Psalm 40 with Augustine – Hoping in the Lord

Blessed is the one who trusts in the LORD, who does not look to the proud, to those who turn aside to false gods (v. 4). Let the Lord your God be your hope. Hope for nothing else from the Lord your God; but let the Lord your God himself be your hope. Many people hope to obtain riches from God's hands, and many earthly honors. Instead, seek after God himself. Indeed, despising everything else, make your way to him! Forget other things; remember him. Leave other things behind, and press forward to him. Surely he set you right, when you turned away from the right path; he guides you to your destination now that you are on the right path. Let him be your hope who guides you to your destination.

But as for me, I am poor and needy (v. 17). I am not rich because I am not proud. And what would you do, O poor and needy man? Beg at God's door; "Knock and the door will be opened to you" (Matt 7:7). Let him who made you care for you. He who cared for you before you existed, how will he fail to care for you, now that you are what he destined you to be? For now you are a believer, now you are walking in the *way of righteousness*. The members of Christ—the Body of Christ extended everywhere—are asking of God, as one single person, one single beggar! For he too was poor, who "though he was rich, yet for your sake he became poor, so that you through his poverty might become rich" (2 Cor 8:9). He makes the truly poor ones rich, and makes the falsely rich ones poor. First there will come days of hardship, and of greater hardship. They will come even as the Scripture speaks, and as days advance, sufferings also increase. Let no one promise himself what the Gospel does not promise.

Psalm 41 with Caesarius of Arles – Confession as the Key to Healing

Have mercy on me, LORD; heal me, for I have sinned against you (v. 4). God will heal you if you only admit your wound. You lie under the physician's hands. Patiently request his aid. If he bathes, or burns, or cuts it, bear it calmly. Do not even pay any attention to the pain, provided you are cured. You will be cured if you present yourself to the doctor. Not that he does not see you if you hide, but confession is the very beginning of restoration to health. "Let a righteous man strike me—that is a kindness; let him rebuke me—that is oil on my head. My head will not refuse it, for my prayer will still be against the deeds of evildoers" (Ps 141:5). What does this mean? It would be better for me if the righteous person who sees my sin would correct me, not spare me, tell me that I have done wrong, be furious over my sin, in order to free me from it. They may seem to speak harshly, but within they are full of kindness, according to the words: "Let a righteous man strike me— that is a kindness." When the righteous person therefore strongly rebukes, it shows kindness, for it all arises from parental pity and not hostile cruelty. Since they do not want you to die in sin, they love you all the more when they perform surgery. They are unwilling to allow your other body parts to decay from the rottenness of sin. They draw a blade, but do not be afraid or dread it. The knife is not applied against you, but against your wound.

> **Caesarius of Arles on Psalm 41**
>
> *"Confession is the very beginning of restoration to health."*

What fuels the sinner but the admiration of a flatterer? If anyone sharply rebukes another, they seem to rave at their sin and freely to tell them what evil they have done. If the other person, perhaps, imitates the one who is chiding him, they will also get angry at their sin. Now, if we are true spiritual physicians and attend carefully to the remedy of your souls, we should not flatter anyone, nor should you do so to us. Let us confess our sins, not excuse them. You have done wrong and are guilty; confess it, and you will be forgiven.

Psalm 42 with Augustine – Longing for God

As the deer pants for streams of water, so my soul pants for you, my God. My soul thirsts for God, for the living God (vv. 1–2). Who says this? It is ourselves, if we are willing! And why ask who it is, when it is in your power to be the one you are asking about? Such "longing" is not found in all who enter the Church: let all who have "tasted" the sweetness "of the LORD" (Ps 34:8) and who relish Christ, say: *As the deer pants for streams of water, so my soul pants for you, my God.*

My tears have been my food day and night, while people say to me all day long, "Where is your God?" (v. 3). My tears, he says, have not been bitterness, but my food. Those very tears were sweet to me: being thirsty for that fountain; since I was not yet able to drink from it, I have eagerly made my tears my food. For he did not say, "my tears became my drink," so he would not seem to have longed for them as for streams of water, but still retaining that thirst by which I am pulled towards the streams, my tears became my food, while I am not yet there.

Why, my soul, are you downcast? Why so disturbed within me (vv. 5, 11). And, as it seems to answer, "Should I not be disturbed, since I am surrounded by great evil? Should I not be disturbed, since I long for what is good, thirsting and laboring for it?" What should I say, but *hope in God, for I will yet praise him.* This is the answer to a disturbed soul, and would gladly account for its disturbance from the evils that abound. Meanwhile dwell in hope, for "hope that is seen is no hope at all. Who hopes for what they already have? But if we hope for what we do not yet have, we wait for it patiently" (Rom 8:24–25).

Psalm 43 with Augustine – Patience to Endure

Vindicate me, my God, and plead my cause against an unfaithful nation (v. 1). I do not dread your judgment, because I know your mercy. Vindicate me, he cries. Now, meanwhile, in this life, you do not yet separate my place because I am to live with the "weeds" even to the time of the "harvest" (Matt 13:30). You do not separate my rain from theirs or my light from theirs. *Plead my cause* (v. 1). Let a difference be made between the one who believes in you, and the one who does not. Our weakness is the same; but our consciences are not: our sufferings are the same; but our longings are not. "The longings of the wicked will come to nothing," (Ps 112:10) but as for the desire of the righteous, we might well doubt, if he were not sure who promised. He who promises is the object of our desires: He will give us himself. He already has!

Patience is needed in order to endure until the harvest, a certain distinction without separation, for they are together with us, and therefore not yet separated, but the weeds are still weeds, and the corn still corn, and therefore they are already distinct. Since then a kind of strength is needed, let us request it from him who invites us to be strong.

Psalm 44 with Augustine – A Prayer for Rescue

At the time when the Church was suffering under the persecution of the Gentiles, Paul quoted from this psalm to encourage patience: *For your sake we face death all day long; we are considered as sheep to be slaughtered* (v. 22; Rom 8:36). Let us then hear in this psalm the voice of the martyrs; and see how good is the cause they plead.

You have rejected and humbled us (v. 9). You have done this not before our own consciences, but in the sight of people. For there was a time when Christians were persecuted; when in every place they were outcasts, when in every place "Christian!" was an insult. Where then is *my King and my God, who decrees victories for Jacob?* (v. 4) Where is he who did all those works, which *our ancestors have told us?* (v. 1) Where is he who will do all those things which he revealed to us by his Spirit? Is he changed? No.

Rise up and help us; rescue us because of your unfailing love (v. 26), that is to say, not for the sake of my good works, but because you have offered to do it, not because I am worthy for you to redeem me. For this very thing, *that we had not forgotten you* (v. 17); that *our hearts had not turned back* (v. 18); that *we have not spread out our hands to a foreign god* (v. 20); how could we have been able to achieve this, except with your help? How could we have strength for it, except through your appealing to us within, exhorting us, and not forsaking us? Whether we suffer hardship, or rejoice in prosperity, redeem us, not for our merits, but for your name's sake.

Psalm 45 with Mary Sidney Herbert – A Royal Wedding

My heart indites an argument[1] of worth,
the praise of him that doth the scepter sway;[2]
My tongue the pen to paint his praises forth,
shall write as swift, as swiftest writer may.
Then to the king these are the words I say:
Fairer art thou than sons of mortal race;
because high God hath blessed thee for ay,[3]
thy lips, as springs, do flow with speaking grace.

Thy honored sword gird to thy mighty side,
O thou that dost all things in might excel;
With glory prosper, on with triumph ride,
since justice, truth, and meekness with thee dwell.
So that right hand of thine shall teaching tell[4]
such things to thee, as well may terror[5] bring,
and terror such, as never erst befell[6]
to mortal minds at sight of mortal king.

---

1 Indites an argument – writes on a theme

2 Sway – yield

3 Ay – ever

4 Tell – recount

5 Terror – deep awe

6 Never erst befell – never before happened

Sharp are thy shafts[7] to cleave their hearts in twain[8]
whose heads do cast[9] thy conquests to withstand;
Good cause to make the meaner[10] people fain[11]
with willing hearts to undergo[12] thy hand.
Thy throne, O God, doth never-falling stand;
Thy scepter, ensign[13] of thy kingly might,
to righteousness is linked with such a band,
that righteous hand still holds thy scepter right.

Justice in love, in hate thou holdest wrong;
This makes that God, who so doth hate and love:
Glad-making oil[14] that oil on thee hath flung,
which thee exalts thine equals far above.
The fragrant riches of Sabean grove,
myrrh, aloes, cassia, all thy robes do smell;[15]
When thou from ivory palace dost remove[16]
thy breathing odors all thy train excel.[17]

---

7   Shafts – arrows

8   Cleave . . . in twain – divide in two

9   Cast – plot

10 Meaner – common

11 Fain – gladly

12 Undergo – submit to

13 Ensign – emblem

14 Glad-making oil – ointment that makes glad

15 Smell – infuse with fragrance

16 Remove – leave

17 Thy breathing odors all thy train excel – the fragrance will fill the air

Daughters of kings among thy courtly band,
by honoring thee of thee do honor hold;[18]
On thy right side thy dearest queen doth stand
richly arrayed[19] in cloth of Ophir gold.
O daughter, hear what now to thee is told:
Mark[20] what thou hear, and what thou mark'st obey;
Forget to keep in memory enrolled
the hours, and folk, where first thou saw the day.[21]

So in the king, thy king, a dear delight
thy beauty shall both breed, and bred maintain;
For only he on thee hath lordly right,
him only thou with awe must entertain.
Then unto thee both Tirus[22] shall be fain[23]
presents present, and richest nations more,
with humble suit[24] thy Royal grace to gain
to thee shall do such homage[25] as they owe.

---

18 By honoring thee of thee do honor hold – your subjects are themselves honored

19 Arrayed – dressed

20 Mark – take note of

21 Forget . . . where first thou saw the day – forget your childhood

22 Tirus – Tyre

23 Fain – willing

24 Suit – petition

25 Do such homage – give honor

This Queen that can a king her father call,
doth only she[26] in upper garment shine?
Nay underclothes, and what she weareth all—[27]
gold is the stuff the fashion art divine.
Brought to the king in robe embroidered fine,
her maids of honor shall on her attend;
With such, to whom more favor shall assign
in nearer place their happy days to spend.

Brought shall thee be with mirth and marriage joy,
and enter so the palace of the king;
Then let no grief their mind, O queen, annoy,
nor parents left thy sad remembrance sting.
Instead of parents, children thou shalt bring,
of partad'gd[28] earth the kings and lords to be.
Myself thy name in lasting verse will sing;
The world shall make no end of thanks to thee.

---

26 Only she – she only

27 What she weareth all – everything she wears

28 Partad'gd – divided into portions

Psalm 46 with Gertrude the Great – Delighting in God

Come and see what the LORD has done (v. 8).

At this point, arouse your soul to delight in God:

O my soul, now lift your eyes; look upon and regard the might of your king, the grace of your God, [and] the charity of your salvation to which you have come near. Be at leisure now; taste and see how dulcet[1] and how remarkable is the spouse whom you have chosen above thousands.

See what and how great is that glory for which you have condemned the world.

See what that good is like for which you have waited.

See what the homeland is like for which you have sighed.

See what the prize is like for which you have labored.

―――――

See who your God is, what he is like and how great he is, whom you have cherished, whom you have adored and for whom you have always wished.

O God of my life, I do not know how I may worthily praise you or with what I may reward you, my beloved, for all the good with which you have rewarded me. Consequently, I offer you in me, and me in you, my cherished Jesus, as a burnt offering of praise to you. I have nothing further. This itself that I am and live in you, this I give to you totally.

―――――

1   Dulcet – sweet

You are my life. You are my sufficiency. You are my glory. You are the proof of mercy that is resplendent[2] in my soul. To you be praise and supreme thanksgiving. Oh, when will I burn up the marrow of my soul on your altar and, in this holy fire that continuously burns there, inflame my heart and immolate[3] myself totally as a sacrifice of praise to you.

Ah! O God, my holy gentleness, widen my heart in you, and extend my soul in order that all my viscera[4] may be filled with your glory. Oh, when will my soul be told: Turn to your rest because the Lord has been the one to do you good? Oh, when will I hear that merriest voice: Come, enter into the inner chamber of your spouse? Oh, when will I rest and fall asleep in you, Jesus, my most dulcet[5] peace, that I may see your glory?

---

2   Resplendent – glorious shining

3   Immolate – burn

4   Viscera – inner organs

5   Most dulcet – sweetest

Psalm 47 with Augustine – Imitating Abraham's Faith

He chose our inheritance for us, the pride of Jacob, whom He loved (v. 4). Esau was born first, and Jacob last; but Jacob was preferred to the firstborn, who through gluttony lost his birthright. So it is written, He longed for the stew, and his brother said to him, "First sell me your birthright" (Gen 25:31). Esau loved what his appetite desired more than what he had earned by being born first, so he laid aside his birthright.

The nobles of the nations assemble as the people of the God of Abraham (v. 9). The God of Abraham, and the God of Isaac, and the God of Jacob. Accordingly the Jews proudly said, "Abraham is our father" (John 8:39), priding themselves in their father's name, carrying his flesh, but not holding to his faith. But the Lord said to them, "If you were Abraham's children, then you would do what Abraham did" (John 8:39). Again, the nobles of the nations: not the nobles of one people, but the nobles of all people have assembled. Belonging to these nobles was that Centurion too, who you heard about when the Gospel was read. For he was a Centurion with honor and power among men. Admiring his faith, Jesus denounces the Jews' unbelief. "I say to you that many will come from the east and the west," not belonging to the nation of Israel, "and will take their places at the feast with Abraham, Isaac, and Jacob in the kingdom of heaven" (Matt 8:11). They are not Abraham's descendants; yet they will come and sit down with him in the kingdom of heaven, and be his children. How? By following his faith. "But the subjects of the kingdom," that is, the Jews, "will be thrown outside, into the darkness, where there will be weeping and gnashing of teeth" (Matt 8:12). Those who are born of Abraham's flesh shall be condemned to outer darkness, and those who have imitated Abraham's faith shall sit down with him in the kingdom of heaven.

Psalm 48 with Mary Sidney Herbert – Jerusalem, the City of God

He that hath eternal being
glorious is, and glorious shows,
in the city he hath chose,
where stands his holy hill.
Hill Zion, hill of fairest seeing,
city of the king most great,
seated in a northly seat,
all climes[1] with joy doth fill
in each palace she containeth.
God a well-known rock remaineth.

One day kings—a day appointed
there with joined force to be,—
See they it? The things they see,
amaze their mated[2] minds.
Flying, trembling, disappointed,
so they fear, and so they fare,
as the wife, whose woeful care
the pangs of child-bed[3] finds
Right as ships from Tarshish going,
crushed with blasts of Eurus[4] blowing.

---

1 Climes – climates, regions

2 Mated – amazed

3 Child-bed – childbirth

4 Eurus – east wind

Now our sight hath matched our hearing
in what state God's city stands,
how supported by his hands
God ever holds the same.
In thy temple's midst appearing
we thy favor Lord attend;[5]
Righteous Lord, both free from end,
thy fame doth match thy name;
thy just hand brings Zion gladness,
turns to mirth[6] all Judah's sadness

Compass[7] Zion in her standing,
tell[8] her towers, mark[9] her forts;
Note with care the stately ports[10]
her royal houses bear.
for that age's understanding,
which shall come, when we shall go,
glad in former time to know,
how many what they were.
For God is our God forever,
us 'til death forsaking never.

---

5   Attend – await

6   Mirth – joy

7   Compass – go around

8   Tell – count

9   Mark – take note of

10 Ports – entrances

Psalm 49 with Theodoret of Cyrus – The Folly of Earthly Riches

Why should I fear when evil days come? (v. 5). I fear and dread the day of judgment, on which the righteous Judge will repay everyone according to their works (2 Tim 4:8). Now, aware of this, keep fear before your eyes regarding your own behavior. But if you were to ask why I am afraid, listen closely: it is an evil day, about which countless speeches are made in the inspired Scriptures. The cause of my fear is the life of lawlessness, through which I strayed from the straight and narrow. *Those who trust in their wealth and boast of their great riches* (v. 6): while I tremble in fear at the expected day, you in your affluence pay no attention to it, being instead puffed up with luxury of your possessions and trusting in temporary things as though permanent. *The foolish and the senseless also perish, leaving their wealth to others. Their tombs will remain their houses forever, their dwellings for endless generations* (v. 11), robbed not only of wisdom but also of influence and all wealth, they will meet their end, removed from their lavish homes to graves, and forced to occupy them forever. After this he provides explanation and advice for those condemned to a life of poverty and worn out through the arrogance of the rich. *Do not be overawed when others grow rich, when the splendor of their houses increases; for they will take nothing with them when they die, their splendor will not descend with them* (vv. 16–17). Do not consider present prosperity any great thing, he is saying. Wealth that catches all eyes is not lasting. Those who raise their eyebrows and are puffed up over it will soon leave it all behind and die, *though while they live they count themselves blessed* (v. 18). Some people declare the one with abundant wealth blessed while alive, but once dead they call him three times more miserable.

Psalm 50 with Augustine –
Living in Light of the Coming Judgment

From Zion, perfect in beauty, God shines forth. Our God comes and will not be silent; a fire devours before him, and around him a tempest rages (vv. 2–3). Those who have begun to feel the sweetness of wisdom and truth know how great a punishment it is to be separated from the face of God: but those who have not tasted that sweetness, if they do not yet yearn for the face of God, let them fear fire; let punishments terrify those who are not won over by rewards. If what God promises is of no value to you, tremble at what he threatens. The sweetness of his presence will come. For now, you are not changed, you are not awakened, you do not sigh or yearn. You embrace your sins and the delights of your flesh, you are heaping kindling upon yourself, the fire will come. Threats should not compel you to do evil, they should not prevent you from doing good. But by the threats of God, by threats of everlasting fire, you are discouraged from doing evil, invited to do good. Why does it upset you, except because you do not believe? Let everyone then examine their hearts, and see what faith remains there. If we believe in a coming judgment, let us live well. Now is the time of mercy; the time of judgment is coming. Even then people will repent, but it will not help. Let there be repentance now, while there is fruit of repentance; let there be sorrow of heart and tears now, lest he come and uproot you. For when he uproots you, a fiery judgment follows.

Let not the poor tremble beneath God's warning. What God requires from us, he first provides; only be devoted. God does not demand what he has not given, and to all people he has given what he demands. *Call upon me in the day of trouble: I will deliver you, and you will honor me* (v. 15). For this purpose I have allowed the day of trouble to come to you: because perhaps if you were not troubled, you would not call on me.

Psalm 51 with Katharina Schütz Zell – A Prayer of Confession

Prayer [51:1–2] O God, be gracious to me according to Your goodness, wipe out and forgive my sins according to Your great mercy. O God, wash me now again and purify me from my sins through the blood of Jesus Christ Your little Lamb. *Lament* [51:3–4a] For I recognize again my misdeeds, and my sin is ever unceasingly before my inward eyes. I cannot forget it, because I have sinned against You Yourself and I have done evil before You (from whom nothing is hidden). *Speech-Narration* [51:4b] Therefore You would also be just in the word of Your law, which You have given and which I have not kept. You may also not be rebuked even if You have tested and judged our thoughts (and see) how gladly we always seek an escape and want to excuse ourselves. *Lament and Confession* So I must confess that You are faithful and I am wicked and lying. [51:5] See, Lord, how could it be otherwise? Indeed I was begotten from sinful seed and my mother also conceived me in sin. That sin, however, I, O Lord, have allowed to reign in me— that sin which I could well have killed through Your grace of the free Spirit. . . .

Katharina Schütz Zell on Psalm 51

"O my God! I have gotten myself into this mess, but I can never get out of it without You!"

Lament [51:6] O my God! I have gotten myself into this mess, but I can never get out of it without You! But since You, Lord, desire truth, and since (besides that) by Your special mercy You allow me to know that same secret truth, so that I should confess in truth before You and pray to You to forgive my sins—*Prayer* so I, a miserable person, ask You, my Lord and God, from my whole heart and longing, with all the might that You have given to me: turn Your mercy toward me and for the sake of Your reputation do not allow me to lack Your former well-known goodness. Have mercy on me, O God, have mercy on me! . . . [51:14, 16–17] O God, You are my God and savior. Save me indeed from my sins of blood-guilt, which You know are in me and which I now confess before you.

Speech-Narration I would gladly free myself from [my sins] before You, with payment and offering of my body and life as sacrifice. Since, however, that does not please You and is not enough to pay for sins, so I know nothing to bring to You except a broken and quiet heart, a heart that is sad and sorrowful before You because it has so provoked You. *Prayer* So be gracious to me, O Lord, only for the sake of Your good will, Your great name and Your fatherly mercy, in Jesus Christ the holy, innocent, living sacrifice who redeems me from eternal anguish and fear. Amen.

Psalm 52 with Aquinas –
Turning Away from Sin and toward God

In justification, two things are necessary: namely, a turning away from sin, and a conversion to God. And so, two things are in sin, as a contrary; namely, a turning away from God, and a turning towards sin. . . . First, he indicates the wickedness of sinners; second, he indicates the evil things that are done by sinners. . . . So, this psalm is divided into two parts. In the first part, he relates the wickedness of the sinner, who clings to iniquity. In the second, he relates the justice of the holy people, thus, *But I, as a fruitful olive tree.* Regarding the first, he does two things. First, he speaks of the fault of the evil people. Second, of their punishment, so, *Therefore will God destroy thee for ever.* But, it should be known, that in the man who clings to sin, three things follow in an order. The first is the delight of the sin. The second is the thought of the sin: for we think within those things that we take delight in. The third is the glorying on his part of having perpetrated the sin. For one takes joy quite naturally when one does what one loves. It proceeds, therefore, in this way from the final end to the first, from the glory of the evil people in the act of sin. Second, from the thought about the sin, whence, *All the day long.* Third, from the love of the sin, whence, *you have loved.* . . .

The just shall see. Here it is the fruit of the punishment that is set down: for God punishes here, and assigns punishments according to their usefulness for the just. First, according to the fear of punishment, so, *and fear.* And this can be metaphorically of the condition of the present life, in which the just fear by having reverence for God, and fall away from the condition in which they are in: Romans

11: "Be not highminded, but fear." But those who are in the kingdom of their father do not fear to fall from any condition, for they are confirmed in the perfection of grace, for they are not separated, but fear with filial[1] reverence: "The fear of the Lord is holy," etc. (Psalm 18). And God's justice will be revered. But, in the present life, more particularly they fear.

Second, according to their contempt for sin and present prosperity. And first, the derision is set down. Second, the cause of the derision is set down, at, *Behold*. In reference to the first, *At him*, that is against him, namely the sinner, *Shall laugh*, that is, they contemn[2] his confidence and prosperity.

---

1   Filial – devoted

2   Contemn – regard with contempt

Psalm 53 with Augustine – Cultivating the Right Kind of Fear

The fool says in his heart, "There is no God" (v. 1). Who is this fool? If God exists, he is just; if he is just, he despises injustice and sin. But when you think that sin pleases him, you deny God. For if God despises sin, but God does not seem to you to despise sin, and there is no God but one who despises sin, then when you say in your heart, God supports my sin, you say in effect: *"There is no God."*

There they are, overwhelmed with dread, where there was nothing to dread (v. 5). Is there fear if someone loses riches? There is nothing to dread there, and yet in that case people are afraid. But if someone loses wisdom, truly that is worthy of dread, yet the person is not afraid. You have been afraid of losing money, and have willed to lose faithfulness. The martyrs took no property from others, and even despised their own property to avoid losing faith; it was too little to lose money, they lost life, in order that unto everlasting life they might find it (Matt 10:39). They feared where they should have been afraid. But those who have said Christ is not God have feared where there was no fear. For they said, "If we let Him go, the Romans will come and take away from us both place and kingdom" (John 11:48). O folly and recklessness to say, "He is not God"! You have feared to lose earth, but you have lost heaven. You have feared the Romans. Could they take God from you? What remains then? What besides your confession that you wanted to keep, and by keeping you have lost everything? For you have lost both place and nation by killing Christ. For you wanted to kill Christ rather than to lose your place; and you have lost your place, and nation, and Christ.

Psalm 54 with Augustine – The Folly of Betrayal

The title of this psalm has fruit in its long-windedness, if it is understood. And because the psalm is short, let us linger over the title. For every verse depends on this. The title reads: *"When the Ziphites had gone to Saul and said, "Is not David hiding among us?"* Saul was persecutor of holy David. Saul represented a worldly kingdom, belonging not to life but to death. And David himself represented Christ, or of the Body of Christ. What about the Ziphites? There was a certain village, Ziph, whose inhabitants were Ziphites, in whose country David had hidden himself, when Saul wanted to find and kill him. These Ziphites then, when they had learned this, betrayed him to king Saul, his persecutor, saying, *"Is not David hiding among us?"* Their betrayal was of no good to them, and no harm came to David. For their evil plot was discovered, but Saul still could not seize David. Rather in a certain cave in that very country, when Saul had been given into his hands, David spared him, and did not do what was in his power (1 Sam 24:4). But Saul was seeking to do what was not in his power. Let those who have been Ziphites take note.

Would you also wish to be a Ziphite? They flourish in the world, wither in judgment, and after suffering, will be thrown into everlasting fire. Would you also choose this? Are you ignorant of what he has promised you, who has come to you, what he displayed in himself?

Psalm 55 with Augustine – Trusting God in the Storm

Amid many hardships of this world, this psalm's complaint arises from understanding. The one who has no understanding does not lament.

Psalm 55 with Augustine

"Perhaps the reason your heart is troubled is because you have forgotten him in whom you have believed."

There is a storm at sea. There is nothing to do but cry out, "Lord, save me!" (Matt 14:30) Let the one who treads the waves fearlessly stretch out his hand. Let him relieve your dread. Let him confirm your security in him. Let him speak within you, and say to you, "Pay attention to Me, what I have endured." Perhaps you are suffering an evil family member or an outside enemy; which of these have I not suffered? Jews roared outside, within a disciple betrayed me. There a storm rages, but he saves us from weakness of mind, and stormy weather. Perhaps the reason your heart is troubled is because you have forgotten him in whom you have believed. You are suffering beyond endurance because you have not remembered what Christ has endured. But when you have considered what He has suffered, will you not calmly endure? And perhaps rejoicing, because you have suffered similarly to your King. When you have begun to be comforted and to rejoice after thinking, he has arisen, he has commanded the winds; therefore there is a great calm.

As for me, I call to God and the LORD saves me (v. 16). The Body of Christ together with Christ himself in anguish, in weariness, in uneasiness. Rightly do you cry out to the Lord.

Psalm 56 with Augustine –
God as the Ground of Our Confidence

I put my trust in you (v. 3). David has not spoken of his confidence, but of the cause of his confidence. For if I shall not fear, I may also by hardness of heart not fear, for many prideful people fear nothing. All who go about with false heart, sojourning and hiding, do not fear.

List my tears on your scroll (v. 8). You have listened to me begging you. *Are they not in your record?* Because as you had promised this thing, so you have done. You have said you would listen to one weeping. I have believed, I have wept, I have been listened to; I have found you merciful in promising, true in repaying. How great a thing has God given to us, that his own we should be, and he should be ours!

God requires praise from you. God requires your confession. But from your field will you give anything? He has provided rain in order that you may have produce. From your accounts will you give anything? He has provided that which you will give. What will you give that you have not received from him? For what do you have that you have not received? (1 Cor 9:7) Will you give from the heart? He has also given faith, hope, and love. This you must bring forth. This you must sacrifice. But evidently all the other things the enemy is able to take away against your will; except this, unless you are willing. A person will lose these things even against his will; wishing to have gold, will lose gold; wishing to have a house, will lose their house. But no one will lose faith, except those who despise it.

Therefore, let us not despair. Let us pray for all who cause us to suffer. Let us never depart from God. Let him be our inheritance, our hope, and our safety. He is here a Comforter, there a Rewarder, everywhere Maker-alive, and the Giver of life.

Psalm 57 with Athanasius – Corruption Does Not Save

One thing you can count on: Corruption does not save those who get into it. On the contrary, it sets itself up against them, tears them down, and brings about their doom. Woe to those people against whom this prophecy is written! For the evil they pursue is sharper than a two-edged sword, and it will first kill those who lay hold of it. As the psalmist points out, their *teeth are spears and arrows, [their] tongues are sharp swords* (v. 4).

But the wonderful part is that the one these people plan to harm actually suffers nothing, while they, on the other hand, are pierced by their own spears. That is because inside themselves they have built up anger, wrath, malice, guile, hatred, and bitterness. Although they may not be able to turn these evil thoughts upon others, they find themselves eaten up by their own internal poison. It works out as the psalmist prays, "But their swords will pierce their own hearts" (Ps 37:15). There is also a similar proverb: "The evil deeds of the wicked ensnare them; the cords of their sins hold them fast" (Prov 5:22). As the Spirit said, "The fool says in his heart, 'there is no God'" (Ps 14:1). Their actions correspond with their thoughts: "They are corrupt, and their deeds are vile' (Ps 14:1). The unrighteous person, then, corrupts their own body in every possible way: stealing, committing adultery, cursing, getting drunk, and doing similar things.

Psalm 58 with Augustine – Truth Overcomes

The truth cries, *Do you rulers indeed speak justly? Do you judge people with equity?* (v. 1). Is not speaking about justice easy for everyone? Who cannot easily answer what is just? Everyone knew the golden rule even before the Law was given, in order that there might be some rule even for those to whom Law had not been given (Matt 7:12). Let it not be a justice of lips, but also of deeds. For if you act differently than you speak, you speak good things, but are judged evil.

Before your pots can feel the heat of the thorns—whether they be green or dry—the wicked will be swept away (v. 9). The bramble, a prickly plant which has many thorns, is at first an herb, and while it is an herb, it is soft and beautiful, but thorns are coming. New sins are pleasant, and they do not prick at first. After miserable delights and pleasures the evident tortures come forth. Let those who love any object question themselves. If they cannot get it, let them see if they are racked with longing, and when they have obtained that which they long for unlawfully, let them notice if they are afraid. But even now the bramble of sin produces thorns of judgment. Fire has fallen upon them, and they are unable to see the sun. That is, the wrath of God consumes the wicked while still living: fire of evil lusts, of empty honors, of pride, of their covetousness. Whatever is weighing them down prevents them from knowing the truth, so that they seem to be unconquered. They are not brought into subjection even by truth herself. For what is more glorious than to be brought in subjection and to be overcome by truth? Let truth overcome the willing, for it shall even overcome the unwilling.

Psalm 59 with John Calvin and Philip Melanchthon – Deliverance from Enemies

Deliver me from my enemies, O God! (v. 1) They rise up against him, referring not simply to the fierceness of their assaults, but their great superiority of power; and yet he asks that he may be lifted up on high, above the reach of this overwhelming attack. He teaches us that we should trust God's ability to deliver us even in emergencies, when our enemies have an overwhelming advantage. In the following verse, while he expresses the extremity to which he was reduced, he also considers the injustice and cruelty of his persecutors. I have already observed that our confidence in our approach to the throne of grace will be proportional to the degree in which we are conscious of our integrity; for we feel greater freedom in pleading a cause which is the cause of God himself. He is the vindicator of justice, the supporter of the righteous cause everywhere, and those who oppress the innocent must rank themselves among his enemies. David therefore bases his first request upon his complete lack of earthly assistance, exposed as he was to plots on every side, and attacked by an imposing conspiracy. His second request rests upon a declaration of his innocence. It may be true that afflictions are sent by God to his people as a punishment for their sins, but as far as Saul was concerned, David could rightly exempt himself from blame, and appeals to God on behalf of his integrity, which lay under suspicion from unjust slander.

––––––

The question here is whether it is permitted to curse enemies, as is often done in the Psalms? I respond yes, if all four of these things are true: First, the cause

which blasphemers protect must be condemned as
severely as possible. Second, those spreading blasphemy
must be condemned because they stubbornly persevere
in sin. Third, because without the help of God truth cannot
conquer, it is necessary to ask God to repress errors and
those committing the errors. This is prayed for when one
curses the unfaithful, and yet it is an intensely faithful
and necessary prayer. Fourth, such curses in the prophets
should be read not as human anger but rather as the
voice of the Holy Spirit, expressing the ultimate way of
thinking about blasphemies and consoling the church
so that it may know the truth that it will conquer, and God
will repress and root out unfaithful teaching and those
who teach blasphemy.

Discussion Questions

 Can you think of an example in your own context where people suppose, "God supports our sins" (Psalm 53)? What does Augustine say about this?

 What might Augustine mean in his reflection on Psalm 55 when he says, "The one who has no understanding does not lament"? Do you agree with him? Why or why not?

 After reading Psalm 40, how would you characterize your prayer life? Do you seek God himself, or only what God can give you?

 Ambrose's reflection on Psalm 39 implies that sometimes the right thing to do is nothing. Do you find it difficult to remain silent when others try to provoke you? What helps you resist the urge to react?

 Is there something hindering you from a closer bond with God? When was the last time you confessed your sins to him (Psalm 41)? How could you make confession a more regular practice?

Chapter 4
Psalms 60–80

Psalm 60 with John Calvin –
Defeat of Rebellious Nations

In triumph I will parcel out Shechem and measure off the valley of Sukkoth (v. 6). The places he names are those possessed later in David's reign, and which were still possessed by Saul's son Ish-Bosheth when this psalm was written. Since a severe struggle was necessary to acquire them, he asserts that they would certainly be brought under his subjection in due time, as God had graciously promised it. So with *Gilead . . . and Manasseh* (v. 7). As Ephraim was the most populous of all the tribes, he appropriately terms it his helmet, that is, of his dominions. He adds that *Judah* would be *his scepter,* for "The scepter will not depart from Judah, nor the ruler's staff from between his feet" (Gen 49:10).

Moab is my washbasin (v. 8). In proceeding to speak of foreigners, he observes a wide distinction between them and his own citizens. The descendants of Abraham he would govern as siblings, and not as slaves; but he was allowed to exercise greater harshness upon the ungodly and the uncircumcised, so they could be subjected to his rule. By this he offers no model to conquerors who would inflict lawless oppression upon nations taken in war, for they lack the divine warrant and commission that David had. He was invested with the authority of a king, as well as the character of an avenger of the Church, especially its more ruthless enemies who had thrown off every feeling of humanity and persisted in harassing a people descended from the same ancestors as themselves. He remarks boldly that the Moabites would be a vessel in which he should wash his feet. With the same view he says *on Edom I toss my sandal*. This expresses disrespect, and suggests that since they had insulted the chosen people of God, they should now be reduced to servitude.

God had pledged his word that every nation opposing him would be defeated, and in the face of remaining difficulties and dangers he advances with certainty of success. Two things are implied in the expression, *with God we will gain the victory* (v. 12). First, that if God withdraws his favor, any supposed human strength will soon fail; and on the other hand, that those whose faith is only in God are armed with courage to overcome every difficulty. To show that it is no mere half credit which he gives God, he adds that *he will trample down our enemies*. Even in our controversy with other humans, we are not free to share the honor of success with God. Those who attribute the least fraction of strength to themselves apart from God only ruin themselves through their own pride.

Psalm 61 with Mary Sidney Herbert – A Prayer for Protection

To thee I cry,
my crying hear!
To thee my praying voice doth fly.
Lord, lend my voice a listening ear,
from country banished,
all comfort vanished,
to thee I run when storms are near.

Up to thy hill
Lord, make me climb;
which else to scale exceeds my skill;
For in my most distressed time
thy eye attended[1] me,
thy hand defended me,
against my foe my fortress still.

Then where a tent
for thee is made,
to harbor still[2] is my extent;
and to thy wings protecting shade
myself I carry will,
and there I tarry[3] will,
safe from all shot against me bent.[4]

---

1   Attended – watched over

2   To harbor still – take shelter always

3   Tarry – linger

4   Bent – aimed

What first I crave
first granting me,
that I the royal rule may have
of such as fear and honor thee.
Let years as manifold[5]
as can be any[6] told,
thy king, O God, keep from the grave.

Before thy face,
grant ever he
may sit, and let thy truth and grace
his endless guard appointed be.
Then singing pleasantly,
praising incessantly,[7]
I daily vows will pay to thee.

---

5   Manifold – many

6   As can be any – as any that can be

7   Incessantly – without stopping

Psalm 62 with Augustine – The Justice of God

Trust in him at all times, you people; pour out your hearts to him (v. 8), by imploring, by confessing, by hoping. Do not hold back your hearts. What you pour out does not perish. *For God is our refuge.* If He protects us, why do you fear to pour out? "Cast your cares on the LORD and he will sustain you" (Ps 55:22). What do you fear among whisperers, slanderers hateful to God, where they are openly attacking, where they are secretly lying in wait, falsely praising, truly in conflict, what do you fear of them? *God is our refuge.* Do they equal God? Are they stronger than He? *God is our refuge, do not worry.*

Do not trust in extortion (v. 10), for my hope is in God. *Or put vain hope in stolen goods.* You are not rich. But will you rob? What do you find? What do you lose? O losing gains! You find money, you lose righteousness. Therefore, you proud and lying people, neither rob, nor set your heart upon riches. No longer love pride, or seek lying. *Do not set your heart on them.* For "blessed is the one who trusts in the LORD, who does not look to the proud, to those who turn aside to false gods." (Ps 40:4) You who would deceive, you who would commit fraud, what do you bring in order to cheat? Deceitful scales, in order to cheat. Do you not know that one person weighs, but Another judges the weight? He does not see who you weigh for, but he sees the one who weighs you and him. Therefore do not wish for fraud or robbery any longer, nor those things for which you have hoped.

Fear is not the enemy. What fear does, he has been empowered to do. Fear the one who does what God wills, and who does nothing unjustly. We might suppose something or other to be unjust. If God has done it, believe it to be just.

Psalm 63 with Gertrude the Great – Thirsting for God

You, God, are my God, earnestly I seek you; I thirst for you, my whole being longs for you (v. 1).

And early in the morning, as if running to meet your God, say this prayer with these three verses:

God, my God; for you I watch at daybreak. For you my soul has thirsted, for you my flesh, how many ways! In a desert land, and where there is no way and no water: so in the sanctuary, have I come before you to see your virtue and your glory.

Ah! O God, love, you alone are my entire and true love. You are my dearest salvation, all my hope and joy and my supreme and best good. My God, my dearest love, in the morning I will stand before you and will see that you yourself are everlasting pleasantness and gentleness. You are what my heart thirsts for. You are the entire sufficiency of my spirit. The more I taste you, the more I hunger [for you]: the more I drink, the more I thirst.

O God, love, the vision of you is for me like the very brightest day: that one day which, in the courts of the Lord, is better above thousands; for this alone sighs my soul, that you have redeemed for yourself. Ah! When will you satisfy me with the gentleness of your mellifluous[1] face? How my soul yearns and pines for the fat[2] of your pleasantness. Behold, I have chosen and chosen above all to be a castaway in the house of my God so that I may be able to aspire to the refreshment of your most dulcet[3] face.

---

1   Mellifluous – soothing

2   Fat – richness

3   Most dulcet – sweetest

Psalm 64 with Saint Basil –
Helpful Fear that Guards Us from Wickedness

"I will teach you the fear of the LORD" (Ps 34:11). When he ordered us to fear the Lord, he also showed the benefit that comes from fear, saying: "Those who fear him lack nothing" (Ps 34:10). The Psalms teach us divine fear. Not every fear is good, but there is also a hostile fear, which the prophet prays may not spring up in his soul, when he says: *Preserve my life from dread of the enemy* (v. 2, ESV).

> **Saint Basil on Psalm 64**
>
> *"The Psalms teach us divine fear."*

Fear of the enemy is that which produces in us a cowardliness with regard to death and misleads us to tremble before distinguished persons. Someone who is easily scared by demons has the fear of the enemy in him. On the whole, such a fear seems to be a passion born of unbelief. For no one who believes that he has at hand a strong helper is frightened by any of those who attempt to throw him into confusion. However, fear that is helpful and produces holiness, fear that springs up in the soul through devotion and not through passion, what kind is it? Whenever you are about to rush headlong into sin, consider that fearful courtroom of Christ, in which the Judge is seated upon a certain high and lofty throne, and every creature stands trembling beside His glorious presence (Matt 25:31–32), and we are about to be led forth, one by one, for the examination of the actions of our life. And beside one who has done many wicked deeds throughout his life certain horrible and dark angels stand, flashing fire from their eyes and breathing fire because of their bitterness, with faces as dark as night because of their dejection and their hatred of man. For the wicked, then, there is the deep pit and the darkness (cf. Matt 8:12) with no escape and light without brightness, which has the power of burning in the darkness but is deprived of its splendor. Next is the poisonous and flesh-devouring class of worms (cf. Isa 66:24), which eat greedily and are never satiated and cause unbearable pains by their ravenous hunger; and lastly, the severest punishment of all, that eternal condemnation and shame. Fear these things, and let this fear teach you to guard your soul from its desire for wickedness.

Psalm 65 with Augustine –
The Beauty of Righteousness

Blessed are those you choose and bring near to live in your courts! We are filled with the good things of your house, of your holy temple (v. 4). What are the good things of the House of God? Think about a lavish house, crowded with numerous good things, abundantly furnished, its gold and silver dishes; its entourage of servants, the many horses and livestock—in a word, how delightful the house filled with pictures, marble, ceilings, pillars, recesses, rooms— all such things are objects of desire, but they are still of the confusion of Babylon. Cut off all such longings, O citizen of Jerusalem, cut them off; if you want to return home, let not captivity delight you. Long for the House of God, and for the good things of that House: but do not long for other things, either in your house or in your neighbor's house.

We are filled with the good things of your house, of your holy temple. You answer us with awesome and righteous deeds (vv. 4–5). These are the good things of that House. He has not said, your holy temple is awesome in pillars, in marbles, in gilded ceilings; but *awesome* in *righteous deeds.* Externally you have eyes that can see marbles and gold. Internally you can see the beauty of righteousness. If there is no beauty in righteousness, why is a righteous old man loved? What does he bring that may please the eyes? Crooked limbs, brow wrinkled, head blanched with gray hairs. Even if he sang well as a young man, all has been lost with age. He can hardly speak clearly for loss of teeth. Nevertheless, if he is righteous, if he does not covet another man's possessions, if he shares with the needy, if he gives good advice, and wisely judges, if he believes the entire faith,—why do we love him? What good thing do we see in him with the eyes of the flesh? Not any. There is therefore a kind of beauty in righteousness, which we see with the eye of the heart, and we love. With these prepare yourself to be satisfied: "Blessed are those who hunger and thirst for righteousness, for they will be filled" (Matt 5:6). And that same temple, *filled with good things*, do not imagine to be anything but yourselves. Love righteousness, and you are the temple of God.

Psalm 66 with Augustine –
Enduring Trials by Hating Sin

For you, God, tested us; you refined us like silver (v. 10).
You have not burned us like hay, but like silver. By applying
fire to us, you have not turned us into ashes, but washed
off uncleanness. And see how God expresses anger with
those whose soul he has brought to life. *You brought us
into a prison* (v. 11), not so we would be caught and die,
but so we would be tried and delivered from it. *And laid
burdens on our backs.* For having been lifted up to no good
purpose, we were bowed down in order to be lifted up
for good. *You let people ride over our heads* (v. 12). All these
things the Church has suffered in various persecutions:
Her individual members have suffered this; they suffer it
even now. For there is not one who in this life is exempt
from these trials. And it is a good thing to consider ourselves
to be sinners, and thus endure those set over our heads:
in order that we may confess to God that we deserve to
suffer. For why do you angrily suffer what is done by one
who is just? God seems to be angry when he does these
things, but do not fear, for he is a Father. He is never angry
enough to destroy. These tribulations are the rods of his
correction, so that he does not need to punish us further.
How sweet tribulation often is, how necessary!

*If I had cherished sin in my heart, the Lord would not have
listened* (v. 18). Judge yourself. Look into the hidden
chamber of your heart, where you and he who sees are
alone. Let sin be displeasing to you, in order that you
may be pleasing to God. Do not love it, but rather despise

it, that is, condemn it, and turn away from it. Whatever pleasing thing it has promised to allure you to sin; whatever grievous thing it has threatened to drive you on to evil doing; all is nothing, all passes away. It is worthy to be despised, in order that it may be trampled upon, not gazed upon lest it be accepted.

Psalm 67 with Augustine – The Blessing of God

May God be gracious to us and bless us (v. 1). Let us bless the Lord, and let God bless us. When God blesses us, we grow, and when we bless the Lord, we grow, both are profitable to us. He is not increased by our blessing, nor is he lessened by our cursing. The one who curses the Lord is lessened. The one who blesses the Lord grows.

And make his face shine on us. God does not shine his face as if we had ever been without light, but he shines it upon us, so that what was hidden from us is opened, and that which was hidden, is illuminated.

How can we draw him to ourselves? By living well, by doing well. Let past things not please us and present things not hold us. Let us not refuse to listen. So we are not kept back by the past, so that we are not entangled by the present, so that we are not prevented from meditating on future things, let us reach forth toward those things which are ahead. Let us forget things past (Phil 3:13). And that for which we work now, for which we groan now, of which now we speak, which in part, however small, we perceive, and are not able to receive, we shall receive. We shall thoroughly enjoy it in the resurrection of the righteous.

Psalm 68 with Cassiodorus –
The Wicked Consumed and the Righteous Rejoice

May God arise, may his enemies be scattered . . . May you blow them away like smoke—as wax melts before the fire, may the wicked perish before God (vv. 1–2). In these two verses the punishment of sinners is foretold by two images. Smoke is a dark, thick mass which rises from the flames of this world that perish; the further it rises, the thinner it becomes through the empty air. Sinners are appropriately compared to smoke, for they bring forth from the fire of their wickedness smoke-bearing activities. Through the action of pride this "smoke" rises to higher levels but inevitably vanishes through their own self-exaltation. The second comparison which describes them follows. Wax is a soft, pliant substance gathered from honeycombs which melts under the fire's heat so that its substance is utterly dissipated. This image is appropriate for the wicked, for at God's judgment sinners disappear before his presence as the frail wax is consumed by the nearness of fire. They will perish before the presence of God, because they will never attain his grace and benefits.

But may the righteous be glad and rejoice before God; may they be happy and joyful (v. 3). Just as earlier the punishment of sinners was pronounced, so now the future reward of the just is recounted. By feasts we mean choice and abundant supplies of food with which the body is refreshed and the appetite satisfied. This is the image used for nourishment of the faithful and fattening the righteous, who are filled but still long for more, and are stuffed with the delights of heaven. These delights are found *before God*, where happiness is always desirable and genuine. What exaltation we experience under the

gaze of the great Judge, when the One we justly fear
in this world is the object of our joy when he is present
before us, and we have been set free by his kindness!
The psalmist added: *may they be happy and joyful*, so that
the fact that they are glad can delight them. They know
that their joy will never end, and they gain a sweeter delight
in it because they do not feel that they will lose it. So the
impending happiness of that blessedness is signified in
what we may call glistening melodies.

The God of Israel gives power and strength to his people.
Praise be to God! (v. 35) No one should lose confidence
because of human weakness, and believe that they are
failing to attain such great rewards. The psalm affirms by
truthful promise that the Lord will give the power of
patience and the strength of faith to his faithful so that
they can attain eternal rewards.

Psalm 69 with John Calvin – Praying in Distress

Save me, O God, for the waters have come up to my neck (v. 1).
Under the metaphor of waters, the psalmist represents his
condition as so distressing that it brought him to the
brink of despair. Yet we know that he often overcame
dreadful temptations with extraordinary courage.
From that we may infer the bitterness of his distress
at that time. We know from biblical history that Saul
sent numerous and powerful armies after him. He speaks
of the mortal hatred they expressed toward him, when
he tells us they were intent upon his destruction, eagerly
desiring to have him cut off by a violent death. And yet
he vows that he did nothing to deserve such unrelenting
persecution. If at any time we experience persecution,
let us determine to have the support arising from the
testimony of a good conscience, and to be able to protest
freely before God, that our enemies' hatred is without
cause. Let us learn from David's example to prepare
ourselves to bear patiently all losses and troubles, even
death itself, as well as shame and reproach, if at any
time we are loaded with false accusations.

But I pray to you, LORD! (v. 13) When the wicked directed
their witty and scoffing remarks against him, as if weapons
of war, to overthrow his faith, his means of repelling all
their assaults was to pour out his heart to God in prayer.
He kept silent before others, and driven out from the
world, he approached God. Similarly, although the faithful
today may be unable to make any impression upon the
wicked, they will ultimately triumph if they turn away
from the world and directly present their prayers to God.

May the table set before them become a snare (v. 22). Here
we have a series of serious prayers for harm. We must

remember that David did not allow himself recklessly to pour out his wrath, the way most people give way to their own passion when they feel wronged. Instead, being under the guidance of the Holy Spirit, he simply called upon God to exercise justice against the scoundrel. Further, it was not on his own account that he pleaded in this manner; but it was a holy zeal for the divine glory which compelled him to summon the wicked to God's judgment seat.

Psalm 70 with John Cassian – A Prayer for Every Day

This, then, is the devotional formula proposed to you as absolutely necessary for possessing continual awareness of God: *Hasten, O God, to save me; come quickly, LORD, to help me* (v. 1). Not without reason has this verse been selected from all of Scripture. For it takes up all the emotions that can be applied to human nature and with great correctness and accuracy it adjusts itself to every condition and every attack. It contains a prayer to God in the face of any crisis, the humility of a devout confession, the watchfulness of concern and of constant fear, a consciousness of one's own weakness, the assurance of being heard, and confidence in a protection that is always present and at hand. For whoever calls continually on his protector is sure that he is always present. It contains a burning love and charity, an awareness of traps, and a fear of enemies. Seeing oneself surrounded by these day and night, one confesses that one cannot be set free without the help of one's defender. This verse is a wall that cannot be climbed, armor that cannot be pierced, and a very strong shield for all those who labor under the attack of demons. It does not permit those troubled by depression and anxiety of mind or those consumed by sadness to despair of a saving remedy, showing that he whom it invokes is always looking upon our struggles and is not detached from those who pray to him. It warns those of us who are enjoying spiritual successes and are glad of heart that we must never be proud because of our good fortune, which cannot be maintained without the protection of God. The psalm begs him to come to our aid not only at all times but also quickly.

This verse is necessary and useful for each of us in whatever condition we may live. For whoever desires to be helped always and in all things shows that he needs God as a helper not only in hard and sad affairs but also and equally as much in favorable and joyful ones. In neither instance can human weakness endure without God's assistance.

Psalm 71 with Augustine – My Righteous Rock

In your righteousness, rescue me and deliver me (v. 2). Not in my righteousness, but in yours. For what is mine? Sin has gone before. And when I am righteous, it will be your righteousness, for I will be righteous by righteousness given to me by you. It is a small thing that you acknowledge the good thing which is in you to be from God. Therefore say to God what you hear in the psalm, *In you, LORD, I have taken refuge; let me never be put to shame. In your righteousness, not in mine, rescue me and deliver me; turn your ear to me and save me* (vv. 1–2). This is also a confession of humility. He who says, *turn your ear to me*, is confessing that he is lying like a sick person laid at the feet of the Physician.

Be my rock of refuge (v. 3). Do not let the darts of the enemy reach me, for I am not able to protect myself. I will not be safe except in you. Unless you are my rest, my sickness will never be made whole. Lift me from the earth; upon you I will lie, in order that I may ascend to a fortified place. What can be better fortified? When you have fled for refuge to that place, tell me which enemies you will dread? Who will lie in wait, and come against you? *For you are my rock and my fortress.* In order that I may be made firm by you, however I shall have been unstable in myself, I will flee to you for refuge. For the grace of Christ makes me firm and immovable against all temptations of the enemy.

Psalm 72 with Theodoret of Cyrus – Praise for God's Deliverance

He will deliver the needy who cry out, the afflicted who have no one to help. He will take pity on the weak and the needy and save the needy from death (vv. 12–13). All will adore him, freed from the harsh rule of the devil. In particular he keeps the mighty in check with his divine laws, terrifies them with the threat of hell, and ensures they exercise some compassion towards the needy, adding this: *He will rescue them from oppression and violence* (v. 14).

All nations will be blessed through him (v. 17). Here he recalled the promise about Abraham, Isaac, and Jacob: to the three ancestors God promised to bless, in one case all the nations of the earth, in another the tribes of the earth (Gen 12:3; 26:4). *Praise be to the LORD God, the God of Israel, who alone does marvelous deeds* (v. 18). In other words, he is saying, the one who is the object of inspired speech and due to perform the prophesied wonders is also the very God of Israel and Lord of all. *Praise be to his glorious name forever* (v. 19).

Psalm 73 with Augustine – God as My Reward

Surely God is good to Israel! (v. 1) But to whom? *To those who are pure in heart.* To those who are perverse, he seems perverse. Not that God is at all perverse. Far be it! What he is, he is. If you have begun to be perverse, and to you God seems perverse, you are changed, not him.

But as for me, my feet had almost slipped (v. 2). When were the feet moved, except when the heart was not right? But as for the wicked, *pride is their necklace; they clothe themselves with violence* (v. 6). Observe them, proud, undisciplined, on all sides covered with their ungodliness.

Surely in vain I have kept my heart pure and have washed my hands in innocence (v. 13). This I seem to have done for no reason. Where is the reward for my good life? Where are the wages for my service? I live righteously and am in need; and the unjust man prospers. *All day long I have been afflicted* (v. 14). God's afflictions do not leave me. I serve well, but I am punished; he does not serve, but is honored. This is a good question, but these words—*How would God know?* (v. 11)—are also dangerous, offensive, and almost blasphemous.

Augustine on Psalm 73

"Let the people of God cry: God is my portion. Not for just a while, but forever."

My flesh and my heart may fail, but God is the strength of my heart and my portion forever (v. 26). This then has been reserved for me in heaven. What is it? Let us find out our riches, let humankind choose their parts. People are torn with diverse desires: some choose military service, some advocacy, some teaching, some merchandise, some farming, they take their portions in human affairs. Let the people

of God cry: God is my portion. Not for just a while, but
forever. Even if I always have gold, what do I truly have?
And if I did not always have God, how good are the
things I do have? Nevertheless, he promises himself
to me, and he promises that I will have this forever.
Such a great a thing I have, and never lack it! Great joy!
The reward belonging to God is God Himself.

Psalm 74 with Augustine –
The Sweetness of Trusting What We Cannot See

Do not let the oppressed retreat in disgrace (v. 21). For
pride has confounded them. *May the poor and needy praise
your name.* You see how sweet poverty should be to you.
You see that poor and helpless people belong to God, that
"Blessed are the poor in spirit, for theirs is the kingdom
of heaven" (Matt 5:3). Who are the poor in spirit? The
humble—those who tremble at the words of God,
confessing their sins, neither on their own merits, nor
relying on their own righteousness. Who are the poor
in spirit? Those who praise God when they do anything
good, but when they do anything evil, accuse themselves.

Rise up, O God, and defend your cause (v. 22). Because I am
not able to point to my God, they mock me as if I was
following an empty thing. And not only heathen, or Jew,
or heretic, but sometimes even a Christian grimaces
when the promises of God are being preached, when
a future resurrection is being foretold. And still even
they, though already washed with the water of eternal
salvation, perhaps say, "and what human has risen
from the dead?" And, "I have not heard my father speaking
out of the grave, since I buried him!" What shall I do
with such people? Shall I show them what they do not
see? I am not able. And not for their sake should God
become visible. "I see nothing," they say. "What am I to
believe?" Fool, your body is seen, but who sees your
soul? How do I know that you are alive, when I cannot
see your soul? How do I know? They will answer,
"Because I speak, because I walk, because I work." Fool,
by the operations of the body I know you are alive;
can you not know the Creator by the works of creation?

Has God given us all the things he promised, and has he deceived us concerning the day of judgment alone? No, it will come. Let no one say, it will not come, or, it will come, but it is far off. But to them it is near at hand. If they have done what the devil suggests, and have despised what God has commanded, the judgment day will come, and they will find what God has threatened to be true, and false what the devil has promised.

Psalm 75 with Augustine – No Place to Flee from God

Do not lift your horns[1] against heaven (v. 5). This the psalmist saw many people do in their hearts. He also added, *no one from the East or the West or from the desert can exalt themselves. It is God who judges* (vv. 6–7). God is judge of your sins. If he is God, he is everywhere. Where will you hide from the eyes of God, so that in some region you may speak and he may not hear?

> **Augustine on Psalm 75**
>
> *"Wherever you flee, there he is."*

If God judges only from the East, go West, and say what you want against God. If from the West, go East, and speak there. If he judges from the forsaken heights of the mountains, go into the midst of the people, where you may murmur to yourself. From no particular place does he judge—everywhere is secret, everywhere open; no one is allowed to know him as he truly is, and no one is permitted not to know him at all. Take care what you do. You are speaking sin against God. Do not think God to be somewhere in particular. He is with you as you have been with him. How have you been? Good, if you have been good; but he will seem evil to you if you have been evil; but a Helper, if you have been good; an Avenger, if you have injured others. There in your "secret" place you have a judge. Willing to do something evil, from the public you retire into your house, where no enemy may see; from those places of your house which are open and before human eyes, you remove yourself into a bedroom; you fear a witness even in your bedroom, so you retreat into your heart, there you plot—but he is more inward than your heart. Wherever you flee, there

---

1 "Do not lift your horns" – exalt yourself

he is. Are you not present wherever you flee? But since there is one who is even more inward than yourself, there is no place you may flee from God angry, but to God reconciled. There is no place at all you may flee. You want to flee from him? Flee to him instead. What then shall we do? "Let us come before His face," in confession. Then the one you angered will come gently.

Psalm 76 with Augustine – The Way to Peace with God

Do you want to see God? First confess, and then there will be a place for God in you; because "there has been made in peace a place for him." As long as you do not confess your sins, in a way you are quarrelling with God. For how are you not disputing with him, when you praise that which displeases him? He punishes a thief, while you praise theft. He punishes a drunken man, while you praise drunkenness. You are disputing with God. You have not made a place for him in your heart, because his place is in peace. And how do you begin to have peace with God? You begin by confession, so that the same thing may displease you as displeases him. Your evil life displeases him. If it pleases you, you are separated from him. If it displeases you, through confession you are united with him.

Augustine on Psalm 76

"Govern the earth which you already possess—your heart."

When you, God, rose up to judge, to save all the afflicted of the land (v. 9). Who are the afflicted? Those who have not mounted on snorting horses, but in their humility have confessed their own sins. Confession unites us to Christ.

He is feared by the kings of the earth (v. 12). The kings of the earth are fearsome, but he is above all, and he terrifies the kings of the earth. Be a king of the earth, and God will be fearsome to you. How will you be a king of the earth? Rule the earth, and you will be a king. Do not set before your eyes vast provinces with a desire to build an empire wherever you may spread your kingdoms. Govern the earth which you already possess—your heart.

Psalm 77 with Augustine – Desiring God

I cried out to God for help (v. 1). But many cry to the Lord
for the sake of getting riches and avoiding losses, for the
safety of their friends, for the security of their house,
for temporal happiness, for secular dignity, lastly, even for
physical health, which is the inheritance of the poor.
For things like this many cry to the Lord; hardly anyone
cries for the Lord himself. For it is an easy thing to desire
something from the Lord, and not to desire the Lord himself,
as if his gifts could be sweeter than the giver. He listens
to you when you seek him, but not when you seek anything
else from him. It has been said of some, "They cried for
help, but there was no one to save them—to the LORD, but
he did not answer" (Ps 18:41). Why? Because their voice
was not to the Lord. And what then has happened to them?
"They all lose heart; they come trembling" (Ps 18:45).
They have trembled about the loss of present things, for
they were not full of him upon whom they did not call.

When I was in distress, I sought the Lord (v. 2). Who are
you who do this? In the day of hardship take care what
you seek. If a jail is the cause of hardship, you seek to
get out of jail. If fever is the cause of hardship, you seek
health. If hunger is the cause of hardship, you seek
fullness. If loss is the cause of hardship, you seek gain.
If exile is the cause of hardship, you seek home. And
why should I name all things? In the day of your hardship
seek God, not some other thing from God. Out of
hardship, seek God himself, so that for this purpose
God may take away hardship, so you may cling to
him without anxiety.

You are the God who performs miracles (v. 14). You are indeed a great God, doing wonderful things in body and in soul. The deaf have heard, the blind have seen, the weak have recovered, the dead have risen, the paralyzed have been strengthened. But these miracles were at that time performed on bodies, let us see those worked on the soul. Sober are those who were recently drunk, believers are those who recently worshipped idols—their goods they bestow on the poor who robbed others.

Psalm 78 with Augustine – Loving God above All Things

Whenever God slew[1] them, they would seek him (v. 34) not for the sake of eternal life, but fearing to end their fleeting life too soon. Those who sought him were not those whom he had slain, but those who were afraid of being slain according to their example. *They remembered that God was their Rock, that God Most High was their Redeemer* (v. 35). But all this is for the sake of acquiring good things on earth, and for avoiding evil things. For those who sought God for the sake of earthly blessings, sought not God, but material things. They worshipped him with fear, not free love. Thus God is not worshipped, for that thing is worshipped which is loved. Since God is found to be greater and better than all things, he must be loved more than all things in order to be worshipped.

> **Augustine on Psalm 78**
>
> *"Since God is found to be greater and better than all things, he must be loved more than all things in order to be worshipped."*

But then they would flatter him with their mouths, lying to him with their tongues; their hearts were not loyal to him, they were not faithful to his covenant (vv. 36–37). He found one thing on their tongue, another thing in their heart, for to him the secret things of men are naked, and without obstacle he saw what they truly loved. Therefore when the heart seeks God for his sake, it is right with him. For one thing David desired of the Lord, that he may dwell in the house of the Lord forever, and may meditate on his beauty (Ps 27:4). As for the crooked generation, even when they seemed to seek God, they loved only with lying mouths, but their hearts were not right with

---

1   Slew – killed

God, because they loved only those things which they needed God's help to acquire.

But he brought his people out like a flock; he led them like sheep through the wilderness. He guided them safely, so they were unafraid; but the sea engulfed their enemies (vv. 52–53). This happened for the greater good, that we are inwardly delivered from the power of darkness. Then we are spiritually transferred into the Kingdom of God and with respect to spiritual pastures we become God's sheep, walking in this world as if it was a desert, since our faith is invisible. But we are being led home in hope, for "in this hope we were saved" (Rom 8:24).

Psalm 79 with Augustine – A Plea for Mercy

The remembrance of former affliction in this psalm is not to inform God about what has happened but to ask, *How long, LORD? Will you be angry forever? How long will your jealousy burn like fire?* (v. 5). The psalmist is asking God not to be angry until the end, that this devastation may not continue forever, but that he moderate his punishments. Recognize that the anger and jealousy of God are not his emotions, as some people suppose who do not understand the Scriptures, but his anger means the avenging of sin; jealousy means the demanding of purity. By pursuing holiness the soul will not despise the law of her Lord, and perish by unfaithfulness to the Lord. When humans operate in anger or jealousy they are violent, but God expresses them calmly.

For the glory of your name, deliver us (v. 9) in order that we may not glory in ourselves, but in the Lord. *And forgive our sins for your name's sake*, not for our sake. For what else do our sins deserve, but appropriate punishments? But *forgive our sins for your name's sake*. Thus you deliver us from evil things while you help us act justly and are merciful to our sins. For "no one living is righteous before you" (Ps 143:2). But sin is iniquity. And "if you, LORD, kept a record of sins, Lord, who could stand?" (Ps 130:3).

Psalm 80 with Augustine – Correcting False Loves

How long, LORD God Almighty, will your anger smolder against the prayers of your people? (v. 4). You were angry at the prayer of your enemy, will you still be angry with the prayer of your servant? You have converted us. We know you. Will you still be angry? Evidently, yes, you will be angry, but as a father correcting, not as a judge condemning. Do not think the wrath of God has passed away because you have been converted. The wrath of God has turned away from you, but only so that it does not condemn forever. But he punishes, he does not spare, because he punishes every child he receives (Heb 12:6). If you refuse to be punished, why do you desire to be received?

What do you love that prevents you from loving God? Tell me. Is there anything you can love which he has not made? Look around at all creation, see whether in any place you are held with the snare of desire, and hindered from loving the Creator, except by that very thing which he who you neglect has created. But why do you love those things, except because they are beautiful? Can they be as beautiful as their maker? You admire these things, because you do not see him. Instead, through those things which you admire, love him who you do not see. Those who do not worship God are dead. In himself he is good, not because he gives good things, which he gives even to bad people. "You will revive us," for we were dead. When we clung to earthly things we were dead, when we bore the image of mortals. You will renew us. We will love you. You will be the sweet forgiver of our sins, you will be the entire reward of the justified. Restore us, LORD God Almighty; make your face shine on us, that we may be saved (v. 19).

Discussion Questions

In his reflection on Psalm 65, Augustine warns us against longing for things other than God and his righteousness. What does your culture encourage you to value more than God?

What do you think of Augustine's claim that God's anger is not an emotion but rather the avenging of sin (Psalm 79)? Is it possible for human anger to be non-violent?

In his reflection on Psalm 64, Basil speaks of "Fear that is helpful and produces holiness, fear that springs up in the soul through devotion and through passion." Have you experienced this kind of fear? If so, what is it like?

According to Augustine, how should we live if we want God to "make his face shine on us" (Psalm 67:1)? If you were to take inventory of your actions, which ones work against this illumination?

According to Calvin, under what circumstances does the psalmist pour out his heart to God (Psalm 69)? What regular practices can help you resist the urge to engage in a battle of words?

BIBLICAL STUDIES

Chapter 5

Psalms 81–101

Psalm 81 with Augustine – Burning Idols

You shall have no foreign god among you (v. 9). Why would you adore what does not exist? *For I am the LORD your God* (v. 10) "who brought you out of Egypt" (Exod 20:1). Not to them alone, for we were all brought out of the land of Egypt. We have all passed through the Red Sea. Our enemies pursuing us have perished in the water. Let us not be ungrateful to our God; let us not forget God who abides, and create in ourselves a new god. God says, *open wide your mouth and I will fill it*. You suffer distress in yourself because of the new god set up in your heart. Break the proud image. Cast the idol down from your conscience: open wide your mouth, in praise, in loving, *and I will fill it*, because with me is the fountain of life.

But my people would not listen to me (v. 11). For God would only speak these things to his own people. For, "we know that whatever the Law says, it says to those who are under the Law" (Rom 3:19). Israel would not submit to me. O ungrateful soul! *So I gave them over to their stubborn hearts* (v. 12), not according to the healthfulness of my commands, but, according to the affections of their heart. I gave them up to themselves. The Apostle also says, "God gave them over in the sinful desires of their hearts" (Rom 1:24).

Therefore if you love something you possess, yet do not commit violence for its sake, or bear false witness for its sake, or swear falsely for its sake, or deny Christ for its sake, then you have a Christian foundation. But because you still love it and are saddened if you lose it, you have built on that foundation, not with gold, or silver, or precious stones, but with wood, hay, and straw. Therefore you will be saved, when that which you have built begins to burn. For let no one who builds on this foundation with adulteries, blasphemies, sacrileges, idolatries, think he shall be "saved through fire," as though they were the "wood, hay, straw" (1 Cor 3:12). Since that person builds the love of earthly things on the foundation of the kingdom of heaven, their love of temporal things will be burned and they will be saved through the right foundation.

Psalm 82 with Gregory of Nazianzen – Learning from Bad Examples

How long will you defend the unjust and show partiality to the wicked? (v. 2). Often the righteous were given into the hands of the wicked, not that the wicked would be honored, but so the righteous could be tested. And though the wicked come to an awful death, nevertheless for the present the godly are mocked, while the goodness of God and the great treasuries of what is in store for each of them after this life are concealed. Then indeed word and deed and thought will be weighed on the righteous scales of God, as he arises to judge the earth, gathering together counsel and works, and revealing what he had kept sealed up. Of this let the words and sufferings of Job convince you, who was a truthful, blameless, righteous, worshipper of God, with all those other qualities which are testified of him. Yet he was struck with one calamity after another. Although many in history have suffered, and some have even been terribly afflicted, yet none can be compared with Job in misfortunes. For he not only suffered, without being allowed space to mourn for his losses in their rapid succession, the loss of his money, his possessions, his large and beautiful family, blessings which all men cherish; but was at last hit with an incurable disease horrible to look at. To crown his misfortunes, he had a wife whose only comfort was evil advice. He had also among his friends truly miserable comforters, as he calls them, who could not help him. For when they saw his suffering, in ignorance of its hidden meaning, they assumed his disaster was punishment for wickedness rather than the proof of his godliness. And they not only thought this, but were not even ashamed to rebuke him in his distress at a time when, even if he had been suffering for wickedness, they ought to have treated his grief with words of consolation.

Psalm 83 with Mary Sidney Herbert – A Desperate Call for Deliverance

Be not, O be not silent still;
Rest not, O God, with endless rest.
For lo, thine enemies
with noise and tumult rise;
Hate doth their hearts with fierceness fill,
and lift their heads who thee detest.

Against thy folk their wits they file[1]
to sharpest point of secret sleight;[2]
A world of traps and trains[3]
they forge in busy brains,
that they thy hid ones may beguile,[4]
whom thy wings shroud from searching sight.

"Come let us of them nothing make;
let none them more a people see;
Stop we their very name
within the mouth of fame."
Such are the counsels these men take;
Such leagues they link,[5] and these they be.

---

1   File – sharpen

2   Sleight – trick

3   Trains – deceitful lures

4   Beguile – mislead

5   Leagues they link – conspiracies they enter into

First Edom's sons, then Ishmael,
with Moab, Agur, Gebal's train;
with these the Amonites,
the fierce Amalekites,
and who in Palestina dwell,
and who in tents of Tyre remain.

Ashur, though further off he lie,
assisteth Lot's incestuous brood.[6]
But Lord, as Jabin thou
and Sisera didst bow;
as Midian did fall and die
at Endor walls, and Kyson flood;

As Oreb, Zeeb, and Zeba strong,
as Zalmuna who led thy foes
(who meant, nay, said no less
then that they would possess
God's heritage) became as dung.
So Lord, O so, of these dispose.

Torment them, Lord, as tossed balls,
as stubble scattered in the air,
or as the branchy brood
of some thick mountain wood,
to naught,[7] or naught but ashes falls,
when flames do singe[8] their leafy hair.

---

6   Incestuous brood – children born of incest

7   Naught – nothing

8   Singe – burn

So with thy tempest them pursue,
so with thy whirlwind them affright,[9]
so paint their daunted[10] face
with pencil of disgrace,
that they at length to thee may sue,[11]
and give thy glorious name his right.

Add fear and shame, to shame and fear,
confound them quite,[12] and quite deface;
and make them know that none,
but thou, and thou alone,
dost that high name Jehovah[13] bear,
high placed above all earthly place.

---

9   Affright – frighten

10 Daunted – intimidated

11 Sue – plead (for mercy)

12 Confound them quite – thwart completely

13 Jehovah – the LORD

Psalm 84 with Augustine –
God as Our Only Object of Desire

Being placed under pressure, we are crushed for this purpose: so that our misplaced love that draws us towards those worldly, secular, unstable, and perishable things might itself perish. Having suffered torments and hardships in this life, and an abundance of temptations, we may begin to seek that rest which is not of this life, nor of this earth. Then the Lord becomes, "a refuge for the oppressed" (Ps 9:9), for the one who is destitute, without aid, without help, without anything on which to rest. For God is present to those who are poor. For though people abound in money on earth, they are filled more with fear than enjoyment. Such people, though they have something, are still poor. But those who have none of this wealth, but only desire it, are counted also among rich men who will be rejected. God does not consider our actual power, but rather our desire.

The poor then are deprived of the world's substance, for even though it abounds around them, they know how fleeting it is. Crying out to God, having nothing in this world with which to delight themselves, they experience abundant pressures and temptations. Yet their desires are good! For God remains their only object of desire. Now they do not love the earth. For they love the one who made heaven and earth, but are not yet with him. Their desire is delayed so it may increase; it increases so they may receive it. For it is not a little thing that God will give to those who desire, nor do they need only minor preparation to be made fit to receive such a great good: God will not give anything he has made, but rather himself who made all things. Prepare yourself to receive God, who you want to possess him forever, desire for a long time.

Blessed are those who dwell in your house; they are ever praising you (v. 4). If you have your own house, you are poor; if you have God's, you are rich. In your own house you will fear robbers; of the house of God, he himself is the wall. Therefore those who dwell in your house possess the heavenly Jerusalem, without constraint, without pressure, without difference and division of boundaries—all have it, and each have all. Great are those riches. No one crowds each other. There is no lack there. Our immortal bodies will be sustained by contemplating God. How will it change us? "We shall be like him, for we shall see him as he is" (1 John 3:2). We will never grow tired of the praise of God, of the love of God. If love could fail, praise could fail. But if love is eternal, as beauty is inexhaustible, do not fear that you are not able to praise and love him forever. Let us long for that life.

Psalm 85 with Augustine – Peace and Rejoicing in God

O God, will you not revive us again? (v. 6). Not as if we turn to you of our own accord, without your mercy, and you make us alive. But our very conversion is from you, so we may be made alive. *That your people may rejoice in you.* For when we wanted to find joy in ourselves, we found distress. But now because God is all our joy, we will rejoice securely. Let us rejoice in him who cannot perish.

Augustine on Psalm 85

"For whatever he gives us now, then he will give us himself instead; this will be full and perfect peace."

He promises peace to his people (v. 8). What is peace? Where there is no war. Without war there is no contradiction, no resistance, nothing to oppose. Are we already there? There is conflict with the devil. All the faithful wrestle with the prince of demons. And how do they wrestle with one they cannot see? As they wrestle with their own desires, he suggests sins, and by not consenting to his suggestions, they fight. What peace do people have here—opposed by troubles, desires, wants, weariness? This is no true peace. One day there will be pure peace among the children of God, all loving one another, seeing one another full of God, since God will be all in all. God will be our common vision, our common possession, our common peace. For whatever he gives us now, then he will give us himself instead; this will be full and perfect peace. Our joy, our peace, our rest, the end of all troubles, is none but God.

Love and faithfulness meet together; righteousness and peace kiss each other (v. 10). Do righteousness, and you will have peace. That way righteousness and peace may kiss each other. If you do not love righteousness, you will not have peace, for righteousness and peace love one another. Everyone wants peace, but not all act righteously. Love righteousness, too. If you do not love the friend of peace, peace will not love you or come to you.

The LORD will indeed give what is good, and our land will yield its harvest (v. 12). He will give you the sweetness of doing righteousness, so that righteousness will delight you, when previously unrighteousness delighted you. You who delighted in drunkenness will rejoice in sobriety. You who rejoiced in theft will seek to give to one who has less. You who delighted in entertainment will delight in prayer. You who delighted in frivolous and dirty songs will delight in singing hymns to God; in running to church, you who ran to the theatre. Where does that sweetness come from? *God will give what is good.*

Psalm 86 with Gertrude the Great – Unequaled Glory

God of my life, oh when will I enter into the tabernacle of your glory in order that I, too, may proclaim to you the most splendid alleluia and that my soul and my heart may confess to you in the presence of all your saints that you have magnified your mercies toward me. My God, my very bright inheritance, oh when, after the snares of this death have been destroyed, will I personally see you without mediation, and praise you? Oh when will I dwell in your tabernacle forever in order that I may assiduously[1] praise your name and sing to your magnificence a new hymn about your multitudinous[2] mercies?

There is none among the gods like you, my Lord, nor is there anything equal to the lofty riches of your wondrous glory. Who will search into the abyss[3] of your wisdom, and who will count out the unlimited treasures of your most copious[4] mercy? Truly nothing is as wondrous as you, my God, immortal king, nothing as glorious. Who will unfold the glory of your majesty? Who will [ever] be able to be sated[5] with the sight of your brightness? How will the eye suffice to see or the ear to hear in wondering at the glory of your countenance?

God, my God, you alone are wondrous and glorious. You alone are great and praiseworthy, alone dulcet[6] and lovable, alone beautiful and lovely, alone radiant and full

1   Assiduously – constantly

2   Multitudinous – many

3   Abyss – depths

4   Copious – abundant

5   Sated – satisfied

6   Dulcet – sweet

of delight. And you alone are so wondrous and glorious; your equal is not found in all the glory of heaven and earth. For my heart, your wondrous light is lovable above all glory because it alone can bring gladness to my spirit and exchange the tediousness of this life for exultation and joy.

Psalm 87 with Augustine –
Dwelling in God's Presence for Eternity

As they make music they will sing, "All my fountains are in you" (v. 7). As if all the joyous and rejoicing ones shall dwell in that city. On our journeys here we suffer bruises; our last home will be the home of joy alone. Labor and groans will perish, prayers pass away, hymns of praise succeed. That will be the dwelling of those who are happy. No longer will there be the groans of those who ache, but the gladness of those who enjoy. The one we long for will be present. "We shall be like him, for we shall see him as he is" (1 John 3:2). There our whole task will be to praise and enjoy the presence of God. And what more could we ask for, when he alone satisfies us who made all things? We will dwell and be dwelt in; and shall be subject to him, that God may be all in all. Let this then be the only object of our desire, when we have reached this pass. Let us prepare ourselves to rejoice in God—to praise him.

In that day, works of charity will be unnecessary; there will be no misery; you will find no one in need, no one naked; no one will meet you tormented with thirst; there will be no stranger, no sick to visit, no dead to bury, no rivals to set at peace. What will you find to do? Shall we plant new vines, plough, and make voyages—all to support the necessities of the body? No, deep quiet shall be there. All toilsome work that necessity demands will cease. Since the necessity will be dead, its works will perish too.

What then will life be like? Many pleasures do I behold here, and many rejoice in this world—some in one thing, others in another—but there is nothing to compare with that delight. Let us prepare for other delights, for a kind of shadow is what we find here, not the reality. Let us praise the Lord as far as we are able, but with mingled mourning: for while we praise we long for him, but do not have him yet. When we have him, all our sorrows will be taken from us, and nothing will remain but praise, unmixed and everlasting.

Psalm 88 with Augustine – Proof of Human Weakness

LORD, you are the God who saves me; day and night I cry out to you; . . . I am overwhelmed with troubles and my life draws near to death (vv. 1–3). These feelings of human weakness our Lord took upon him, as he did the flesh of human weakness, and the death of human flesh, not by necessity, but by the free will of his mercy, that he might transform his own body, which is the Church to be like him. If any of them happened to be in sorrow and pain, they would not think that they were separated from his favor. The point is that the body learns from its Head that these sorrows are not sin, but proof of human weakness.

The Church is "poor," as she hungers and thirsts in her wanderings for that food with which she will be filled. She says, *from my youth I have suffered* (v. 15). She experiences the wrath of God, but it is not lasting, since it is only the unbelieving about whom it is written that "God's wrath remains on them" (John 3:36). The terrors of God disturb the weakness of the faithful, because of the possibility of judgment (even though it actually does not happen). It is wise to fear. Sometimes these terrors frighten the reflective soul with the surrounding evil because they seem to flow around us on every side like water, and to encircle us in our fears. But what is the purpose? That the prayers of this holy body may in the light of faith delay God's wrath until our salvation comes, which we await with patience and faithfulness. Then the Lord will not repel our prayers, as there will no longer be anything to be requested. Everything that has been rightly asked will be obtained. He will not turn his face away from us, since we shall see him as he is (1 John 3:2). We will not be poor, because God will be our abundance, all in all (1 Cor 15:28). We will not suffer, as there will be no more weakness. We will not experience even the temporary wrath of God, as we will be in his abiding love. His terrors will not frighten us, because his promises will bless us.

Psalm 89 with John Chrysostom –
Patience for Sinners and Strictness for the Godly

Indeed, God is good to everyone, but he shows his patient endurance especially to those who sin. And if you want to hear a paradoxical statement—paradoxical because it is not normal, but true for the great faithfulness it reveals—listen. God seems to be severe to the righteous but good to sinners, and quick to forgive. He restores the one who sinned and tells him: "Return to me . . . and I will return to you" (Zech 1:3). Elsewhere he promises that salvation is available with repentance: "As surely as I live, declares the Sovereign LORD, I take no pleasure in the death of the wicked, but rather that they turn from their ways and live" (Ezek 33:11). To the righteous he says: "If a righteous person turns from their righteousness and commits sin and does the same detestable things the wicked person does, will they live? None of the righteous things that person has done will be remembered. Because of the unfaithfulness they are guilty of and because of the sins they have committed, they will die" (Ezek 18:24). O such strictness toward the righteous! O such abundant forgiveness toward the sinner! He finds so many different means, without himself changing, to keep the righteous in check and forgive the sinner, by usefully distributing his rich goodness. And listen how: if he frightens the sinner who persists in sins, he brings him to desperation and to the exhaustion of hope. If he blesses the righteous, he weakens the intensity of his virtue and makes him neglect his zeal, since he considers himself already blessed. For this reason, he is merciful to the sinner and he frightens the righteous. For *he is more awesome than all who surround Him* (v. 7). And who are they but the saints? *In the council of the holy ones, God is greatly feared* (v. 7). If God sees someone who has fallen, he extends a loving hand. If he sees someone standing, he brings fear upon him. And this reveals righteousness and righteous judgment. God establishes the righteous person by fear, and he raises up the sinner with generosity.

Psalm 90 with Basil the Great – Flee Sin and Run to God

Those who acknowledge God often err in the judgment of their affairs, making demands for useful things foolishly, asking for some things as good, which frequently are not for their advantage, and fleeing others as evil, though at times they bring great assistance to them. For example, is someone sick? Because they are fleeing the pain from the sickness, they pray for health. Did they lose their money? They are exceedingly pained by the loss. Yet, frequently the disease is useful when it will restrain the sinner, and health is harmful when it becomes the means for sin to one who possesses it. In the same manner, money also has already enabled some to live wildly, while poverty has taught self-control to many who had begun badly. Do not flee, then, what you do not need to flee. Sin is the one thing you must flee, and God is the one refuge from evil you must seek. Do not trust in princes. Do not be exalted in the uncertainty of wealth. Do not be proud of bodily strength. Do not pursue the splendor of human glory. None of these things saves you. All are transient, all are deceptive. There is one refuge, God. "Cursed is the one who trusts in man" (Jer 17:5) or in any human thing.

Now, it is the privilege of many to say: "God is our refuge and strength" (Ps 46:1) and *Lord, you have been our dwelling place* (v. 1). But there are few people who do not admire human interests but depend wholly on God and place all hope and trust in him. And our actions convict us whenever in our afflictions we run to everything else rather than to God. Is a child sick? You look around for an enchanter, or finally, you go to a doctor and to medicine, having neglected him who is able to save. If a dream troubles you, you run to the interpreter of dreams. And, if you fear an enemy, you cunningly recruit some man as a supporter. In short, in every need you contradict yourself—in word, naming God as your refuge; in act, drawing on help from useless and empty things. God is the true aid for the righteous person.

Psalm 91 with Gertrude the Great – The Protection of God

Whoever dwells in the shelter of the Most High will rest in the shadow of the Almighty. I will say of the LORD, "He is my refuge and my fortress, my God, in whom I trust" (vv. 1–2).

Psalm: He who lives in the aid [of the Most High].

Antiphon:[1] He who lives in the aid of the Most High will remain under the protection of the God of heaven.

Prayer: Keeper of my soul and my refuge of the day of evil, in every temptation shade me with your shoulders of defense; enclose me with the shield of truth. May you yourself be with me in all my tribulation. [You who are] my hope, from every danger to body and soul always defend and protect me. Ah! And after this exile,[2] show me yourself, my dulcet[3] salvation. Amen.

---

1 Antiphon – musical recitation

2 This exile – life on earth

3 Dulcet – sweet

Psalm 92 with Augustine – Gratitude in All Circumstances

Let no Christian hope for present blessings or promise themselves the happiness of the world, because they are a Christian, but let them use the happiness they have. When it is present, let them give thanks for the consolation of God. When it is lacking, let them give thanks to the divine justice. Let them always be grateful to the Father, who soothes and caresses them, and grateful to their Father when he punishes and teaches. God always acts in love, whether he caresses or threatens. Let them say: *It is good to praise the LORD and make music to your name, O Most High* (v. 1).

The righteous will flourish . . . in the courts of our God. They will still bear fruit in old age, they will stay fresh and green (vv. 12–13). Do not be seduced by the prosperity of the wicked. Do not admire the flower of grass. Do not admire those who are only happy for a season, but miserable for eternity. If you wish to flourish like a tree, and not to wither like grass when the sun is hot, what will you declare? *The LORD is upright; he is my Rock, and there is no wickedness in him* (v. 15). How can there be no unrighteousness? One person commits major sins; he is well, he has children, a large house, pride, and honors; another person, innocent, attending to his own affairs, not robbing, doing nothing against anyone, suffers in chains, in prison, tosses and sighs in poverty. How is it that there is no unrighteousness in God? Is this not unfair? Because God is eternal, for the present he spares the bad, bringing them to repentance. Meanwhile he punishes the good, instructing them in the way to the kingdom of heaven. Fear not. The evil man will eventually hear, "Depart into everlasting fire." At that time you will be elevated to his right hand. Therefore, do not let those things move you. Be quiet, and demonstrate *the LORD is upright; he is my Rock, and there is no wickedness in him.*

Psalm 93 with Martin Luther –
God's Wonderfully Strange Works

According to our psalm, *the LORD on high is mighty* (v. 4) can be understood like Ps 68:35: "You, God, are awesome in your sanctuary; the God of Israel gives power and strength to his people"; or Ps 65:4–5: "You answer us with awesome and righteous deeds"; and Ps 4:3: "Know that the LORD has set apart his faithful servant for himself." That is to say, he turns his servant over to every kind of suffering and death and trouble, and yet saves him at the same time. And when he abandons him the most, then he rescues him the most. And when he condemns, he saves most of all. In this way he has carried out his wonderful plan (according to Isa 28:21), while his work is strange, he does his own work. This he said in the preceding psalm: "How great are your works, LORD, how profound your thoughts! Senseless people do not know, fools do not understand" (Ps 92:5–6). And the next psalm will have the same, when it says, "Blessed is the one you discipline, LORD, . . . you grant them relief from days of trouble" (Ps 94:12–13). Therefore also in this psalm, since he had said that the persecutions of the saints are great, he marvels that through them God saves by the foolishness of the cross, and very many are offended at Him.

Psalm 94 with Augustine – God as Avenger

The LORD is a God who avenges (v. 1). Do you think he does not punish? You murmur because the bad are unpunished. Do not murmur, so you will not be among the punished. One has committed theft, and lives: you murmur against God because of this. If you want another to correct the thief's hand, first correct your tongue. You would have him correct his heart towards others; correct your heart towards God, so that when you desire God's vengeance and it comes, it will not find you first. Watch your slightest daily sins. Rivers are filled with the smallest drops.

How long, LORD, will the wicked be jubilant? They pour out arrogant words; all the evildoers are full of boasting (vv. 3–4). God's people sometimes see the wicked flourishing and are led to follow them in their actions because they see that apparently it does not profit them to live well in humility. You are working in a vineyard; execute your task, and you will receive your pay. You would not demand payment from your employer before your work was finished; do you demand it from God before you work? This patience is part of your work, and your pay depends on your work. But if you are treacherous, take care, so you will not suffer punishment because you have chosen to be a treacherous worker. When such a worker begins to do wrong, he watches his employer's eyes, who hired him for his vineyard, so he may loiter when his eye is turned away, but the moment his eyes are turned towards him, he works diligently. But God, who hired you, does not look away. You cannot work treacherously. The eyes of your Master are always on you. Seek an opportunity to deceive him, and loiter if you can. If any of you had such ideas when you saw the wicked flourishing, and if such thoughts caused your feet to slip in the path of God, this psalm speaks to you.

He will repay them for their sins (v. 23). Therefore let the righteous bear with the ungodly. Let the temporary suffering of the righteous bear with the temporary freedom of the wicked; for "the righteous person will live by his faithfulness" (Hab 2:4). But if we live by faith, let us believe that we will inherit rest after our present toil, and that they will suffer eternal torments after their present honors. And if faith works by love, let us love our enemies also, and as far as we can, have the will to profit them. For then we will prevent their injuring us.

Psalm 95 with Augustine –
The Banquet of Joy and the Fire of Destruction

Come, let us sing for joy to the LORD (v. 1). He calls us
to a great banquet of joy, not one of this world, but in the
Lord. For if there were not in this life a wicked pleasure
which is to be distinguished from a righteous joy, it would
be enough to say, *Come, let us sing for joy*, but he has
briefly distinguished it: *to the LORD*. What is it to rejoice
rightly? To rejoice in the Lord. You should rejoice in the
Lord faithfully, if you wish to trample safely upon the world.

We began with exulting joy, but this psalm ends with
great fear: *So I declared on oath in my anger, "They shall
never enter my rest"* (v. 11). It is a great thing for God
to speak; how much greater is it for him to swear? You
should fear a man when he swears, lest he do something
on account of his oath against his will. How much more
should you fear God, when he swears, seeing he can swear
nothing rashly? He chose the act of swearing to confirm
his words. And who does God swear by? Himself, for
he has no one greater by whom to swear (Heb 6:13). By
himself he confirms his promises, by himself he confirms
his threats. Let no one say in their heart: his promise
is true; his threat is false. As his promise is true, so is his
threat sure. You should be equally assured of rest, of
happiness, of eternity, and of immortality if you have
executed his commandments, as you are of destruction,
of the burning of eternal fire, of damnation with the
devil, if you have despised his commandments.

Psalm 96 with Origen –
Condemning the Worship of Demons

All the gods of the nations are demons [v. 5, LXX]. And it is
not we alone who speak of wicked demons, but almost all
who acknowledge the existence of demons. Therefore, it
is not true that all obey the law of the Most High. All who
fall away from the divine law, whether through carelessness,
or through depravity and vice, or through ignorance of what
is right, do not keep the law of God, but rather "the law
of sin" (Rom 7:23). In the opinion of most of those who
believe in the existence of demons, some of them are
wicked; and these, instead of keeping God's law, break it.
But, according to our belief, demons were not demons
originally, but they became so in departing from the true
way; so that the name "demon" is given to those beings
who have fallen away from God. Accordingly, those who
worship God must not serve demons. We may also learn
the true nature of demons if we consider the practice of
those who call upon them by charms to prevent certain
things, or for many other purposes. For this is the method
they adopt, by means of incantations and magical arts to
invoke the demons, and induce them to further their wishes.
For this reason, the worship of all demons is inappropriate
for us who worship the Supreme God. The service of demons
is the service of so-called gods, for *all the gods of the nations
are demons*. The same thing also appears from the fact that
the dedication of the most famous of the so-called sacred
places, whether temples or idols, was accompanied by
magical incantations performed by those who zealously
served the demons with magical arts. For this reason
we are determined to avoid the worship of demons even
as we would avoid death; and we hold that the worship
that the Greeks render to "gods" at altars, images, and
temples, is in reality offered to demons.

Psalm 97 with John Calvin –
God, the Fountain of Righteousness

The LORD reigns, let the earth be glad (v. 1). God's throne is founded in justice and judgment. This is the benefit we derive from it. The greatest misery that we can conceive is living without righteousness and judgment. The psalmist mentions it as a matter of praise exclusively due to God that when he reigns, righteousness is revived in the world. He denies that we can have any righteousness, until God brings us into submission to his word, by the gentle but powerful influences of his Spirit. A great proportion of people stubbornly resist and reject the government of God. For that reason, the psalmist was forced to show God's severe qualities, to teach the wicked that their opposition will not pass unpunished. When God draws near to people in mercy, and they fail to welcome him with reverence and respect, this implies blasphemy.

Let those who love the LORD hate evil (v. 10). Those who fear God are here encouraged to practice righteousness. The psalmist shows from God's very nature that we cannot be acknowledged as his servants unless we depart from sin and practice holiness. God is the fountain of righteousness, so he hates all sin—or do you suppose that he can deny himself? We have fellowship with him only when we separate ourselves from unrighteousness.

We have seen that the LORD's people are often treated with the utmost cruelty and injustice, and would seem to be abandoned to the fury of their enemies. The psalmist reminds us for our encouragement that God, even when he does not immediately deliver his children, upholds them by his secret power. In the concluding verse he exhorts the LORD's people to gratitude, that looking upon God as their Redeemer, they should lead a life corresponding to the mercy they have received, and rest contented under all the evils they encounter, with the consciousness that they enjoy his protection.

Psalm 98 with Peter Chrysologus – Celebrating God's Kindness

Shout for joy to the LORD, all the earth (v. 4). What is it that an understanding of this great joy is likely to make clear? Why is it that, after God gave commandments so great, so terrifying, and so awesome, he now invites the earth to shout joyfully? *Shout for joy to the LORD, all the earth*, the text reads. What other reason is there than the following? The awesome God later chose the role of a very gentle shepherd. He assumed this character in order to act as a merciful shepherd and gather together, like straggling sheep into one fold, those wandering peoples, those straying nations, those tribes scattered far and wide. Yes, more, he wanted to lead back to milk and grass and restore those wild nations which were sluggish after eating the flesh and drinking the blood of carcasses. Briefly, he desired to make them again gentle sheep.

Shout for joy to the LORD, all the earth, he says, and by this command he imposes his shepherdly control on all the earth. The resounding trumpet draws the soldier forth to war. Just so does the sweetness of this joyous call invite the sheep to pasture. How fitting it was to lessen the chaos of fighting by shepherdly kindness, in order that grace so gentle might save the nations which their own natural wildness had long been destroying.

Psalm 99 with John Calvin – A Display of God's Power

The LORD reigns, let the nations tremble (v. 1). The people who were formerly called upon to rejoice are now commanded to tremble. For as the Jews were surrounded by enemies, it was extremely important that God's power was magnified among them, so they might know that, under his guardianship, they were constantly and completely safe from the hatred and fury of every foe. The prophet here intends that God, in freeing his chosen people, should give such a tangible display of his power that it would strike all the nations with dismay, and make them feel how wildly they had rushed into their own destruction. For God is said to reign over humans when he exalts himself by his magnificent displays of power. But while the aid he gives to them remains invisible, unbelievers act presumptuously, just as if there was no God.

Great is the LORD in Zion (v. 2). It is proper that we should not forget the reason that God is great in Zion: because he destroys and annihilates all the enemies of his Church. When the psalmist goes on to say, he is exalted over all the nations, he does not mean that he presides over them to promote their welfare, but to ruin their plans, baffle their designs, and subvert all their power.

They called on the LORD and he answered them (v. 6). God, with a special reference to his gracious covenant, bestowed great benefits upon the descendants of Abraham—the Jews—from the beginning. And, therefore, as often as they experienced the faithful love of God, it was proper for them to call to mind his former faithful love.

LORD *our God you answered them* (v. 8). The prophet
here reminds those whose prayers God had heard that his
grace and their faithfulness harmonized. Consequently,
encouraged by their success in prayer, their descendants
should call upon God, not merely pronouncing his name
with their lips, but keeping his covenant with all their
heart. He further reminds us that if God does not display
his glory so abundantly in every age, the fault is with
humans themselves, who gradually lose the faith of their
ancestors. It is not strange that God should withdraw his
hand when he sees faithfulness turning cold on the earth.

Psalm 100 with Augustine – Rejoicing in the Creator

Shout for joy to the LORD, all the earth (v. 1). Those working in the fields are most likely to shout for joy. Reapers or vinegrowers, or those who gather the fruits of the earth sing in exultation, delighted with abundant produce and rejoicing in the very richness and exuberance of the soil. Among the songs they utter in words, they add joyful cries without words.

How do we celebrate? When we offer as praise that which is beyond words. For we observe the whole creation, the earth and the sea, and all things that are within them. Who created all these things? Who made them? Who made you? I have observed the whole creation, as far as I could. I have observed the physical creation in heaven and on earth, and the spiritual in myself. And can I even comprehend myself? How then can I comprehend what is above myself? Yet the sight of God is promised to the human heart, and we are instructed to purify our hearts.

Look at the things that are made. Admire them. Seek their creator. If you are unlike him, you will turn away; if you are like him, you will rejoice. And when, being like him, you have begun to approach him, and to feel God, the more you will love since God is love, you will begin to perceive what you were trying to say, and could not say. Will you then be silent in the praises of God, and will you not offer up thanksgivings to him who made himself known to you? You praised him when you were seeking, will you be silent when you have found him? By no means; you will not be ungrateful. Honor, reverence, and great praise are due to him.

Augustine on Psalm 100

"Your praise of him is like food: the more you praise him, the more you acquire strength, and he becomes more sweet."

For the LORD is good (v. 5). Do not think you will grow tired of praising him. Your praise of him is like food: the more you praise him, the more you acquire strength, and he becomes more sweet. *His love endures forever.* For he will not cease to be merciful after he has freed you. He will protect you even until eternal life.

Psalm 101 with Cassiodorus –
The Love and Justice of God

I will sing of your love and justice; to you, LORD, I will sing praise (v. 1). The Lord's power is always either loving or bringing justice. But his mercy is never found without judgment, nor his judgment without mercy. Both are joined in an interlinked association; no act of his ever comes to light which is not seen to be full of all the virtues. Just as the psalmist speaks here of mercy and justice, so elsewhere instead of these two he links justice and peace, or love and truth, or justice and judgment, so that everywhere he shows God as devoted and just. This way of speaking is typical of divine Scripture. On the glorious occasion of his coming, he first mentions mercy when he says: "Come, you who are blessed by my Father; take your inheritance" (Matt 25:34); this is not without fairness, for he keeps his promises to the faithful. But next follows judgment, when he said to the wicked: "Depart from me, you who are cursed, into the eternal fire" (Matt 25:41), though this action is not unloving; he is known to show punishment only after much patience. Thus you see that the two concepts are reconcilable with each other and shine forth in their due places. Sinners who give up hope of being forgiven must listen to the Lord of mercy, whereas the proud who think that their wickedness will not be punished must visualise him as judge. So here the totality is sung briefly but fully, for in these two words—love and justice—all the Lord's works and the building up of the entire Church are clearly told.

Discussion Questions

 In his reflection on Psalm 100, Augustine suggests we will never get tired of praising God. How does this fit with the concept of the afterlife that your community anticipates?

 In his reflection on Psalm 89, Chrysostom states, "God always seems to be severe on the righteous, but good to sinners and quick to forgive them." Do you agree? Can you think of exceptions?

 Have you ever wrestled with God's fairness when the wicked around you prosper while you struggle? Do Augustine's words about Psalm 92 bring reassurance?

 Why does God use an oath in Psalm 95 when we are told not to swear in James 5:12?

 In his reflection on Psalm 87, Augustine urges us to "prepare ourselves to rejoice in God." What tangible practices might help us do this before we gather for corporate worship?

Chapter 6

Psalms 102–119:32

Psalm 102 with Augustine – The Promise of Forgiveness

The title is, *A prayer of an afflicted person who has grown weak and pours out a lament before the LORD*. Let us hear and recognise ourselves in these words. Why do you call? In what trouble? With what need? O poor one, from what destitution do you ask relief? From what need do you knock, that it may be opened for you?

In my distress I groan aloud and am reduced to skin and bones (v. 5). I also groan because many groan for the wrong reason. If someone loses money, they groan; but do not groan if they lose faith. I find more cause for groaning for the loss of faith than the loss of money. Someone commits fraud and rejoices. But with what gain, and with what loss? They have gained money and lost righteousness. We wish to reform them, and when we cannot, we groan.

Because God gives people room for repentance, and because he promises forgiveness, people do evil deeds.

They disregard consequences, because everything is forgiven when they are converted. If there is only license for sin, and no forgiveness for sins, then where will you be? Where will you go? People sin more under the hope of forgiveness. They also sin more if they lose hope of being forgiven. Do you not observe the promiscuous cruelty in which gladiators live? Because they are destined for the sword, they choose to satisfy their lust before they pour out their own blood. Would you not do the same? I am already a sinner, already an unjust man; I am one already doomed to damnation, and there is no hope of pardon. Why should I not do whatever pleases me, even if it is unlawful? Why not fulfill any longings I may have, if nothing but torments are in store for me? Would you not speak this way to yourself, and from this very despair become even worse? Rather than this, he who promises forgiveness corrects you, saying, "As surely as I live . . . I take no pleasure in the death of the wicked; but rather that they turn from their ways and live" (Ezek 33:11). For in order that people might not live worse because of despair, he promised a harbor of forgiveness. Therefore, repent! *I eat ashes as my food and mingle my drink with tears* (v. 9). By this banquet you will reach the table of God. Do not despair; pardon has been promised to you.

Psalm 103 with Gertrude the Great – Cleansing from Sin

At the first verse, *praise the LORD, my soul* (v. 1), I was granted to lay down upon the wounds of your sacred feet the scouring[1] rust of sin and all attachments to the worthless pleasures of the world. Then, at the second verse, *Praise the LORD, my soul, and forget not all his benefits* (v. 2), I was to wash away all the stains of fleshly and ephemeral[2] pleasure in the fountain of your cleansing love, whence[3] blood and water flowed for me. At the third verse, *who forgives all your sins* (v. 3) like the dove who builds her nest in the cleft of[4] the rocks, I was to find rest for my soul (Song of Sol 2:14; Ps 83:4–5) in the wound of your left hand. Then, at the fourth verse, *who redeems your life from the pit* (v. 4), approaching your right hand, I was to draw confidently from the treasures which it held all that I lacked for the perfection of every virtue.[5] Thus honorably adorned, through the fifth verse, *who satisfies your desires with good things* (v. 5), I was purged[6] from the infamy of sin. My deficiencies were made good by your sweetest and most longed-for presence. Now indeed I, who was of myself unworthy, was made worthy enough to rejoice in your chaste embrace. In this way you granted the petition of my prayer, the grace to read in these wounds your suffering and your love. . . . May glory, honor, and power with joyful praise be given to you in all eternity!

---

1 Scouring – fast moving

2 Ephemeral – fleeting

3 Whence – from which

4 Cleft of – crack between

5 "The perfection of every virtue" – the full development into maturity of Christian character

6 Purged – cleansed

Psalm 104 with Ambrose – Creation's Wonders Reveal the Creator

He made the moon to mark the seasons, and the sun knows when to go down (v. 19). Consider that the sun, the moon, and the stars, though they light up the sky and shine with brilliant splendor, are yet creatures. Whether they rise or fall in their daily duties, they serve the will of the eternal Creator, bringing forth the beauty with which they are clothed and shining by day and by night. How often is the sun covered by clouds or taken from the gaze of the earth when the ray of its light dims or an eclipse occurs, and as Scripture says: *the sun knows when to go down* (v. 19). It knows when it should shine in full light or weakened light. The stars, which are engaged in service to this world's advantage, disappear when they are covered by clouds. They do not do so willingly, surely, but in hope, because they hope for gratitude for their labor from him who made them. Thus, they persevere for his sake, that is, for his will.

Ambrose on Psalm 104

"This world is an example of the works of God, because, while we observe the work, the Worker is revealed to us."

This world is an example of the works of God, because, while we observe the work, the Worker is revealed to us. Let us consider the arts: There are those which are practical. These relate to the movement of the body or to the sound of the voice. When the movement or the sound has passed away, there is nothing that survives or remains for the spectators or the hearers. Other arts are theoretical. These display the vigor of the mind. There are other arts of such a nature that, even when the processes of creation cease, the result remains visible. As an example of this we have buildings or woven material which, even when the craftsperson is silent, still exhibit skill, so that testimony is presented of the artist's own work. In a similar way, this work is a distinctive mark of divine majesty from which the wisdom of God is made manifest. When he sees this, raising the eyes of his mind at the same time to invisible things, the psalmist says: *How many are your works, LORD! In wisdom you made them all* (v. 24).

Psalm 105 with Wolfgang Musculus – Remembering His Covenant

Sing to him, sing praise to him; tell of all his wonderful acts (v. 2). He sings because God has entrusted the word and mission of this covenant to a thousand generations. *He remembers his covenant forever, the promise he made, for a thousand generations* (v. 8). What sort of thing has been entrusted? The covenant begins with mortals, and he entrusts the word of the covenant to a thousand generations. I find two dimensions to this covenant. The first is that those things which concern the people of the covenant are preserved—that is, the tablets of the covenant on the Ten Words have been handed down. The other is that the grace of this covenant will be announced, spread, and communicated not only to the present generation but also to the following ones, and that up to a thousand generations. The prophet primarily sings about the mission of the covenant—by which God requires that what he established with Abraham and his descendants may also be offered to later generations so that nothing deprives them of this grace of the covenant.

Psalm 106 with Augustine – Human Forgetfulness

Remember me, LORD, when you show favor to your people
(v. 4): so we may be among those with whom you are well
pleased, since God is not well pleased with all of them.
*That I may enjoy the prosperity of your chosen ones, that
I may share in the joy of your nation* (v. 5). Show us your
salvation so we may see the happiness of your chosen
and rejoice with your people.

*But they gave no thought to your miracles; they did not
remember your many kindnesses* (v. 7). He rebukes both
their understanding and memory. Understanding is what
they needed in order to meditate on the eternal blessings
God had in store. They also needed memory, so they
would not forget his earthly wonders, and might faithfully
believe. By the same power they had already experienced,
God would free them from enemy persecutions. But they
forgot the help he gave them in Egypt to crush their
enemies through such wonders. We should especially
notice how the Scripture condemns their failure to
understand that which should have been understood,
and the failure to remember that which should have
been remembered. *Yet he saved them for his name's sake,
to make his mighty power known* (v. 8), not because
they deserved it.

But they soon forgot what he had done (v. 13): For they
should have thought that such great works of God towards
them had a purpose, namely, an invitation to wait with
patience for the endless happiness to come; but they hurried
to entertain themselves with earthly things that give no
one true happiness because they do not quench longing.

Psalm 107 with John Calvin – Gratitude for God's Providence

Let them give thanks to the LORD for his unfailing love (vv. 8, 15, 21, 31). Those who were delivered from slavery and imprisonment, and after a long and painful journey, arrived safely home are exhorted to offer gratitude to God. These he calls *the redeemed of the LORD*, because in wandering through the uncharted desert and howling wilderness, they would not have been able to return home if God had not appeared as their guard and guide. He does not refer to all travelers, but to refugees who felt themselves to be in imminent danger. Or it may be that he refers to those who were imprisoned by enemies, pirates, or other robbers. He reminds them that it was no coincidence that they were pursued in that manner, and later brought back to their home country, but that all their wanderings had been under the providence of God. So let the redeemed of the LORD, who have returned from captivity to their own land, come and take part in the celebration of God's praises. Let them declare his loving-kindness which they have experienced in their deliverance.

John Calvin on Psalm 107

"We will never be able to arrive at a calm state of mind until we are taught to rest with complete confidence in the providence of God."

They cried out to the LORD in their trouble (vv. 6, 13, 19, 28). Those who wander in desert places often suffer from hunger and thirst because they have found no place to lodge. When all hope of deliverance fades, they cry unto God. If a person falls into the hands of robbers or pirates, and is not instantly murdered, but giving up all hope of life, expects death every moment; surely their deliverance is a striking proof of the grace of God, which shines more brightly in proportion to how few make their escape. Therefore, if a great number die, this circumstance should not diminish the praises of God. The prophet condemns all those who are ungrateful, those who after they have been saved, very soon lose sight of the deliverance provided for them. To strengthen the charge, he brings forward their sighs and cries, as a testimony against them. For when they are in distress, they confess earnestly that God is their deliverer. How does it happen that this confession disappears when they are enjoying peace and quiet? We will never be able to arrive at a calm state of mind until we are taught to rest with complete confidence in the providence of God.

Psalm 108 with Cyril of Alexandria – Almighty God Over All Things

By belief "in One God," we cut off the error of false religions who believe in multiple gods, arming ourselves against the Greeks and all opposition on the part of heretics. . . . Of the Greeks, some have said that God is the soul of the world; others that His power does not extend to earth, but only to heaven. Some, working under a similar delusion, pervert the text: *your faithfulness reaches to the skies* (v. 4), and have dared to limit the providence of God to skies and heaven and to alienate from God the things on earth, forgetting the psalm which says: "If I go up to the heavens, you are there; if I make my bed in the depths, you are there" (Ps 139:8). For, if there is nothing higher than heaven, and the depths are deeper than the earth; he who rules the lower regions reaches the earth also. But heretics, as we said before, do not acknowledge one Almighty God. For he is Almighty who rules over all things and exercises authority over all.

Psalm 109 with John Calvin – God Fights Our Battles

My God, whom I praise, do not remain silent (v. 1). In these words, which introduce the psalm, David declares that he relies on God alone to prove his integrity. When David was attacked in a cruel and hostile manner, he did not unlawfully return evil for evil, but committed himself to the hand of God, fully satisfied that he alone could guard him from all evil. It is a great and desirable achievement for a person to restrain their passions by directly and immediately making their appeal to God's courtroom at the very time when they are abused without cause, and when the very injuries are calculated to arouse them to revenge. For some people aim to live in terms of friendship with the good, but when they come in contact with evil people, they imagine they are free to return injury for injury. All the godly are susceptible to this temptation. The Holy Spirit, however, restrains us, so that though often provoked by the cruelty of our enemies to seek revenge, we abandon all fraudulent and violent behavior, and give ourselves to God alone through prayer. We are instructed by David's example to do the same if we wish to overcome our enemies through the power and protection of God.

In Psalm 69:12, we have a parallel passage: "Those who sit at the gate mock me, and I am the song of the drunkards. But I pray to you, LORD!" Although David was aware that the whole world was opposed to him, he could still cast all his cares upon God, and this was enough to calm his mind. And as the Holy Spirit taught David and all the godly to offer up prayers like these, it must follow that those who imitate them will be promptly helped by God when he sees them disrespected and rudely persecuted.

David, free from all excessive passion, prayed under the influence of the Holy Spirit. The ungodly, who disdain God and who are constantly plotting the overthrow of the unsuspecting and the good, deserve the punishment of having *someone evil to oppose them* (v. 6). And since by means of intrigue and treachery they are constantly aiming at exterminating the good, they are rightly punished by God, who raises up against them an enemy who will never leave their side. Believers must be on their guard, so they do not pray this too hastily. Let them rather leave room for the grace of God to demonstrate itself on their behalf. For it may turn out that the person who shows us deadly hatred today may become our friend by tomorrow through that grace.

Psalm 110 with John Calvin and Philip Melanchthon – God's Anointed Protects His People

The LORD says to my lord: "Sit at my right hand" (v. 1). It is true that earthly kings may be said to sit at God's right hand, if they reign by his authority. However, here something more exalted is expressed, for this king is chosen in a peculiar manner and elevated to a powerful rank next to God. Of this dignity only glimpses appeared in David, while in Christ it shone forth in full splendor. And as God's right hand is elevated far above angels, it follows that he who is seated there is exalted above all creatures. We cannot say that angels were brought down from their high position to be put in subjection to David. The result is that by the spirit of prophecy Christ's throne is exalted far above all principalities in heavenly places. Therefore the Son, through whom the Father governs the world, is represented as invested with supreme dominion.

Until I make your enemies a footstool for your feet (v. 1). By these words the prophet affirms that Christ would subdue all his enemies' raging opposition which attempts to subvert his kingdom. At the same time, David suggests that the kingdom of Christ would never enjoy peace until he conquered his numerous enemies. But even if the whole world directed their energy to overthrowing Christ's royal throne, David here declares that it would remain unmoved and unmoveable, while all those who rise up against it shall be ruined. From this we learn that, however numerous those enemies may be who conspire against the Son of God, none will succeed against God's unchanging purpose. On the contrary, they will bow at Christ's feet. And since this prediction will not be accomplished before the last day, the kingdom of

Christ will first be attacked by many enemies until the
end of the world. That is why the psalmist says, *"Rule in
the midst of your enemies!"* (v. 2).

———

*The Lord is at your right hand; he will crush kings on the
day of his wrath. He will judge the nations, heaping up the
dead and crushing the rulers of the whole earth* (vv. 5–6).
These words describe the defense of the church in this life
and afterward a total deliverance. If we compare this to
the present dangers and miseries of the church, which has
been protected through all time, a more brilliant point
has been made: even if devils, political and religious empires,
kingdoms, the hatred of ungodly nations, and the fury of
heretics and false religions try to destroy the church, the
Messiah will still protect and preserve her. Finally, when
all these enemies have been suppressed and the empires
of the world destroyed, then will she be entirely free.

Psalm 111 with John Calvin – God's Faithful Justice

Glorious and majestic are his deeds (v. 3). Every act of God is full of glorious majesty. The psalmist specifies what this beauty and magnificence consist of by stating that his righteousness is visible everywhere. It is not the purpose of God to display his power and sovereignty in such a way that it would only terrify us. Instead, he also gives us a display of his justice in such an inviting way as to captivate our hearts. This tribute to the works and ways of God is introduced in opposition to the noisy lies of the ungodly, which they try to use to the utmost extent of their power, to disfigure and deface the glory of God. And having called upon us to contemplate his justice, now, in a similar way, and almost in the same terms, he celebrates the grace and mercy of God, mainly in relation to his works, because the justice he displays in the preservation and protection of his people arises from his unmerited favor which he shows them.

John Calvin on Psalm 111

"The law is prominent because, by declaring the eternal love of God, it became the means of giving life."

The works of his hands are faithful and just (v. 7). In the first part of the verse the psalmist exclaims that God is known to be faithful and upright in his works, and then he goes on to celebrate the same truth throughout the law. A beautiful harmony characterises all the sayings and doings of God, because everywhere he shows himself to be just and faithful. We have a memorable proof of this fact in the redemption of his ancient people. Among humans it is reckoned to be more important for one to be found fair in practice than in what they say; yet, as the law was the very life and safety of the people, the psalmist appropriately declares, *all his precepts are trustworthy. They are established for ever and ever, enacted in faithfulness and uprightness* (vv. 7–8). And surely, without God uniting the people to him by the sacred chain of the law, the fruit of their redemption would have been very small, and even that benefit would soon have been lost. We should observe, then, that the law is prominent because, by declaring the eternal love of God, it became the means of giving life.

Psalm 112 with Augustine – The Generosity of Forgiveness

Blessed are those who fear the LORD, who find great delight in his commands (v. 1). God, who alone judges both truthfully and mercifully, will see how far we obey his commandments. *Their children will be mighty in the land; . . . Wealth and riches are in their houses* (vv. 2–3). For their house is their heart, where, with the praise of God, they live in greater riches with the hope of eternal life than with flattering people in palaces of marble, with splendidly adorned ceilings, with the fear of everlasting death. For *their righteousness endures forever* (v. 9). This is their glory, these are their riches, while purple, and fine linen, and grand banquets, even when present, are passing away (Luke 16:24).

> **Augustine on Psalm 112**
>
> *"You will not grow poor by giving, for heavenly treasure is a safer possession."*

Good will come to those who are generous and lend freely (v. 5). It is generally called mercy when another is assisted in distress, yet there is a difference when you spend no money, and do no bodily labor, but by forgiving what each one has sinned against you, you gain pardon for your own sins also. "Forgive," he says, "and you will be forgiven; give, and it will be given to you" (Luke 6:37–38). While you forgive so you may be forgiven, you are merciful; while you give so it may be given unto you, you lend. You will not lose honor by forgiving: for it is a commendable triumph to conquer anger. You will not grow poor by giving, for heavenly treasure is a safer possession.

Psalm 113 with Gertrude the Great – A Humble Heart

He raises the poor from the dust and lifts the needy from the ash heap (v. 7).

First, then, come to the face of your God in the spirit of humility in order that he may show you the grace of his countenance. And say:

I speak to my Lord, although I am dust and ashes. O my God, exalted and sublime, look upon that which is humble far below (v. 7); my soul and spirit grow faint at the limitless good you have done. Open to me the treasure of your most gracious heart, where the sum of my desires is stored. Open the grace of your mellifluous[1] countenance for me that I may pour out my soul under your gaze (Ps 142:2). Open to me that most dulcet[2] favor of my peace in you, which will exhilarate my soul and loosen my tongue in your praise.

Ah! O love, enter for me before the gaze of the great God and there announce the clamoring[3] of my desire because, in thirsting for God, all of my own virtue has already dried up. Ah, drag and draw my spirit upwards to you because already my flesh and my heart are growing faint for God, my salvation. Ah! Present me to the Lord, my king, because my soul has already melted with loving and waiting for my spouse. O love, now very quickly fulfill my desire; if you delay I, already growing faint, will die for love.

---

1 Mellifluous – soothing

2 Dulcet – sweet

3 Clamoring – crying out

Psalm 114 with John Calvin – Remembering God's Deliverance

This psalm contains a short account of that deliverance by which God brought his people out of Egypt and brought them to the promised land, providing proof of his power and grace that should be remembered forever. This wonderful deliverance was designed so the descendants of Abraham would surrender themselves fully to God, who graciously adopted them as his holy and treasured people (Exod 19:5–6).

When Israel came out of Egypt (v. 1). Since the exodus was a remarkable pledge and symbol of God's love for the children of Abraham, it is not surprising that it is remembered so often. In the beginning of the psalm, the prophet informs us that the people God purchased at such a high price are no longer their own: *Judah became God's sanctuary, Israel his dominion* (v. 2). In delivering his people, God constructed a kingdom for himself and gained respect for his sacred name. If they do not constantly reflect upon such a remarkable instance of his kindness, their ingratitude is inexcusable.

After the people passed through the Red Sea, God gave another splendid demonstration of his power in the wilderness. The glory of God did not appear on one day only, at the departure of the people. It constantly shone in his other works, as when a stream suddenly poured out of the dry rock (Exod 17:6). Waters may be found trickling out from among rocks and stony places, but to make them flow out of a dry rock was unquestionably miraculous.

Psalm 115 with Augustine – The Folly of Idol Worship

Our God is in heaven (v. 3). Not in the heavens, where people see the sun and moon, works of God which they adore, but "in heaven above," which surpasses all heavenly and earthly bodies. *Their idols are silver and gold, made by human hands* (v. 4). That is, although we cannot display our God to human eyes, we should recognize him through his works. Do not be seduced by your pride, because you can point to the objects of your worship—bronze, wood, and clay idols. As it says in Scripture concerning idol worshippers, "They say to wood, "You are my father," and to stone, "You gave me birth" (Jer 2:27). But do not think that someone who speaks to gold and silver rather than to wood or stone is wiser. Both employ human hands to create a false god out of that material which a true God created.

For they have mouths, but cannot speak; eyes, but cannot see. They have ears, but cannot hear, noses, but cannot smell. They have hands, but cannot feel, feet, but cannot walk, nor can they utter a sound with their throats (vv. 5–7). Even their artist surpasses them, since he has the ability of shaping them by the motion of his arms, though you would be ashamed to worship the artist. You surpass them, though you have not made them, since you do what they cannot. Even a beast surpasses them, for they see, and hear, and smell, and walk, and some even feel with their hands. Even the dead surpass a god who neither lives nor has lived. *Those who make them will be like them, and so will all who trust in them* (v. 8). *But you who fear him, trust in the LORD* (v. 11).

Psalm 116 with Augustine – Correcting Misplaced Love

I love the LORD, for he heard my voice; he heard my cry for mercy. Because he turned his ear to me, I will call on him as long as I live (vv. 1–2). I love because he will hear; he will hear, because he turned his ear to me. But how do you know that God has turned his ear to you when you simply say, "I have believed"? These three things, therefore, "remain: faith, hope, and love" (1 Cor 13:13). Because you have believed, you have hoped; because you have hoped, you have loved.

I was overcome by distress and sorrow. Then I called upon the name of the LORD (vv. 3–4). For I did not experience trouble and beneficial sorrow; trouble, where he gives aid, to whom it is said, "Give us aid against the enemy, for human help is worthless" (Ps 60:11). For at first, I thought I might rejoice in the help of humans, but it proved useless. When I had heard from my Lord, "Blessed are those who mourn, for they will be comforted" (Matt 5:4), I did not wait to mourn until I lost those earthly blessings in which I rejoiced. Instead, I paid attention to that very misery of mine which caused me to rejoice in such earthly things, which I both feared to lose and could not retain. I looked at my misplaced love firmly and courageously, and I saw that I was not only agonized by the troubles of this world, but bound by its good fortune. In this way *I was overcome by distress and sorrow which had escaped me, I called upon the name of the LORD: "LORD, save me!*

Psalm 117 with Cassiodorus – The Whole World Praises

Praise the LORD, all you nations; extol him, all you peoples (v. 1). Collective praise is expressed together by all the faithful, and is seen to be fitting for the entire church assembled from different parts of the world. All nations in common are exhorted among the people so that none at the Lord's judgment may claim that they were not included. *For great is his love toward us, and the faithfulness of the LORD endures forever* (v. 2). The reason why the Lord must be praised throughout the world is because he has fulfilled his promises made through the holy prophets by his coming to us. His mercy towards Christians is confirmed and will never be changed, for he who granted it, as we rightly believe, protects us. This tiny psalm is enclosed in the most spacious conciseness. What more expansive feeling can be spoken than that the Creator must be praised all over the world?

Psalm 118 with Augustine – Trusting God Alone

We are taught in this psalm to *give thanks to the LORD* (v. 1). The praise of God could not be expressed in fewer words than these, *for he is good* (v. 1). But, when my enemies have been brought to contempt, do not let my friend present himself to me as a good person, to get me to rest my hope on him: for *It is better to take refuge in the LORD than to trust in humans* (v. 8). Do not let any one, even a "good angel," seem trustworthy to me: for "no one is good—except God alone" (Mark 10:18), and when a human or an angel appears to aid us, he does it through them. Therefore *It is better to take refuge in the LORD, than to trust in princes* (v. 9).

The LORD's right hand has done mighty things! (v. 16). Nevertheless, the body of Christ, the holy Church, the people he adopted, suffered humiliation. *The LORD has chastened me severely, but he has not given me over to death* (v. 18). Do not let the boastful wicked imagine that they have power to do anything to us. They would not have that power if it had not been given to them from above. Likewise, often the father of a family commands his children to be corrected even though he designs an inheritance for them. What is our inheritance? Is it of gold, or silver, or jewels, or farms, or pleasant estates? Consider how we enter into it, and learn what it is. *Open for me the gates of the righteous* (v. 19). What is within? *I will enter and give thanks to the LORD.* This is the confession of praise full of wonder. This is the everlasting bliss of the righteous; those who dwell in the LORD's house are blessed, praising him forevermore (Ps 84:4).

Psalm 119 with Gertrude the Great – Determination to Follow God's Commands

I run in the path of your commands, for you have broadened my understanding (v. 32).

Prayer: Ah, lovingly-kind Jesus, although the will [to do what is good] is in me, I do not find [the strength] to accomplish it. Therefore, by the cooperation of your grace and through the spotless law of your love, turn my soul from the frailty of the human condition toward you in such a way that I may untiringly run in the way of your commandments and cling inseparably to you. Be with me, my Lord, aiding me always and making me strong in the work that I have taken up for the love of your love.

And now, where will I go from you? Both in heaven and on earth, I now know nothing except you. My God, praise of Israel, you who dwell in the sanctuary (Ps 22:3), in whom I live and move and have my being (Acts 17:28), in you alone I trust. In you my heart is laid wide-open (2 Cor 6:11; Ps 119:32) because you are my entire and only joy and all my desire. The ray of your daylight has awakened my sleeping spirit.

Sustain me, my God, according to your promise, and I will live; do not let my hopes be dashed (v. 116).

Let me not be confounded in my expectation but grant me to find rest for my soul in you. I have found nothing more desirable, I have judged nothing more lovable, I have wished for nothing more dear than to be held tight,

O love, in your embrace, to rest under the wings of my Jesus, and to dwell in the tabernacle of divine charity.

O love, O radiant noonday, I would die a thousand times to be at rest in you. If only you would bend to me your face of such beautiful cherishing-love, O dearest one.

Discussion Questions

 Writing about Psalm 102, Augustine says "People sin more under the hope of pardon." Can you think of examples where this is the case in your life?

 Inspired by Psalm 119, Gertrude laments, "although the will [to do what is good] is in me, I do not find [the strength] to accomplish it." How does this compare to the apostle Paul's teaching in Romans 7–8?

 Psalm 115:5–7 talks about worshipping idols. Is there anything in your life that takes priority over God?

 What does Augustine say about forgiveness in his reflection on Psalm 112? Is there someone in your life to whom you need to show this form of generosity?

 Psalm 119 lists dozens of benefits of God's Word. What habits might make Scripture engagement a more frequent practice in your life?

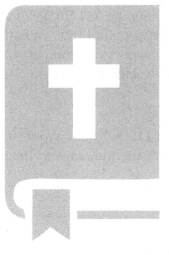

BIBLICAL STUDIES

Chapter 7
Psalms 119:33–130

Psalm 120 with Augustine – A Pilgrim's Cry for Peace

Woe to me that I dwell in Meshek (v. 5). My journey has departed far from you; my pilgrimage has become a far one. I have not yet reached that country where I will someday live with no wicked person to threaten me. I have not yet reached that company of angels, where I will fear no offence. But why am I not there yet? Because my journey is a pilgrimage. And when is it far off? Sometimes, when people go abroad, they live among better people than they would perhaps live with in their own country. But it is not like this when we go far from that heavenly Jerusalem. For a person changes their country, and this foreign sojourn is sometimes good for them. In travelling they find faithful friends whom they could not find in their own country. They had enemies, so they were driven from their country; and when they travelled, they found what they did not have at home. (By this I do not mean

Jerusalem, where all are good, all are righteous and holy, all gaze at the face of God. What a country! A great country indeed, and wretched are the wanderers from that country).

Augustine on Psalm 120

"You will not be able to prove how truly you sing, unless you have begun to do what you sing."

The psalmist, when ascending to Jerusalem, said, *I live among the tents of Kedar!* (v. 5). The tents of Ishmael are called those of Kedar. Genesis tells us that Kedar belongs to Ishmael (Gen 25:13). Isaac therefore is with Ishmael. That is, those who belong to Isaac live among those who belong to Ishmael.

Too long have I lived among those who hate peace. I am for peace (vv. 6–7). But you will not be able to prove how truly you sing, unless you have begun to do what you sing. However much I say this, in whatever ways I explain it, in whatever words I use, it does not enter into the heart of one who takes no action. Begin to act in peace, and see what we speak. Then tears flow forth at each word, then the psalm is sung, and the heart does what is sung in the psalm.

Psalm 121 with Augustine –
Trusting the One Who Never Sleeps

He who watches over Israel will neither slumber nor sleep (v. 4). Choose him who will neither sleep nor slumber, and your foot will not slip. God never sleeps. If you wish to have a guardian who never sleeps, choose God for your guardian. "Do not let my feet slip," you say, but he also says to you, "Let not the one who watches over you slumber." Perhaps you were about to turn to a human as your guardian. Who can you find who will never sleep? The psalmist tells you: *He who watches over Israel will neither slumber nor sleep* (v. 4). Do you wish to have a guardian who neither slumbers nor sleeps? Then do not trust in any human.

The LORD will keep you from all harm (v. 7). From harm by the sun, from harm by the moon, from all injury he will preserve you. He is your defence at your right hand, who will not sleep nor slumber. And for what reason? Because we are amid temptations: *The LORD will keep you from all harm—he will watch over your life; The LORD will watch over your coming and going both now and forevermore* (v. 8).

Psalm 122 with John Calvin – Praying for Unity

Jerusalem is built (v. 3). Here David begins to celebrate Jerusalem in order to encourage the people to persevere steadfastly in their obedience. Instead of being drawn here and there, the minds of the godly were to be kept constantly fixed on that city, which facilitated holy unity. It is not surprising to find David endorsing so earnestly the place God had chosen, knowing that the success of the Church depended on the children of Abraham worshipping God there in purity, according to the appointed observances of the law. The success of the Church also depended on the peoples' acknowledgment of the royal throne which God had established there by his own authority and had taken under his own protection.

When it is said that *Jerusalem is built like a city that is closely compacted together*, it refers not only to the walls, or towers, or ditches of that city, but especially to the good order and holy administration that distinguished it from other cities. Jerusalem is a compact city to encourage the faithful, instead of gazing in all directions around them, to rest contented with the city which God had chosen, since they could nowhere find its equal. The excellence of Jerusalem's construction represents its peaceable state. Thus the mutual agreement which reigns among the citizens of a city is compared to buildings compacted together by a skillful and elegant workmanship, so that they are joined together perfectly. By this David teaches us that the Church can only remain in a state of safety when holy unity prevails, being joined together by faith and love.

Pray for the peace of Jerusalem (v. 6). David now exhorts
all serious worshippers of God to pray for the prosperity
of the holy city. In order to stir them up to do this, he
promises that the divine blessing will descend upon them.
The reason why he was so deeply concerned about the
prosperity of Jerusalem was because the welfare of the whole
Church was inseparably connected with that kingdom
and priesthood. Now each of us would perish miserably
if the whole Church was ruined, so it is not surprising
to find David urging all the children of God to cultivate
this diligent concern for the Church. Let us always begin
our prayers by pleading that the Lord would be pleased
to preserve this sacred community.

Psalm 123 with Augustine – True Riches

Have mercy on us, for we have endured no end of contempt (v. 3). All you who live faithfully with Christ must suffer rebuke, and must be despised by those who do not choose to live faithfully, all whose happiness is earthly. You are ridiculed because you hope for what you do not see; and those who seem to hold what they see, scorn you. Yet since we hope for those things which are to come, and sigh for future happiness, *we have endured no end of contempt* by those who seek or enjoy happiness in this world. *We have endured no end of ridicule from the arrogant, of contempt from the proud* (v. 4). Perhaps they mock when they are happy, when they boast in their great wealth! When they boast of their false honors, then they mock us.

To this we must add that sometimes those who are unhappy mock us. Did not the robber mock, who was crucified with our crucified Lord (Luke 23:39)? He wishes to deprive God of governing this world, and steer creation himself, to distribute pains and pleasures, punishments and rewards. Miserable soul!

Christians should not be wealthy, but should acknowledge themselves poor. If they have riches, they ought to know that they are not true riches. And what is the wealth of our righteousness? However much righteousness there may be in us, it is a sort of dew compared to that fountain. Compared to that abundance it is only a few drops. Let us only desire to be filled with the full fountain of righteousness; let us long to be filled with that abundant richness: "They feast on the abundance of your house; you give them drink from your river of delights" (Ps 36:8). But while we are here, let us understand ourselves to be destitute and in need. Let our whole hunger, our whole thirst, be for true riches, and true health, and true righteousness. What are true riches? That heavenly dwelling in Jerusalem. For who is called rich on this earth? When a rich man is praised, what is meant? He is very rich: nothing is lacking for him. But in that City there will be true riches, because there will be nothing lacking for us there; for we will not be in need of anything, and there will be true health.

Psalm 124 with Augustine – The Praising Multitude

We have sung a psalm: *Praise be to the LORD, who has not let us be torn by their teeth* (v. 6). This is a proper expression of gratitude for the gifts of God. And when can human gratitude ever match such divine gifts? When the blessed martyr shed his sacred blood in this place, I do not know whether there was as big a crowd here of people raging against him, as there is now a multitude of people praising him. I repeat—I am delighted, after all, to see in the house of the Lord people gathering so faithfully in this place. But even if there was a larger crowd, *Praise be to the LORD, who has not let us be torn by their teeth.* When they killed, they imagined they had conquered; in fact, they were being conquered by the people who were dying, and they rejoiced. If they were being conquered, they were naturally raging. So the raging crowd has departed, and the praising multitude has taken its place. Let them say, let the praising multitude say, *Praise be to the LORD, who has not let us be torn by their teeth.* Whose teeth? The teeth of the enemies, the teeth of the godless, the teeth of those persecuting Jerusalem, the teeth of Babylon, the teeth of the enemy city, the teeth of the crowd gone stark raving mad in their wickedness, the teeth of a crowd persecuting the Lord, forsaking the Creator, turning to the creature, worshiping things made by hand, ignoring the one by whom they were made.

Psalm 125 with Augustine –
God's Everlasting Inheritance

As the mountains surround Jerusalem, so the LORD surrounds his people, both now and forevermore (v. 2). He surrounds his people, and he has walled his people with a spiritual fortification, so they may never be shaken. If the mountains stand around Jerusalem, and the Lord stands around his people, the Lord binds his people into one bond of love and peace, so that they who trust in the Lord, like mount Zion, will never be shaken.

The scepter of the wicked will not remain over the land allotted to the righteous, for then the righteous might use their hands to do evil (v. 3). At present the righteous suffer, and at present the unrighteous sometimes dominate the righteous. In what ways? Sometimes the unrighteous achieve worldly honors. When they have achieved them, and have been made either judges or kings, the honor must be shown to them due to their power. For God has ordained that every worldly power may have honor, and sometimes from those who are better than those in power. But the ungodly will not always have power over the righteous. The rod of the ungodly is felt upon the righteous for a season but it will not be there forever. A time will come when Christ, appearing in his glory, will gather all nations before him (Matt 25:32–33). And there you will see many slaves among the sheep, and many masters among the goats; and again many masters among the sheep, many slaves among the goats. For not all slaves are good, nor are all masters evil. There are good masters who believe, and there are evil. There are good servants who believe, and there are evil. But as long as good servants serve evil masters, let them endure for a season, so the righteous may prepare themselves to possess their everlasting inheritance.

Psalm 126 with Augustine – Sow Mercy and Reap Peace

Those who sow with tears, will reap with songs of joy (v. 5). In this life, which is full of tears, let us sow good works. Works of mercy are our seeds: seeds of which the apostle Paul says, "Let us not become weary in doing good, for at the proper time we will reap a harvest if we do not give up" (Gal 6:9). Speaking of giving itself, he says, "Whoever sows sparingly will also reap sparingly" (2 Cor 9:6). Whoever sows plentifully, will reap plentifully; and whoever sows nothing, will reap nothing. Why do you long for large estates, where you may sow plentifully? There is not a wider field on which you can sow than Christ, who desires for us to sow in him. Your soil is the Church; sow as much as you can. But—you object—you do not have enough to do this. Have you the desire? What you have would be nothing, if you did not have a good will. So do not lose confidence because you have nothing, if you have a good will. Sow mercy and reap peace.

Zacchaeus had a strong will; Zacchaeus had great charity (Luke 19:1–8). Did that widow who cast her two coins into the treasury, sow little (Luke 21:1–4)? No, she sowed as much as Zacchaeus. For she had fewer resources, but an equal will. She gave her two coins with as good a will as Zacchaeus gave half of his estate. If you consider what they gave, you will find their gifts different; if you look to the source, you will find them equal; she gave whatever she had, and he gave what he had. Even beggars whose profession is asking for money have something to offer one another in times of trouble. The one who can walk lends their feet to the lame. The one who can see lends their eyes to the blind. The one who is young and healthy lends strength to the old or the weak by carrying them.

The one is poor, the other is rich. Sometimes the rich man is found to be poor in some way, and something is given to him by the poor. Love one another. Pay attention not only to yourselves, but also to those in need around you. But because these things take place in this life with troubles and cares, do not give up. What you sow in tears, you will reap in joy.

Psalm 127 with Gertrude the Great – Full Surrender to God

He grants sleep to those he loves (v. 2).

Hide me, most loving Jesus, in the hiding-place of your face from all those plotting crafty devices against me, and let my soul not be confounded when it speaks with its enemies at the gate; but fill it full of gladness with your mellifluous[1] face.

O God, love, you are the consummation[2] and the end of all good: to the very end, you cherish what you choose; whatever comes into your hand, you do not toss out but preserve most diligently for yourself. Ah! By right of possession make all my being . . . your own forever. Spare me now no longer, but wound my heart to the spirit's very marrow until you leave no spark of life within me. Rather, take away with you my entire life, reserving for yourself my soul in you.

Who will grant me to be consummated[3] in you, O charity, and to be delivered by your death from the prison of this body and to be freed from this sojourn? How good, O love, to see you, have you, and possess you for eternity. On the day I depart this life, may you yourself be present, regardful of great consolation, and may you bless me then in the beautiful dawn of the manifest contemplation of you. Now, O love, I here . . . commend to you my life and, at the same time, my soul: allow me, allow me now to rest and fall asleep in you in peace. Amen.

---

1 Mellifluous – soothing

2 Consummation – fulfillment

3 Consummated – fulfilled

Psalm 128 with Cassiodorus – The Fear of the Lord

Blessed are all who fear the LORD, who walk in obedience to him (v. 1). In his first words he has distinguished fear of the Lord from the terror of this world. His words—*blessed are all who fear the LORD*—reveal that those with troubled mind who are apprehensive of the world's dangers in loss of temporal possessions are not blessed. These dangers make men wretched, torturing them with empty fear, so that they experience no growth but a reduction, no ascent but a headlong fall.

By contrast, fear of the Lord is the offspring of love, is sprung from sweetness. What devoted fear, consoling the timid, refreshing the afflicted, experiencing no absence of joy unless the benefit of such fear is laid aside! Scripture says of this fear: "Come, my children, listen to me: I will teach you the fear of the LORD" (Ps 34:11). How advantageous the fear is by which children are instructed, how splendid the training bestowed with sweet affection! But to prevent your believing that the Lord is perhaps only to be feared when he thunders, or sends lightning, or makes lands quake, or threatens death to lawbreakers, he added: *who walk in obedience to him*. Fear of the Lord not only causes us to abandon wicked deeds, but also establishes us as walking in the most upright faith; those people *fear the LORD who walk in obedience* and perform his commandments with devoted minds.

Psalm 129 with Cassiodorus – The Vindication of God

They have greatly oppressed me from my youth, but they have not gained the victory over me (v. 2). The Church says that she has been fiercely attacked from her youth, so that you may realise that she is never destroyed, in spite of constant attack. She grows under the persecution of the wicked, and expands through her grief. Even though she seems to lose holy ones in this life [through martyrdom], she gains them for the inheritance to come. She cannot be brought to an end, since she is clearly increased by the losses which she endures. This is what the following words make clear: *but they have not gained the victory over me.* Those who had attacked her could not prevail over her; for the attack that develops into further conflict is not yet ended. Victory must not be pronounced when it is certain that the conflict can be renewed.

May they be like grass on the roof, which withers before it can grow (v. 6). Abandoned buildings often sprout momentarily with grass on their tops. Before it can be gathered it withers and dies because it has insufficient roots to give it strength. Hostile sinners are linked with such grass in a most fitting association, for they also often die off here before they are taken from this world's light, for they sprout on the heights of pride where they are not firmly based, whereas if they sprouted in the valley of tears, they would bring their harvest to fullness with the Lord's help.

Psalm 130 with Katharina Schütz Zell – An Earnest Prayer for Grace

[130:1] O God, out of the depths of my heart, of all the most inward and spiritually rich power in me, I cry to You now in my great distress. [130:2] Hear my voice, let Your ears be open to me. Take to heart, give heed to, and receive my plea to You, which I make with earnest sighing and weeping. [130:3] If You should regard sins, to reckon and chastise them and therefore not listen to prayers, who could stand before You, or dare to pray for something, much less hope to obtain it?

Refusing to forgive would be contrary to Your accustomed way of acting, which has come down to us from of old, contrary to Your faithfulness and goodness, which have been experienced and known. [130:4] For with You there is much forgiveness, and You never weary in doing good, if only a person fears You and does not despise Your faithfulness and goodness, but builds on them. This truth You have granted me to know; this truth I confess with thanks because I know it and have experienced it in my many afflictions.

[130:5] So I wish now to keep watch for You; yes, my soul should keep watch for what You will do—with such watching that I may hope in You with my whole heart through the word of Your promise. [130:6a] Yes, indeed, my soul should keep watch in such a way that You will say to her that You are still my God [cf. Ps 42:5–6, 11; 43:5]. [130:6b] This is so, even if indeed the watching goes on from one morning watch to another, from one time to another, from one affliction to another, from one promise to another, from one body to another, yes, from one life to another, and even if we still find the time long. [130:7a] Yes, whoever can believe thus will appropriately be called "Israel," one who overcomes God [cf. Gen 32:28], because he took God at His word: therefore he may hope and will not be put to shame before his enemies.

[130:7b] For with the Lord alone is grace and many and varied ways to redemption in many difficult and secret afflictions, beyond all human knowledge and understanding. [130:8] And He will redeem Israel (the seed of Abraham), the guilty, afflicted, distressed, believing sinner, from all his sins, which are a cause, foundation, and power of all afflictions. Amen.

Discussion Questions

Calvin discusses the importance of peace and unity in the Church in his reflection on Psalm 122. Are peace and unity a priority in your church? How can you tell? In what ways might this be improved?

How does the fear of the Lord transform us to do what is good in Psalm 128? What is the difference between this fear and an unhealthy fear?

Psalm 119 celebrates the law of God almost endlessly! What aspects of God's instructions does the psalmist finds particularly helpful or praiseworthy? How about you? What do you treasure most about the Scriptures?

In his reflection on Psalm 126, Augustine claims, "Even beggars whose profession is asking for money have something to offer one another in times of trouble." What does a beggar have to offer others? What implications could this have for the way "charity work" is done?

Reflecting on Psalm 120, Augustine warns "You will not be able to prove how truly you sing, unless you have begun to do what you sing." Choose a favorite worship song or hymn to discuss as a group. How can you implement this song in your life?

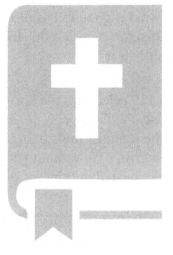

BIBLICAL STUDIES

Chapter 8
Psalms 131-150

Psalm 131 with John Cassian and Martin of Braga – The Danger of Pride and the Value of Humility

Although the disgrace of pride is the last battle we fight, it is nonetheless the source of all sins and wrongful deeds, and it does not do away merely with its opposite virtue— that is, humility—but is actually the destroyer of all the virtues. That is why, although blessed David guarded his heart with great care so that he could boldly declare to him from whom the secrets of his conscience were not hidden: *My heart is not proud, LORD, my eyes are not haughty; I do not concern myself with great matters or things too wonderful for me* (v. 1). He knew nevertheless how difficult it was even for the perfect to keep up this guard, and he did not presume on his own effort alone, but, in order to be able to escape unharmed this enemy's dart, prayerfully implored the Lord's help and said: "May the foot of pride not come against me" (Ps 35:12). And he was terrified and frightened lest there befall him what was said of the proud: "God opposes the proud" (James 4:6).

How great the evil of pride is, that it deserves to have God himself as its adversary! For it is never said of those who are caught up in the other vices that the Lord resists them, or that the Lord is set against the gluttonous, or fornicators, or the angry, or the greedy; this is true of the proud alone. For those vices only turn back upon wrongdoers or seem to be committed against other human beings. This one, however, touches God, and therefore it is especially worthy of having God opposed to it.

———

Now listen briefly while I explain how the virtue of humility may be obtained. First of all, if you intend to start a good work, begin it not with the intention of acquiring praise, but for the love and desire of doing good. Then, when this good task has been completed, guard your heart most cautiously, lest you fall under the influence of human favors and overestimate yourself, trying to please yourself or to look for some fame from any deed. For glory is like a human shadow: if you follow it, it runs away; if you run away, it follows. Always value yourself least of all and remember, whenever any good befalls you throughout your life, ascribe it all to God who gave it, not to yourself who received it. And when you have built in your heart a temple to the Holy Spirit, using these most precious stones of holy humility, then pray in it, using the song of the prophet David. Not in words only, but in deeds shall you sing: *My heart is not proud, LORD, my eyes are not haughty; I do not concern myself with great matters or things too wonderful for me* (v. 1).

Psalm 132 with Augustine – True Humility

Let us go to his dwelling place (v. 7). Whose? The Lord God of Jacob. Those who enter to dwell in it also enter so that he may dwell in them. You enter your house that you may dwell in it; into the house of God, so that he may dwell in you. When he has begun to dwell in you, he will make you happy. For if he does not, you will be miserable.

Also, *her poor I will satisfy with food* (v. 15). Let us be poor, and we shall then be satisfied. Many who trust in the world and are proud worship Christ, but are not satisfied, for they have been satisfied and abound in their pride. These have abundance, and therefore eat, but are not satisfied. They worship Christ, they honor Christ, they pray to Christ; but they are not satisfied with his wisdom and righteousness. Why? Because they are not poor. For the poor, that is the humble in heart, the more they hunger, the more they eat; and the emptier they are of the world, the hungrier they are. Those who are full refuse whatever you give them, because they are full. Give me one who hungers, for "Blessed are those who hunger and thirst for righteousness, for they will be filled" (Matt 5:6).

Sometimes, however, you find a poor man who is proud, and a rich man who is humble. God's poor are therefore poor in spirit, not necessarily in their purse. Sometimes a man has a full house, rich lands, many estates, much gold and silver, but he knows he must not trust in his wealth. He humbles himself before God. He does good with his possessions. In this way his heart is raised to God, so that he is aware that riches do not profit him, but that they even impede his feet, unless he rules and aids them. One who is satisfied with bread is counted among the poor. You find another, a proud beggar, or not proud only because he has nothing, yet still seeking how to exalt himself. God judges him according to his wish for earthly blessings, not according to the means which it is not his luck to have. When they have laid hold of eternal life, then will they be rich, but since they do not have it yet, they should know that they are poor. Thus it is that God counts among his poor all who are humble in heart.

Psalm 133 with John Calvin – The Spirit of Unity

How good and pleasant it is when God's people live together in unity! (v. 1) David thanks God for the peace and harmony which followed a long-standing division in the kingdom, and urged everyone to maintain peace. He praised the goodness of God for uniting people as one who had been so terribly divided. When he first took the throne, most of the nation considered him an enemy to the public good. The division was so deadly that nothing but the destruction of the opposing party seemed to hold out the prospect of peace. However, the hand of God was unexpectedly seen in the harmony that resulted from the surrender of those who had been inflamed with the most violent hatred. David celebrates the spirit of unity between those who had been so bitterly divided.

The Holy Spirit commends a mutual harmony among all God's children, exhorting us to make every effort to maintain it. So long as hatred divides us, we are still brothers and sisters in God, but we present the appearance of a broken and dismembered body. Since we are one in God the Father, unity must be upheld by reciprocal harmony, and brotherly love. However, we cannot extend this relationship to those who stubbornly persist in false teaching, since the condition of receiving them as brothers and sisters would be our renouncing God as Father of all, and from whom all spiritual relationship takes its rise.

Like precious oil poured on the head (v. 2). We have clear proof here that David considers all true unity among believers to come from God. His goal is for everyone to worship God in purity, and call upon his name with one voice. Any unity among people is pointless if it is not infused by true worship. Therefore, we claim that people should be united in mutual affection so that they may be placed together under the government of God. The mention of the priest implies that unity arises from true and pure worship of God.

There the LORD bestows his blessing (v. 3). David adds in closing that God commands his blessing where peace is cultivated. In other words, God shows his pleasure regarding our unity by showering down blessings. Let us then seek to walk in brotherly love, that we may secure the divine blessing. Let us even stretch out our arms to those who differ from us, desiring to welcome them if they will return to the unity of the faith. Do they refuse? Then let them go. We recognize no brotherhood apart from the children of God.

Psalm 134 with John Calvin – Genuine Worship

It is evident that the psalmist addresses priests, since he prescribes the form of benediction which they were to offer up for the people, and this was a duty belonging exclusively to the priests. The Levites are here called servants of God, because of the role they played as specially appointed to watch by night in the temple (Lev 8:35). Notice the psalmist's design in urging the duty of praise so earnestly upon them. Merely to keep nightly watch over the temple, light the lamps, and oversee the sacrifices, was of no importance, unless they served God spiritually, and referred all outward ceremonies to that which must be considered the main sacrifice—the celebration of God's praises. You may think it a very labor-intensive service to stand watch in the temple while others sleep in their own houses, but the worship God requires is something more excellent than this, and demands of you to sing his praises before all the people.

May the LORD bless you from Zion! (v. 3) The psalmist had first told the priests to bless God; now he tells them to bless the people in his name. This does not excuse the people from worshipping God themselves. What God intended was that the priests should lead the way in divine service, and the people follow their example from the temple, and practice it individually in their private houses. The God who blessed them out of Zion is said to be the *Maker of heaven and earth*. Mention of his title as Maker sets forth his power, convincing believers there is nothing that may not be hoped from God. For what is the world but a mirror in which we see his boundless power? But since many, when they hear God spoken of as Creator, tend to think of him as standing at a distance from them, and doubt their access to him, the psalmist also mentions that which was a symbol of God's nearness to his people—*Zion*. This encouraged them to approach him with the freedom and unrestrained confidence of people who are invited to come to the embrace of a Father. By looking to the heavens, then, they were to discover the power of God; by looking to Zion, his dwelling place, they were to recognize his fatherly love.

Psalm 135 with Augustine – Reasons to Praise

Sing praise to his name, for that is pleasant (v. 3). Worship should be very pleasant to us, and we should rejoice because it is pleasant, to which this psalm urges us. For it says, *Praise the name of the LORD* (v. 1). And it adds the reason; why it is right to praise the name of the Lord. Praise the Lord, *you servants of the LORD*. What would be more right? What would be more worthy? What would be more thankful? For you will do nothing out of place, by praising your Lord, as servants.

Why you should praise Him? *For the LORD is good* (v. 3). Briefly in one word the praise of the Lord our God is explained: *Good*, not in the same manner as the things which he made are good. For God made all things very good. He made the sky and earth, and all things in them good. If he made all these things good, what is the one who made them like?

Eventually he offers a loud cry of praise: *Your name, LORD, endures forever* (v. 13), after everything you have done. For what do I see that you have done? Your creation—which you have made in heaven; this lower part—where we live; and your gifts of clouds, and winds, and rain. Your people—you led them from the house of slavery, and performed signs and wonders on their enemies. You punished those who caused your people trouble. You drove the wicked from their land, killing their kings. You gave their land to your people. I have seen all these things, and I am filled with joy, I have said, *Your name, LORD, endures forever* (v. 13).

Psalm 136 with John Calvin – His Love Endures Forever

His love endures forever (v. 1, etc.). The insertion of this phrase over and over in so many abrupt sentences may seem unnecessary, but repeated choruses are both allowed and admired in secular poetry. Why should we object to repetition here, which is for the best reason of all? People acknowledge that divine goodness is the source and fountain of all their blessings, but although Scripture gives it great emphasis, the graciousness of God's generosity is far from being fully and sincerely recognized.

Who alone does great wonders (v. 4). In saying this, the psalmist imagines all God's works from the least to the greatest, in order to awaken our admiration of them. For although these works signal God's inconceivably great wisdom and divine power we tend to undervalue them thoughtlessly. He declares that whatever is worthy of admiration is exclusively made and done by God. We cannot transfer to another being even the smallest portion of the praise he deserves without committing awful blasphemy. There is no sliver of divinity in the whole range of heaven and earth with which it is right to compare him.

Throughout the psalm, the psalmist demonstrates how every age receives the same goodness shown to their ancestors, since God helped his people by a continuous string of deliverances. His rescue during times of overwhelming trouble was a greater proof of his mercy than if he had preserved them in stable times. The emergency awakened their attention. Besides, whenever God delivers his people physically, he also forgives their sins.

He gives food to every creature (v. 25). Finally, he speaks of the fatherly provision of God that extends not only to humans, but to every living creature. We have no reason to be surprised at his kindness and fatherly provision for his own people, since God even stoops to care for cattle, donkeys of the field, the crow, and the sparrow. Humans are worth far more than animals! The psalmist reasons from the lesser to the greater. If God cares for animals, how much greater is the mercy which he shows to his own children.

Psalm 137 with John Calvin –
Justice for Those in Distress

During the Babylonian captivity the established temple worship was ended, and the psalmist complains of the enemy's taunts. The writer of this psalm announces deserved judgment upon the Edomites and Babylonians. True God-fearers were not tempted by the luxuries of Babylon to forget their native inheritance. In spite of their hardships they recognized that they deserved punishment. *By the rivers of Babylon we sat and wept when we remembered Zion* (v. 1). Their tears express humility and repentance, as well as distress. They remember Zion, which proves that they were not charmed by worldly advantages in Babylon, but only the worship of God.

There on the poplars we hung our harps (v. 2). The banks of Babylon's rivers were planted with trees, but this shade, however delightful, could not dispel a grief which was too deep to allow consolation or refreshment. As they sat upon the river banks in the shadows of the trees, this was just the place where they might have been tempted to take up their harps, and soothe their griefs with song; but their minds were too heavily wounded with the Lord's displeasure to deceive themselves with such empty comfort.

Remember, LORD, what the Edomites did on the day Jerusalem fell (v. 7). Vengeance was to be executed upon neighboring nations which had conspired to destroy Jerusalem. Edom is specified either because they showed more hatred and cruelty than the rest, or because their attacks were not so easily endured, considering they were brothers of the Israelites, being descendants of Esau. The Israelites had spared the Edomites at God's command (Deut 2:4). Therefore, it was especially cruel of the Edomites to invite the Babylonians to destroy them. However, the psalmist does not burst into these awful denunciations rashly, but as God's herald, to confirm former prophecies. God had announced through Ezekiel and Jeremiah that he would punish the Edomites (Ezek 25:13; Jer 49:7; and Lam 4:21, 22). Obadiah distinctly gives the reason why— they had conspired with the Babylonians (Obad 1:11). The psalmist prays, under the inspiration of the Spirit, that God would demonstrate the truth of this announcement practically. And when he says, *remember, LORD,* he reminds God's people of his promise to strengthen their belief in his avenging justice, and make them wait patiently for the event.

Happy is the one who seizes your infants and dashes them against the rocks (v. 9). It may seem cruel, but he does not speak under the impulse of personal feeling, and only employs words which God had himself authorized, so that this is the declaration of a just judgment, as when our Lord says, "With the measure you use, it will be measured to you" (Matt 7:2).

Psalm 138 with Augustine – Loving God More Than Life

Though I walk in the midst of trouble, you preserve my life (v. 7). It is true that whatever hardship you are in, you are invited to confess to God, call on him. He frees you, he revives you. Love the other life, and you will see that this life is hardship—whatever prosperity it shines with, whatever delights it abounds and overflows with. We do not yet have that joy most safe and free from all temptation, which God reserves for us in the end. Without a doubt it is hardship.

You stretch out your hand against the anger of my foes; with your right hand you save me (v. 7). Let my enemies rage. What can they do? They can take my money and my clothes and banish me, afflict me with grief and torture, even kill me if they can. Can they do any more? But you have stretched out your hand against everything my enemies can do. For my enemies cannot separate me from you. You avenge me the more, the longer you delay, not to make me despair; for it follows, *with your right hand you save me.*

> ### Augustine on Psalm 138
> *"For whatever good works of mine are there, they are from you; and so they are more yours than mine."*

Your love, LORD, endures forever (v. 8). I do not desire to be freed only temporarily. Your enduring love, with which you have freed the martyrs, has quickly taken them from this life. *Do not abandon the works of your hands.* I do not praise works of my own hands. I fear that when you look into them, you find more sins in them than righteousness. See in me your work, not mine. For if you see mine, you condemn. If you see yours, you crown. For whatever good works of mine are there, they are from you; and so they are more yours than mine.

Psalm 139 with Augustine – Searching for Runaways

Where can I go from your Spirit? (v. 7). Where in the
world can anyone flee from that Spirit who fills the world?
The psalmist seeks a place to flee from the wrath of God.
What place will shelter God's runaway? People who shelter
runaways ask from whom they have fled; and when they
find anyone a slave of some master less powerful than
themselves, they shelter them without fear, saying, "they
do not have a master who can track them down." But
when they are told of a powerful master, they either do
not shelter the runaway, or they shelter them with great
fear, because even someone with power can be deceived.

Where is God absent? Who can deceive or hide from
God? From whom does God not demand his runaway?
Where will that runaway go from the face of God? *If
I go up to the heavens, you are there; if I make my bed in the
depths, you are there* (v. 8). At length, miserable runaway,
you have learned that you cannot make yourself far from
the one you flee. Behold, he is everywhere; where will you
go? If by sinning I go down to the depths of wickedness,
and do not confess, saying, "Who sees me?" you are
also present to punish. Where will I go to flee from your
presence, that is, to find you not angry? *If I say, "Surely
the darkness will hide me and the light become night around
me," even the darkness will not be dark to you; the night will
shine like the day, for darkness is as light to you* (vv. 11–12).
Thanks to him who searched for me when I was a runaway,
who struck my back with strokes of punishment, who by
calling me brought me back from destruction, who made
my night light.

Psalm 140 with Augustine – Protection from Evildoers

Rescue me, LORD, from evildoers (v. 1). Many unrighteous people seem to be harmless. They are not fierce or savage. They do not persecute or oppress. Yet they are unrighteous, because they are luxurious, drunkards, given to pleasure. Every unrighteous person is wicked, whether gentle or fierce. Whoever falls in their way, whoever is taken by their snares, will find out that what seems harmless is harmful indeed. They may be silent, they may hide their enmity, but they cannot love you. Since they cannot love you, and since those who hate you seek your harm, do not let your tongue and heart be slow to say to God,

Keep me safe, LORD, from the hands of the wicked; protect me from the violent (v. 4). Here they wear their real colors and are known. Here we do not need to understand, but to act. We need to pray, not ask who they are. Everyone has enemies in business who seek to cheat them in trade, to rob them of money. Everyone has some neighbor as an enemy who devises how to bring mischief upon their family, to destroy their property in some way, who surely devises this and tries to accomplish it by deceit, by fraud, by devilish devices. No one can doubt it. Do not guard against them to protect your property. However, be sure that if they lie in wait for you and draw you to themselves they will not separate you from the Body of Christ and make you part of their gang. For as Christ is the head of the good, so the devil is their head.

Surely the righteous will praise your name (v. 13), Lord, when you plead the cause of the righteous, and when you maintain their right. The righteous will attribute nothing to their own merits, but everything to your mercy.

Psalm 141 with Martin of Braga –
The Practice of Humility

Discipline your mind carefully so that, when the crowd flatters you on all sides with only pleasant words, saying to you what they should say to God, you may realize that this praise does not properly belong to you. The only thing praiseworthy is that which will remain with you even after you have departed from this life.

> **Martin of Braga
> on Psalm 141**
>
> *"Humility will tell you just how much of the things that people ascribe to you in praise is really yours and how long it will last. Humility does not allow you to be attentive to lies."*

Therefore whenever great flattery has exceeded the limits proper to humans, recall that well-known lesson of David, in which he shunned the poison of flatterers with these words: *Let a righteous man strike me— that is a kindness; let him rebuke me—that is oil on my head* (v. 5) The "oil of the sinner" is flattery, which uses a smooth, suave anointing to brighten up, as though with cosmetics, the head of the inner self, that is, the heart. This is why David said that it was better for him to be corrected or advised by a righteous person than to be praised by any flatterer. It was right that he should denote the flatterer as a "sinner," since hypocrisy is the greatest and most detestable crime in the sight of God—to hold one thing in the heart, to speak another with the lips. As he also says in another psalm: "His words are more soothing than oil, yet they are drawn swords" (Ps 55:21). He describes the righteous person as "The one who . . . speaks the truth from their heart, whose tongue utters no slander" (Ps 15:2–3). Practice humility, then, take it for your companion, set it as your guide when flatterers entice.

Humility will tell you just how much of the things that people ascribe to you in praise is really yours and how long it will last. Humility does not allow you to be attentive to lies.

Psalm 142 with Augustine – Deliverance from Distress

I cry to you, LORD; I say, "You are my refuge" (v. 5).
When I endured, when I was in trouble, *you are my refuge.*
Therefore I endure. *My portion is not here, but in the land
of the living.* God gives a portion in the land of the living;
but he does not give anything without himself. What
will he give to one who loves him except himself?

Listen to my cry, for I am in desperate need (v. 6)—
humbled by persecutors, humbled in confession. He
humbles himself in human eyes, in the sight of his
enemies. Therefore he is lifted up by God both visibly
and invisibly. Invisibly the martyrs are already lifted up;
they will be lifted up visibly "when the perishable has
been clothed with the imperishable" (1 Cor 15:54) in the
resurrection of the dead; when this very part of him,
against which alone the persecutors of the church could
rage, shall be renewed. "Do not be afraid of those who
kill the body but cannot kill the soul" (Matt 10:28). And
what perishes? What do they kill? Why then are you
anxious about the rest of your members, when you will
not lose even a hair? (Luke 21:18) *Rescue me from those
who pursue me.* From whom do you think he prayed to be
delivered? People who persecuted him? Is it so? Are mere
people our enemies? We have other enemies, invisible,
who persecute us in another way. People persecute to kill
the body; another persecutes to ensnare the soul (Eph 2:2).

There are then other enemies of ours too, from whom
we should pray for deliverance, so they will not lead us
astray, either by crushing us with troubles of this world,
or by alluring us with its enticements. Who are these
enemies? Let us see whether they are plainly described
by any servant of the Lord, by any soldier, now perfected,

who has engaged with them. Hear the Apostle saying, "our struggle is not against flesh and blood:" (Eph 6:12) as though he would say: Do not hate people. Do not think of them as enemies. Do not think they are hurting you. These people who you fear are flesh and blood.

Set me free from my prison (v. 7), bring me out of distress. For to one who rejoices, even a prison is wide; to one in sorrow, a field is narrow. Therefore he prays to be brought out of distress. For though hope grows, yet in reality at present he suffers. It is not the body that weighs down the soul or makes the prison, but the corruption of the body. *Set me free from my prison, that I may praise your name.*

Psalm 143 with Augustine – Righteousness from God

In your faithfulness and righteousness, come to my relief (v. 1). Note the emphasis on *your righteousness*. For it is a commendation of grace that none of us should think of our righteousness as our own. It is the righteousness of God, which God has given us to possess. You are perverse when you attribute what you have done wrong to God and what you have done right to yourself. You will be right when you attribute to yourself what you have done wrong and attribute to God what you have done right. For when I look at myself, I only find my sin to be my own.

> **Augustine on Psalm 143**
>
> *"You will be right when you attribute to yourself what you have done wrong and attribute to God what you have done right."*

Do not hide your face from me (v. 7). You turned it away from me when I was proud. For once I was full, and in my fullness I was puffed up. "When I felt secure, I said, 'I will never be shaken'" (Ps 30:6), not knowing your righteousness, and establishing my own. But from you came whatever security I had. And to prove to me that it was from you, "when you hid your face I was dismayed" (Ps 30:6–7).

Teach me to do your will, for you are my God (v. 10). Glorious confession! Glorious rule! *For you are my God.* To another I would hurry to be re-made, if I was made by another. But you are my all. Shall I seek a father to get an inheritance? You are not only the Giver of my inheritance, but my Inheritance itself. "LORD, you alone are my portion" (Ps 16:5). *Teach me*, for it cannot be that you are my God, and yet I am to be my own master. *May your good Spirit lead me on level ground* (v. 10). For my bad spirit has led me into a crooked land. And what have I deserved? What can be reckoned as my good works without your aid, through which I may obtain and be worthy to be led by your Spirit into the right land?

Listen, then, with all your power, to the commendation of Grace, by which you are saved without price. *For your name's sake, LORD, preserve my life in your righteousness* (v. 11). Not in my own, not because I have deserved, but because you have mercy.

Psalm 144 with Mary Sidney Herbert – God's Protection

Praised be the Lord of might,
my rock in all alarms,
by whom my hands do fight,
my fingers manage arms.
My grace, my guard, my fort,
on whom my safety stays,[1]
to whom my hopes resort
by whom my realm obeys.

Lord what is man that thou
should'st tender so his fare?[2]
What hath his child to bow
thy thoughts unto his care?
Whose nearest kin[3] is nought,
no image of whose days
more lively can be thought,
than shade that never stays.

Lord bend thy arched skies
with ease to let thee down;
and make the storms arise
from mountain's fuming[4] crown,
Let follow flames from sky,
to back their stoutest stand;[5]
let fast thy arrows fly,
dispersing thickest band.[6]

---

1   Stays – rests

2   Tender so his fare – have such regard for his welfare

3   Kin – relative

4   Fuming – smoking

5   Stoutest stand – strongest display of power

6   Band – group of men

Thy heavenly help extend
and lift me from this flood;
let me thy hand defend[7]
from hand of foreign brood,
whose mouth[8] no mouth at all,
but forge of false intent,
Where to their hand doth fall
as aptest[9] instrument.

Then in new song to thee
will I exalt my voice;
then shall, O God, with me
my ten-stringed lute rejoice.
Rejoice in him, I say,
who royal right preserves
and saves from sword's decay
his David that him serves.

So then our sons shall grow
as plants of timely spring,
whom soon to fairest show[10]
their happy growth doth bring.
As pillars both do bear
and garnish[11] kingly hall,
our daughters straight and fair,
each house embellish shall.

---

7 Let me thy hand defend – let your hand defend me

8 Mouth – mouth is

9 Aptest – most fitting

10 Fairest show – most beautiful display

11 Garnish – decorate

Our store[12] shall ay[13] be full,
yea shall such fullness find,
though all from thence we pull[14]
yet more shall rest[15] behind.
The millions of increase
shall break the wonted fold;[16]
Yea, such the sheepy prease,[17]
the streets shall scantly[18] hold.

Our herds shall brave[19] the best;
Abroad, no foes alarm;
At home to break our rest,
no cry, the voice of harm.
If blessed term I may[20]
on whom such blessing fall,
then blessed blessed they
their god Jehovah call.[21]

---

12 Store – storehouse

13 Ay – always

14 From thence we pull – from there we take out

15 Rest – remain

16 Wonted fold – the existing sheepfolds

17 Prease – crowd

18 Scantly – barely

19 Brave – show themselves equal to

20 If blessed term I may – If I may call "blessed"

21 Their god Jehovah call – those who call on the LORD their God

Psalm 145 with Augustine – The One Worthy of Praise

I will exalt you, my God the King; I will praise your name for ever and ever (v. 1). Now begin to praise, if you intend to praise forever. Those who will not praise in this temporary age will be silent when forever has come. But so no one will seek another age in which to praise, he says, *Every day I will praise you* (v. 2). No day will pass by on which I will not praise you. It is no wonder, if on a joyful day you bless the Lord. What if a day of sorrow has dawned, as is natural in this life—will you cease to praise God? Will you cease to bless your Creator? If you cease, you have lied in saying, *every day.* But if you do not cease, even in difficulty on your day of sorrow, in God it will be well with you.

Great is the LORD, and most worthy of praise (v. 3). Do not think that he whose greatness has no end can ever be praised enough by you. Since his Greatness is without end, let your praise also be without end.

Do you praise what he has made but not the one who made it all? In what you can see, what is it that you praise? The form, the usefulness, some virtue, some power? If beauty delights you, what is more beautiful than the maker? If usefulness is worthy of praise, what is more useful than he who made all things? If excellence is praised, what is more excellent than he who made all things? For if you love these more than him, you will not have him. Truly you should love them, but love him more, and love them for his sake.

They tell of the glory of your kingdom, and speak of your might (v. 11). How powerful is God, who has made the earth! How powerful is God, who has filled the earth with good things! How powerful is God, who has given life to each of the animals! How powerful is God, who has given different seeds to the womb of the earth, so various plants might spring up, such beautiful trees! How powerful, how great is God!

Therefore if God is good, who has given you what you have, how much more blessed will you be when he has given you himself! You have desired all these things from him. I urge you: desire him also. For these things are not truly sweeter than he is, nor in any way are they to be compared to him. Those who prefer God to all the things they have received, in which they rejoice, *call on him in truth* (v. 18).

Psalm 146 with Augustine – Hope for the Oppressed

Praise the LORD, my soul (v. 1). For sometimes in the hardships and temptations of this present life, whether we want it or not, our soul is troubled. But to remove these troubles, he suggests joy, not yet in reality, but in hope; and says to us when troubled and anxious, sad and sorrowing, *Blessed are those . . . whose hope is in the LORD their God* (v. 5).

He remains faithful forever. He upholds the cause of the oppressed (vv. 6–7). He avenges those who suffer unjustly. For whatever you suffer lawfully is not unjust; you should not say, I have suffered wrong, for I have suffered such a thing in such a place, and such a thing for such a reason. Consider whether you have suffered unjustly. Robbers suffer many things, but they do not suffer unjustly. Wicked men, evildoers, house-breakers, adulterers, seducers, all these suffer many evils, yet is there no injustice in their suffering. It is one thing to suffer wrong; it is another to suffer hardship, or penalty, or annoyance, or punishment. Consider where you are; see what you have done; see why you are suffering; and then you see what you are suffering. Consider what you have done. If you have done right, you are suffering wrong; if you have done wrong, you are suffering right.

Psalm 147 with Augustine – Genuine Praise

How pleasant and fitting it is to praise him (v. 1). How? If he is praised by our good lives, then praise will be pleasant to him. Praise is not fitting in the mouth of a sinner. If praise is not fitting in the mouth of a sinner, neither is it pleasant, for only what is fitting is pleasant. For praise may be pleasant to someone when they hear someone praising with neat and clever sentiments and with a sweet voice; but let our praise be pleasant to God, whose ears are open not to the mouth, but to the heart; not to the tongue, but to the life of the one who praises.

Great is our Lord and mighty in power; his understanding has no limit (v. 5). He who numbers the stars cannot himself be numbered. Whatever this world contains, though it is infinite to humans, is not infinite to God. His understanding surpasses all calculators. It cannot be counted by us. Let human voices be hushed, human thoughts still. Let them not stretch themselves out to incomprehensible things, as though they could comprehend them, but as though they were to take part in them, for partakers we shall be. Let no one doubt it—Scripture says those things which are now impossible will not be impossible for us. *The LORD delights in those who fear him, who put their hope in his unfailing love* (v. 11).

Psalm 148 with Augustine – Practicing Whole-Bodied Praise

The subject of our meditation in this present life should be the praise of God; for the everlasting occupation of the life after this one will be the praise of God. No one can become fit for the life after this one who has not practiced for it. So we praise God now, but we pray to him, too. Our praise is marked by joy, our prayer by groans. For the time being all the evil men sing with us, Hallelujah. However, if they persevere in their wickedness, they may sing the song of our life after this one, but they will not be able to enter into it, because they would not practice it before it came, and lay hold of what was to come.

> **Augustine on Psalm 148**
>
> *"Praise with your whole selves: that is, do not let your tongue and voice alone praise God, but your conscience also, your life, your deeds."*

"Hallelujah." "Praise the Lord," you say to your neighbor, and they say it to you, when all are urging each other, all are doing what they urge others to do. But praise with your whole selves: that is, do not let your tongue and voice alone praise God, but your conscience also, your life, your deeds. For now, when we are gathered together in the Church, we praise. When we each go out to our own business, we seem to cease praising God. Let us not cease to live well, and then we continually praise God. Therefore, pay attention not only to the sound. When you praise God, praise with your whole selves. Let your voice, your life, your deeds, all sing.

Psalm 149 with Augustine – Sing with Your Life

My brothers and sisters, my children, holy and heavenly seed, you who have been born again in Christ and have been born from above, listen to me—or rather, listen to God through me: *Sing to the LORD a new song* (v. 1). "Well, I am singing," you say. Yes, you are singing; of course you are singing. I can hear you. But do not let your life give evidence against your tongue. Sing with your voices, sing also with your hearts; sing with your mouths, sing also with your conduct. *Sing to the LORD a new song.* You ask what you should sing about the one you love? For of course you do want to sing about the one you love. You are asking for praises of his to sing. You have been told, *Sing to the LORD a new song.* You are looking for praise songs, are you? *His praise in the assembly of his faithful people* (v. 1). The praise of the one to be sung about is the singer himself. Do you want to sing God his praises? Be yourselves what you sing. You are his praise if you lead good lives. His praise, you see, is not to be found . . . in the madness of the pagans, nor in the errors of the heretics, nor in the applause of the theaters. You ask where it is to be found? Look at yourselves, you are it. *His praise in the assembly of his faithful people.* You ask what to rejoice about when you are singing? *Let Israel rejoice in their Maker* (v. 2), and all he can find to rejoice about is God.

Psalm 150 with Mary Sidney Herbert – Great Praise for God's Greatness

O laud[1] the Lord, the God of hosts commend,
exalt his power, advance his holiness;
With all your might lift his almightiness;
Your greatest praise upon his greatness spend.

Make trumpet's noise in shrillest notes ascend;
make lute and lyre his loved fame express.
Him let the pipe, him let the tabret[2] bless,
him organ's breath, that winds or waters lend.

Let ringing timbrells[3] so his honor sound;
Let sounding cymbals so his glory ring,
that in their tunes such melody be found,
As fits the pomp of most triumphant king.
Conclude: by all that air, or life enfold,[4]
let high Jehovah highly be extolled.

Mary Sidney Herbert on Psalm 150

"Your greatest praise upon his greatness spend."

---

1   Laud – praise
2   Tabret – small drum
3   Timbrells – tambourine
4   Enfold – have within them

Discussion Questions

 Re-read Psalm 145. What are some ways that our culture praises what "God has made but not the one who made it all"?

 How does Calvin interpret Psalm 137:9? Do you find his interpretation helpful?

 How does Augustine understand the reference to the "poor" in Psalm 132? Based on his classification, would you classify yourself as poor or rich? Why?

 John Cassian and Martin of Braga have harsh words to say about human pride (Psalm 131). What practical steps do they recommend for us to guard against pride?

 How does Martin of Braga's reading of Psalm 141 help you understand humility? How does humility help you avoid false praise? How can you cultivate humility?

Afterword

BIBLICAL STUDIES

Afterword

Congratulations on having reached the end of this 150-step walk through Psalms. On this journey we have prayed the Psalms with Augustine and twenty-six of his friends gathered from diverse cultures and centuries. Hopefully you have had opportunity to meet regularly with a friend or group of gospel-coworkers to discuss questions, edify, and encourage one another along the way.

In *Letters of Faith through the Seasons*, James Houston makes a number of interesting observations about letter writing.[1] He emphasizes that writing letters is a way to develop and deepen a culture of friendship. Houston notes that twenty-one of the twenty-nine New Testament books are actually letters to individuals or groups, and that some have described the whole Bible as God's love letter to us (e.g. Kierkegaard). Houston notes that throughout church history letter writing has remained an important ministry. To this day, we have over nine thousand letters preserved

---

1   James Houston, *Letters of Faith Through the Seasons: December to May* (Vancouver, BC: Regent College, 2018).

from the early centuries of the church. Among these many letters we find a long tradition of sisters and brothers writing to one another to encourage each other in the use of Psalms for prayer, pastoral ministry, and public worship.

We close this journey with a letter from a mother to her son written over one thousand years ago. It was written by a godly mother, Dhouda, to her son who was serving in the military sometime around the year 843. Dhouda adapted an earlier letter she had read on the Psalms and she passed it on to her son in her own words.[2] Imagine receiving this letter as if from your own mother. Read it with the openness and honor a godly mother deserves to receive.

> *My dear Son,*
>
> *As your mentor in all things, I stand ready at your side, so that with God's help you may choose the Psalms to recite for the range of your needs.*
>
> *When Psalms are sung with heartfelt intensity, a channel is prepared to the heart so that Almighty God may pour into it the mystery of prophecy or the grace of remorse for those who meditate with spiritual fervor.*
>
> *The sacrifice of divine praise, therefore, provides a way between us and Jesus. While our repentance pours out through psalms, we are opening in our heart this channel through which we may come to Jesus. Surely, it is a good thing for the mind to cleanse itself as much as possible of daily affairs and cling to divine, heavenly, spiritual things, so that the heavenly can be revealed to it. Nothing in this mortal life can make us cling more closely*

---

2   Dhouda adapted an earlier letter on the use of Psalms written by an English pastor named Alcuin (d. 804). Alcuin, in turn, was building on similar letters written by earlier pastors. See for example the letter by the Egyptian pastor Athanasius (d. 373) written to his friend Marcellinus on how to read and pray the Psalms.

to God than divine praises of the Psalms. For no mortal can unfold in words or through the power of the Psalms.

If you study the Psalms intently and drill down to their spiritual meaning, you will discover the Incarnation of the Lord's Word, his Passion, Resurrection, and Ascension. If you study the Psalms intently you will find such intimate prayer that you could never think of it yourself. Furthermore, in the Psalms you will find the innermost confession of your sins in a perfect way to invoke the Lord's divine mercy. In Psalms you also confess your weakness and wretchedness, and in that way appeal to God to show you mercy. You will discover all the virtues in the Psalms if you are worthy before God of having their secrets revealed to you.

If you wish to **repent** of your sins and confess them and ask God's pardon, devote all your attention to slowly reading, not rushing the words, but contemplating them and examining them. Sing these seven psalms of David: Psalms 6, 32, 38, 51, 130, and 143. You will very quickly obtain God's compassion.

If you wish your understanding to grow bright with **spiritual joy** and gladness, recite with an eager spirit the following psalms: Psalms 17, 25, 31, 54, 67, 70, and 86. More quickly and confidently, then, you will be able to gain God's mercy.

If you wish to **praise** almighty God and have his majesty, and to know even a little of all the benefits he has designed to grant the human race from the world's beginning, recite the following psalms: Psalms 103, 104, 105, 147, and 149. You will be offering to almighty God a sweet gift of honey and honeycomb if you praise him continually and magnify him with these Psalms.

If you are afflicted by various **hardships** and attacked on all sides by trials, whether human or spiritual, if it seems God has abandoned you—as he often abandons his saints for a time in order to test them—and the resulting trial seems more than you can endure, recite privately Psalms 12, 22, 61, and 64, and *immediately he will help you so that you can withstand the trial you undergo.*

*If your present life seems abominable to you and your spirit delights in contemplating its heavenly home, and **gazing on almighty God** with burning desire, privately recite Psalms 42, 63, and 84, and the compassionate God will quickly comfort your spirit.*

*If you see yourself **abandoned by God** in your hardships recite with a repentant heart the following psalms: Psalms 13, 31, 34, 44, 56 or 57, and God will gladden you in the midst of your suffering.*

*Once you have recovered your peace, and are in a time of **prosperity**, sing these psalms of praise: Psalms 34, 103, and 145.*

*If you wish in private to devote yourself to **divine praises and heavenly teachings and commands**, recite Psalm 119. While you may continue to ponder and examine the meaning of this alphabetic psalm until the end of your life, I think you will never be able to grasp it perfectly. It contains no verse which does not describe God's way, his law, his commands, God's teachings, his words, his acts of justice and his court of law, or the sayings of God. And for this reason you do not need to squander your efforts by consulting a variety of books.*

In the Psalter alone you have plenty of matter to read, sift over and learn from until the end of your life. . . . If you meditate on these privately and deeply, you will discover, by God's grace, the substance of their inner meaning.

. . . Because singing the Psalms has such great effectiveness, and so many virtues, I encourage and remind you to recite them diligently. . . .

Amen.

Now that you have made it through the psalms with Augustine, with Dhouda, and with your own friends and coworkers in the gospel, consider writing a letter to share what you have learned with a friend. Write to a son or daughter, to a disciple you have been investing in spiritually, to a family member, or perhaps share with a mentor what you are learning. It may help to know that there are some additional resources for learning more about the Psalms in the "resources" section following this afterward. These include additional information on the people you met in this book and some practical ideas on how to develop a growing daily habit of prayer in the Psalms.

Our prayer is that you will continue to read, pray, and talk with friends about the Psalms for the rest of your earthly life. If we don't meet before then, we look forward to talking with you about them in eternity. What a day of rejoicing that will be!

Grace,

Carmen Joy Imes and Hank Voss

Resources for Application

BIBLICAL STUDIES

Soul Work and Soul Care:
Doing "Psalm Work" with Augustine and Friends

By Hank Voss

No one presumes to teach an art until he has first carefully studied it. Look how foolish it is for the inexperienced to assume pastoral authority, since the care of souls is the art of arts!

~ Gregory the Great, c. 590

Your leaders . . . keep watch over your souls and will give an account for their work.

~ Hebrews 13:17a

Each *Sacred Roots Spiritual Classic* has a "Soul Work and Soul Care" resource to illustrate how Christian leaders across cultures and generations have found a particular spiritual classic helpful in pastoral ministry. "Soul work" includes the *personal* work of watering, weeding, pruning, and fertilizing the garden of one's own soul. In a similar way, "soul care" involves the *pastoral* work of nurturing growth in another's friendship with God. When Jesus discusses soul work and soul care, he often uses metaphors from the medical and agricultural professions. Like a doctor for souls, or a farmer caring for an orchard of fruit trees, congregational leaders who hope to serve as soul surgeons can learn much from the wisdom of those who have gone before.

Praying the Psalms with Augustine and Friends: Doing "Psalm Work"

Praying the Psalms with Augustine and Friends introduces the spiritual discipline of "psalm work." Psalm work includes personal, pastoral, and public components. We pray psalms in our personal devotions, use them in pastoral care, and integrate them into our weekly worship (including prayer, teaching or preaching, and singing—also known as "psalmody"). The resources below provide guidance for using Psalms to watch over your own soul and over those for whom you will give an account to God (Heb 13:17). Tables 1 and 2 provide examples of how biblical leaders have used Psalms for soul work and soul care. Table 3 illustrates three ways church leaders have taught their discipleship communities to pray using Psalms during the past two thousand years. Tables 4 and 5 provide a place to record your own progress at praying Psalms across the years and decades God grants. Table 6 provides an overview of different kinds of prayer we learn in the King's treasury.

Table 1: Biblical Examples of Psalm Work from the Life of King David

Hundreds of biblical leaders used the Psalms for personal soul work, pastoral soul care and public worship. Two important examples include King David and Jesus. First, consider King David, a man connected by name to some seventy-five psalms. Seventy-three psalms have a title ("of David") that connects them to David, and the New Testament adds Psalm 2 (Acts 4:25–26) and Psalm 95 (Heb 4:7). Clearly, David loved the praises and prayers found in Psalms. Fourteen of the "David" psalms are connected to specific historical events in David's life. We can imagine these prayers as journal entries or songs written in response to the many dramatic events of his life. King David's example provides precedent for learning to pray specific psalms in relation to specific historical situations. Truly, the Psalms provide believers with a reliable guide as we join David in following the Good Shepherd (Ps 23).

Journal Entry	Topic	Background
Psalm 3	A psalm of David. When he fled from his son Absalom.	2 Sam 15:13–37
Psalm 7	A *shiggaion* of David, which he sang to the Lord concerning Cush, a Benjamite.	2 Sam 16:5–14
Psalm 18	For the director of music. Of David the servant of the Lord. He sang to the Lord the words of this song when the Lord delivered him from the hand of all his enemies and from the hand of Saul. He said:	2 Sam 21:15–23:39
Psalm 30	A psalm. A song. For the dedication of the temple. Of David.	2 Sam 24:1–25; 1 Chron 21:1–22:1
Psalm 34	Of David. When he pretended to be insane before Abimelek, who drove him away, and he left.	1 Sam 21:10–15
Psalm 51	For the director of music. A psalm of David. When the prophet Nathan came to him after David had committed adultery with Bathsheba.	2 Sam 11:1–12:25

Journal Entry	Topic	Background
Psalm 52	For the director of music. A *maskil* of David. When Doeg the Edomite had gone to Saul and told him: "David has gone to the house of Ahimelek."	1 Sam 22:6–23
Psalm 54	For the director of music. With stringed instruments. A *maskil* of David. When the Ziphites had gone to Saul and said, "Is not David hiding among us?"	1 Sam 23:19–24; 26:1–2
Psalm 56	For the director of music. To the tune of "A Dove on Distant Oaks." Of David. A *miktam*. When the Philistines had seized him in Gath.	1 Sam 21:10–15
Psalm 57	For the director of music. To the tune of "Do Not Destroy." Of David. A *miktam*. When he had fled from Saul into the cave.	1 Sam 22:1–2; 24:1–22
Psalm 59	For the director of music. To the tune of "Do Not Destroy." Of David. A *miktam*. When Saul had sent men to watch David's house in order to kill him.	1 Sam 19:1–18
Psalm 60	For the director of music. To the tune of "The Lily of the Covenant." A *miktam* of David. For teaching. When he fought Aram Naharaim and Aram Zobah, and when Joab returned and struck down twelve thousand Edomites in the Valley of Salt.	2 Sam 8:1–14; 1 Chron 18:1–13
Psalm 63	A psalm of David. When he was in the Desert of Judah.	2 Sam 15:13–37
Psalm 142	A *maskil* of David. When he was in the cave. A prayer.	1 Sam 22:1–2; 24:1–22

Table 2: Sample Uses of Psalms in the Gospels and Acts

Jesus provides a second example of how to use Psalms for personal prayer and public ministry. The Gospels record Jesus quoting a psalm from memory while teaching some fourteen times. We often see snapshots of Jesus praying from the Psalms. When Jesus was at his most difficult moments, the Psalms provided his prayers. In the Garden of Gethsemane, Jesus quoted from Psalm 42:6 (Matt 26:38; Mark 14:34). On the cross, Jesus twice prayed from the Psalms, first from Psalm 22 (Matt 27:46) and then Psalm 31:5 (Luke 23:46). Jesus's personal and public ministry were shaped by regular engagement with the Psalms. The table below provides a sample of the frequent use Jesus and the Apostles made of the Psalms.

Psalm	NT Quotation
2:1–2	Acts 4:25–26
2:7	Acts 13:33
6:3	John 12:27
6:8	Matt 7:23; Luke 13:27
8:2	Matt 21:16
16:10	Acts 2:28–31; 13:35
22:1	Matt 27:46; Mark 15:34
22:7–8	Matt 27:39, 41–43
22:15	John 19:28
22:18	Matt 27:35; Mark 15:24; Luke 23:34; John 19:23–24
31:5	Luke 23:46
34:20	John 19:36

Psalm	NT Quotation
35:19	John 15:25
41:9	John 13:18
42:5, 11; 43:5	Matt 26:38; Mark 14:34
62:12	Matt 16:27
69:4	John 15:25
69:9	John 2:17
69:21	John 19:28–30
69:25	Acts 1:20
78:2	Matt 13:35
78:24	John 6:31
82:6	John 10:34
89:20	Acts 13:22
91:11–12	Matt 4:6; Luke 4:10
104:12	Matt 13:32; Mark 4:32; Luke 13:19
110:1	Matt 22:44; Matt 26:64; Mark 12:36; Mark 14:62; Luke 20:42–43; Luke 22:69; Acts 2:34–35
118:22–23	Matt 21:42; Mark 12:10–11; Luke 20:17; Acts 4:11; Eph 2:20–22; 1 Pet 2:4–8
118:25–26	Matt 21:9; Matt 23:39; Mark 11:9; Luke 19:38; John 12:13
132:11	Acts 2:30
146:6	Acts 4:24
148:1	Matt 21:9; Mark 11:10

To learn more about the use of the Psalms within the Bible consider the following resources:

> A good study Bible will include tables, charts, and cross-references to help you identify connections between individual Psalms and their use in other places in Scripture.

> Childs, Brevard S. *Introduction to the Old Testament as Scripture.* Philadelphia: Fortress, 1979.

> Johnston, Philip, and David G. Firth, eds. *Interpreting the Psalms: Issues and Approaches.* Downers Grove: InterVarsity, 2005.

> Spurgeon, Charles Haddon. *The Treasury of David: Containing an Original Exposition of the Book of Psalms: A Collection of Illustrative Extracts from the Whole Range of Literature: A Series of Homiletical Hints Upon Almost Every Verse; and Lists of Writers Upon Each Psalm.* Peabody, MA: Hendrickson, 1990. [Originally published 1869; available for free at *www.ccel.org*]

Table 3: How Churches Pray the Psalms

Every healthy family of believers in church history has embraced regular habits of prayer from the Psalms. The table below illustrates three examples of how to pray Psalms as a regular spiritual discipline. The book of Psalms encourages us to view our life as a journey with God. Consider the three ways to pray the Psalms below as different paces to use on your journey. As we learn to talk with God we can pray the Psalms at a walking, jogging or running pace.

Psalm Work Pace	Daily # of Psalms Prayed	Psalms Prayer Habits
Walking	1	Praying one psalm a day in your morning and evening devotions is a great place to begin. A daily psalm leads you through the whole book of Psalms a little over twice each year. One variation is to pray the same psalm every day for a week. This method leads you through Psalms every three years.
Jogging	5	Praying through Psalms every month is a discipline embraced by millions of Christians today. One of the most famous plans for praying the Psalms monthly was developed by an English Christian leader named Thomas Cranmer (d. 1546). His plan, recorded in a spiritual classic known as The Book of Common Prayer, is used today by millions of Christians around the globe.
Running	21	Many thousands of Christians over the past two thousand years have weekly prayed through the whole book of Psalms. Some, like those influenced by the early Christian leader Cassian (d. 435), would pray twelve psalms in their morning devotions and twelve in their evening devotions. This rhythm allowed them to pray the Psalter weekly. Probably the most influential plan was written by an Italian Christian leader named Benedict of Nursia (d. 547). His plan, described in The Rule of St. Benedict, invites disciples to pause at multiple points during the day in order to pray four or five psalms at a time. Benedict's plan continues to be followed by thousands of Christians in dozens of languages and cultures to this day.

To learn more about the spiritual discipline of praying the Psalms on a daily basis, consider the following resources:

Benedict of Nursia and Basil of Caesarea. *Becoming a Community of Disciples: Guidelines from Abbot Benedict and Bishop Basil.* Edited by Greg Peters. *Sacred Roots Spiritual Classics 2.* Wichita, KS: The Urban Ministry Institute, 2021.

McKnight, Scot. *Praying with the Church: Following Jesus Daily, Hourly, Today.* Brewster, MA: Paraclete, 2006.

Selvaggio, Anthony T., and Joel R. Beeke, eds. *Sing a New Song: Recovering Psalm Singing for the Twenty-First Century.* Grand Rapids: Reformation Heritage, 2010.

Whitney, Donald S. *Praying the Bible.* Wheaton, IL: Crossway, 2015.

Witvliet, John D. *The Biblical Psalms in Christian Worship: A Brief Introduction and Guide to Resources.* Calvin Institute of Christian Worship Liturgical Studies Series. Grand Rapids, MI: Eerdmans, 2007.

Identifying a Personal or Corporate Vision for a Lifetime of Psalm Work

---

The days of our lives add up to seventy years, or eighty, if one is especially strong.

But even one's best years are marred by trouble and oppression. Yes, they pass quickly and we fly away.... So teach us to consider our mortality, so that we might live wisely.

~ Moses, Psalm 90:10a, 12

The consistent example of the great cloud of witnesses includes a daily habit of praying the Psalms (Heb 11). While a daily psalm habit is the norm, there are many different ways this can be done. Below are two tables for planning a strategy for your daily habit of praying psalms.

Table 4: Praying through the Book of Psalms at a Walking, Jogging, or Running Pace

Use the table below to create a personal vision for your life and/or for the pastoral ministry you lead. For example, how many times do you hope to lead your children through an experience of praying the Psalms by the age of 12? What is your vision for how you would like to pray the Psalms over the next decade? We often overestimate what we can accomplish in a day and underestimate what we can accomplish in a decade. Also, pause to consider your vision for the end of your life. If you live to be seventy or eighty, what do you hope will be true of your psalm prayer habits? Will you follow Moses' example and allow the Lord to teach you to live wisely (Ps 90:10, 12)?

Age	# of Times Praying through Psalms in a Year	# of Times Each Decade	Notes: My Practical Experience and Lessons Learned
2–20			
21–40			
41–70			
Totals			

Table 5: My First 100 Times Praying through the Psalms: A Record of Personal Psalm Work

The chart below is a tool to record your personal progress at praying the Psalms. Note your first, second, third, etc., time praying through Psalms. Set a periodic time to review what you have learned, and then build on those lessons the next time you journey through the Psalms. Consider New Year's Day or the anniversary of your baptism as a time to reflect on lessons learned in the past year about praying psalms; use that time to make a new prayer strategy for the coming year.

# of Times Praying through Psalms	Date Completed	My Age	Personal Notes
First Time			
Fifth Time			
Fiftieth Time			
One Hundredth Time			

To learn more about crafting a personal vision for engaging with Scripture over your lifetime, consider the following resources:

Clinton, Robert. *Having a Ministry That Lasts—By Becoming a Bible Centered Leader*. Pasadena, CA: Barnabas, 1997.

Davis, Don. *Master the Bible Guidebook: Charting Your Course through Scripture Memorization*. Wichita, KS: The Urban Ministry Institute, 2008.

Table 6: Learning to Pray with the Psalms

The psalms are a pharmacy for the soul. They provide words to approach God, our healer, in every circumstance of life. By regularly praying them we receive keys to what Charles Spurgeon (d. 1892) described as the King's "treasury." In them we find soul riches for every season

of life. The table below is not an exhaustive catalog of
the Psalms' riches, but it does provide a starting place for
recognizing different kinds of soul medicine. The Psalms
can be used in multiple ways, so there is some overlap in
the samples below.

Type of Prayer	Example Psalms	Notes on How to Pray
Wisdom Prayers	1, 19, 112, 119, 127	The fear of the Lord is the beginning of wisdom. The fear of the Lord is found in seeking the Lord in his Word (*torah*). Praying wisdom psalms teaches us how to approach the Lord in his Word and how to live a wise life that brings him glory.
Lament Prayers	3, 4, 5, 7, 10, 12, 13, 14, 17, 22, 25, 26, 27, 28, 31, 36, 39, 41, 42–44, 52, 53, 54–61, 64, 70, 71, 74, 77, 79, 80, 83, 85, 86, 88, 89, 94, 120, 123, 126, 129, 139, 141, 142	Jesus wept, and we who follow Jesus often find ourselves in seasons of suffering. Lament psalms are one of the most common kinds of prayer in Psalms. They contain both personal and corporate examples of how to pray when we are suffering and experiencing pain.
Confession of Sin	6, 32, 38, 51, 102, 130, 143	The first passages of Scripture that Martin Luther (d. 1546) translated into German were the seven "confession" or "penitential psalms." These seven psalms have been especially important across the history of God's people in teaching us how to regularly confess our sin and truly repent.

Type of Prayer	Example Psalms	Notes on How to Pray
Prayers about Enemies	5, 6, 7, 17, 35, 55, 69, 109, 137, 139	Some thirty psalms provide words to pray when we face enemies. Because Christians follow the example of Jesus, we often pray these psalms about enemies with reference to the temptations, the sins and the spiritual attacks against which we battle. Those who walk in the Spirit face spiritual combat, and followers of Jesus recognize that our enemies are not flesh and blood (Eph 6:10–20).
Prayers for Life's Journey	84, 120–134	Pilgrim prayers like Psalm 84 or the Psalms of Ascent remind us that this world is not our home. Like the witnesses who have gone before (Heb 11), these psalms remind us that our primary citizenship is in the kingdom of God. They help us know how to pray as pilgrims on the way of Jesus.
Holy History Prayers	44, 78, 85, 86, 105, 106	Salvation history psalms help us reflect on God's actions in history. They teach us to remember what God has done in the past in order to be faithful in the present and to persevere into the future. They provide a model for individuals and families of faith to imitate by writing family history psalms recalling God's work in their lives.

Type of Prayer	Example Psalms	Notes on How to Pray
Leadership Prayers	2, 72, 110	Royal psalms were originally written as guides for praying for Israel's kings, and point toward Jesus as the true priest-king of God's people (Ps 110). These psalms teach us to give ultimate trust to God as king, but they also provide wisdom for how to pray for human leaders in the church and the world.
Thanksgiving Prayers	30, 32, 34, 100, 107	These psalms contain both personal and corporate examples. Many overlap with the praise psalms in the next category.
Praise Songs	8, 18, 19, 20, 21, 24, 29, 30, 32, 33, 34, 36, 52, 45, 46, 48, 65, 66, 67, 72, 76, 84, 87, 92, 95, 96, 97, 100, 103, 104, 105, 107, 111, 113, 114, 116, 117, 118, 121, 124, 129, 135, 136, 138, 145–150	The largest category of prayers in the Psalms give praise to God. These prayers teach us how to praise and thank God both as individuals and as a community.
Songs for Church	46, 48, 50, 76, 84, 87, 112	Zion songs teach God's people how to pray for God's people. As we pray these prayers we find our hearts turned to the desires of God's own heart for his people.

To learn more about how to pray different kinds of prayer in Psalms, consider the following resources:

Bonhoeffer, Dietrich. *Psalms: The Prayer Book of the Bible*. Minneapolis: Fortress, 1974.

Johnston, Philip. "Appendix 1: Index of Form-Critical Categorizations." In *Interpreting the Psalms: Issues and Approaches*, edited by Philip Johnston and David G. Firth. Downers Grove: InterVarsity, 2005.

Witvliet, John D. *The Biblical Psalms in Christian Worship: A Brief Introduction and Guide to Resources*. Calvin Institute of Christian Worship Liturgical Studies Series. Grand Rapids, MI: Eerdmans, 2007.

Continuing the Conversation

By Carmen Joy Imes

Who Are These People?

Sorted alphabetically by last name, if they had one, or by first name if they did not:[1]

Alcuin of York (735–804) – Alcuin was an Irish monk and scholar in the Carolingian court from Northumbria. His essay on the usefulness of the Psalms was quoted by Dhuoda in her *Handbook for Her Warrior Son* in 843, which illustrates his lasting influence.

Ambrose of Milan (340–397) – Ambrose was bishop of Milan, Italy. His preaching was one of the most significant influences in Augustine's conversion to Christianity.

Aquinas, Thomas (1225–1274) – Aquinas was a Dominican Friar and priest from Italy known as a Doctor of the Church (that is, a highly respected scholar). He had an immense influence on the church. He is best known for his use of reason in theology, and he left behind many writings on theology and philosophy as well as commentary on the first fifty psalms.

Athanasius of Alexandria (298–373) – Athanasius was bishop of Alexandria, Egypt. Due to theological arguments among church leaders of his day, he was exiled five times. He was a strong defender of the doctrine of the Trinity.

Augustine of Hippo (354–430) – Augustine was born in Numidia, North Africa, and educated in Rome. He lived

---

1   For more information on any of these contributors, see ACCS or RCS. Wikipedia has longer articles on most of them.

a wild life as a young man until his conversion in 386. He was later appointed Bishop of Hippo in North Africa. His autobiography, *The Confessions of Saint Augustine*, was the first of its kind and remains the most read book of all history after the Bible. His five-volume commentary on the Psalms was compiled over three decades. Much of it originated as sermons to his poor and persecuted congregation.

Basil the Great (330–379) – Basil the Great was bishop of Caesarea and brother of Gregory of Nyssa. His mother, Macrina, and sister, Macrina the Younger, also made significant theological contributions to their time. Basil was another strong defender of the doctrine of the Trinity. He worked tirelessly on behalf of the poor and the underprivileged, founding a monastic community that focused on prayer and work.

Caesarius of Arles (470–543) – Caesarius was bishop of Arles (now a city in southern France), known for his ability to preach effectively to a wide range of audiences. His passion was to serve the poor.

Calvin, John (1509–1564) – Calvin was a French pastor and theologian who was very influential during the Protestant Reformation. He is best known for his *Institutes of the Christian Religion*, but he also wrote Bible commentaries on almost every New Testament book and twelve Old Testament books, including the Psalms.

Cassian, John (360–432) – Born in what is now Eastern Europe, Cassian lived for a time in Palestine and then in Egypt before settling in the coastal city of Marseilles (now France). He founded a new monastery for both men and women that sought to pass along the teachings of Egyptian monks to the Western church.

Cassiodorus (485–580) – Cassiodorus was a Roman politician and scholar who founded a monastery that worked to preserve literature in Greek and Latin for the next generation. The first book he assigned to his monks for reading and meditation was the Psalms.

Chrysologus, Peter (380–450) – Peter was a pastor and teacher of the church from northern Italy who is recognized as one of the thirty-six most important by the Roman Catholic Church. He encouraged believers to take communion daily and was known for keeping his sermons short yet profoundly insightful.

Chrysostom, John (347–407) – Chrysostom was born in Antioch (now in Turkey), educated in Greek, and eventually became Archbishop of Constantinople. He was renowned for his eloquent preaching and practical application of the Bible to life. This is evident in his concern for the poor, speaking out against those who abused their wealth.

Cyril of Jerusalem (315–386) – Cyril was bishop of Jerusalem who came to accept the doctrine of the Trinity. He is known for his instruction for new converts to Christianity.

Dhuoda, Carolingian Duchess (fl. 824–844) – Dhuoda was a noblewoman in southern France during the Carolingian Empire who loved books and was well-educated. She left behind a lengthy letter to her son in the military. The letter exhorts William to live well and advises him on his spiritual life, concluding with a catalogue of Psalms borrowed from Alcuin.

Gertrude the Great of Helfta (1256–1301) – Gertrude seems to have been orphaned by age 4 and grew up in a monastery in what is now Germany. She was a bright child, and was well-educated at the monastery. At 25 years old, Gertrude had a vision of Jesus asking her to marry him. She looks back on that day as her conversion. She spent the rest of her life in the monastery, working, writing, and praying for those who flocked to see her.

Gregory of Nazianzus (329–389) – This Gregory was archbishop of Constantinople and a friend of the brothers Basil the Great and Gregory of Nyssa. Together they are known as the Cappadocian Fathers. He is one of the most highly regarded theologians of the early church and is known for his skills in Greek rhetoric.

Gregory of Nyssa (335–394) – This less-famous Gregory was bishop of Nyssa, brother of Basil the Great, and friend of Gregory of Nazianzus. Together, the three of them are known as the Cappadocian Fathers.

Herbert, Mary Sidney, Countess of Pembroke (1561–1621) – Mary was a well-educated English woman who continued her brother Philip's project of re-writing the Psalms as English poetry after he died. Together their work is known as the "Sidney Psalms." She made use of commentaries and translations in Latin, French, English, and possibly Hebrew.

Luther, Martin (1483–1546) – Luther was an Augustinian Friar as well as a German priest and professor who experienced a major personal transformation while reading the book of Romans. This led to his role in the Protestant Reformation, confronting the Catholic Church of his day for teachings that had gone off-track. He is best known for his translation of the Bible into German.

Martin of Braga (520–579) – A well-educated archbishop over the region including Braga (now part of Portugal) who founded a monastery.

Melanchthon, Philip (1497–1560) – Melanchthon was a German professor of Greek and coworker of Martin Luther who helped to reform the church.

Musculus, Wolfgang (1497–1563) – Musculus was a German pastor, Benedictine monk, and professor of theology at Bern during the Reformation. J. S. Bach used his paraphrase of Psalm 23 for one of his chorale cantatas.

Origen of Alexandria (200–254) – Origen was a prolific scholar who was born and worked in North Africa, writing extensively on theology and biblical studies. Among his many books is a commentary on Psalms 1–25.

Sidney, Philip (1554–1586) – Philip was an English nobleman and Member of Parliament who was also a poet and patron of the arts. His premature death at age 31 from a battle injury interrupted his rendition of the Psalms into English poetry, a task completed by his sister, Mary Sidney Herbert, Countess of Pembroke.

Theodoret of Cyrus (393–466) – Theodoret was bishop of Cyrus (or Cyr, now in Syria) remembered for writing many Old Testament commentaries, including one on the Psalms. By the age of 23, both his parents had died and he had given all his money to the poor, becoming a monk. As a pastor, he remained generous and encouraging to those experiencing persecution.

Valerian of Cimiez (fl. 422–439) – Valerian was a monk who became bishop of Cimiez (now in southern France) whose passion was to strengthen discipline in the church. Many of his sermons were preserved, including his sermon on Psalm 12, excerpted here.

Zell, Katharina Schütz (1498–1562) – Katharina participated in her husband Matthew's pastoral duties during the Protestant Reformation. They worked in Strasbourg (now in modern-day France). After his death, she continued the work of visiting the people of their congregation and encouraging others by letter. This book features her paraphrases of Psalms 51 and 130 from her own German diaries, which she sent to Sir Felix Armbruster, a man of high society who was isolated due to disease.

When Did They Live?

Here is a list of contributors in order of when they lived.

Name	Approximate Date (AD)	Psalms
Origen	200–254	96
Athanasius of Alexandria	298–373	1, 57
Cyril of Jerusalem	315–386	108
Gregory of Nazianzus	329–389	82
Basil the Great	330–379	33, 64, 90
Gregory of Nyssa	335–394	6

Name	Approximate Date (AD)	Psalms
Ambrose of Milan	*340–397*	*39, 104*
John Chrysostom	*347–407*	*7–10, 89*
Augustine of Hippo	*354–430*	*3, 5, 16–19, 25–27, 30–31, 34–38, 40, 42–44, 47, 50, 53–56, 58, 62, 65–67, 71, 73–81, 84–85, 87–88, 92, 94–95, 100, 102, 106, 112, 115–116, 118, 120–121, 123–126, 132, 135, 138–140, 142–143, 145–149*
John Cassian	*360–432*	*70, 131*
Peter Chrysologus	*380–450*	*98*
Theodoret of Cyrus	*393–466*	*13, 28, 49, 72*
Valerian of Cimiez	*fl. 422–439*	*12*
Caesarius of Arles	*470–543*	*41*
Cassiodorus	*485–580*	*22, 68, 101, 117, 128–129*
Martin of Braga	*520–579*	*131, 141*
Alcuin of York	*735–804*	*Appendix*
Dhuoda	*fl. 824–844*	*Appendix*
Thomas Aquinas	*1225–1274*	*21, 52*
Gertrude the Great	*1256–1301*	*23–24, 46, 63, 86, 91, 103, 113, 119, 127*
Martin Luther	*1483–1546*	*93*
Philip Melanchthon	*1497–1560*	*59, 110*

Name	Approximate Date (AD)	Psalms
Wolfgang Musculus	1497–1563	105
Katharina Schütz Zell	1498–1562	51, 130
John Calvin	1509–1564	2, 4, 14–15, 20, 29, 32, 59–60, 69, 97, 99, 107, 109–111, 114, 122, 133–134, 136–137
Philip Sidney	1554–1586	11
Mary Sidney Herbert	1561–1621	45, 48, 61, 83, 144, 150

Where Can I Read More?

The selections in this book were adapted from other sources, which are listed below. We have updated vocabulary, standardized punctuation and formatting, shortened sentences (in rare cases, moved sentences within a selection), and replaced Bible quotes with the NIV text (unless otherwise noted). Our goal has been to preserve the original authors' intention and give proper credit to the English translators of each of these works.

Prayer of St. Augustine – Adapted from Augustine, "Prayer of Saint Augustin," (Psalm 150) [ccel.org].

Psalm 1 – Adapted from Athanasius, "The Ninth Letter, A.D. 339: The Wicked Dig a Pit for Themselves," in *The Resurrection Letters*, paraphrased by Jack N. Sparks (Nashville: Thomas Nelson, 1979), 153–54.

Psalm 2 – Adapted from John Calvin, *Commentary on the Book of Psalms*, trans. James Anderson, vol. 1 (Psalm 2) [ccel.org]

Psalm 3 – Adapted from Augustine, *Expositions on the Book of Psalms*, 3.9–10 (NPNF 8:4, 6–8).

Psalm 4 – Adapted from John Calvin, *Commentary on the Book of Psalms*, trans. James Anderson, vol. 1 (Psalm 4) [ccel.org]

Psalm 5 – Adapted from Augustine, *Expositions on the Book of Psalms*, 5.4–6 (NPNF 8:12–13, 15).

Psalm 6 – Adapted from Gregory of Nyssa, "On the Sixth Psalm, concerning the Eighth Day," trans. Brian E. Daley, in "Training for 'the Good Ascent': Gregory of Nyssa's Homily on the Sixth Psalm," in *In Lordly Eloquence: Essays on Patristic Exegesis in Honor of Robert Louis Wilken*, eds. Paul M. Blowers, Angela Russell Christman, David G. Hunter, and Robin Darling Young (Grand Rapids: Eerdmans, 2002), 214–216.

Psalm 7 – Adapted from St. John Chrysostom, *Commentary on the Psalms*, trans. Robert Charles Hill, vol. 1 (Brookline, MA: Holy Cross Orthodox Press, 1998), 116–17.

Psalm 8 – Adapted from St. John Chrysostom, *Commentary on the Psalms*, trans. Robert Charles Hill, vol. 1 (Brookline, MA: Holy Cross Orthodox Press, 1998), 166–67.

Psalm 9 – Adapted from St. John Chrysostom, *Commentary on the Psalms*, trans. Robert Charles Hill, vol. 1 (Brookline, MA: Holy Cross Orthodox Press, 1998), 188–91.

Psalm 10 – Adapted from St. John Chrysostom, *Commentary on the Psalms*, trans. Robert Charles Hill, vol. 1 (Brookline, MA: Holy Cross Orthodox Press, 1998), 202–204.

Psalm 11 – Philip Sidney, *The Psalms of Sir Philip Sidney and the Countess of Pembroke*, ed. J. C. A. Rathmell (New York: New York University Press, 1963), 24 (with updated spelling).

Psalm 12 – Adapted from Saint Valerian, "Homily 5: Insolence of the Tongue," in *Homilies*, trans. George E. Ganss, FC 17 (Washington, D.C.: Catholic University of America Press, 1953), 334–35.

Psalm 13 – Adapted from Theodoret of Cyrus, *Commentary on the Psalms: Psalms 1–72*, trans. Robert C. Hill, FC 101 (Washington, D.C.: Catholic University of America Press, 2000), 104–105.

Psalm 14 – Adapted from John Calvin, *Commentary on the Book of Psalms*, trans. James Anderson, vol.1 (Psalm 14) [ccel.org].

Psalm 15 – Adapted from John Calvin, *Commentary on the Book of Psalms*, trans. James Anderson, vol. 1 (Psalm 15) [ccel.org].

Psalm 16 – Adapted from Augustine, *Expositions on the Book of Psalms*, 16.4–5, 8, 10 (NPNF 8:48–49).

Psalm 17 – Adapted from Augustine, *Expositions on the Book of Psalms*, 17.2–4, 6, 12–13 (*NPNF* 8:49–50).

Psalm 18 – Adapted from Augustine, *Expositions on the Book of Psalms*, 18.2–3, 18–21, 38 (*NPNF* 8:50–54).

Psalm 19 – Adapted from Augustine, *Expositions on the Book of Psalms*, 19.10–11, 14 (*NPNF* 8:55–56).

Psalm 20 – Adapted from John Calvin, *Commentary on the Book of Psalms*, trans. James Anderson, vol. 1 (Psalm 20) [ccel.org].

Psalm 21 – Aquinas, *Commentary on the Psalms, Psalm 20* (g, h), trans. Stephen Loughlin (accessed Aug 14, 2019: http://hosted.desales.edu/w4/philtheo/loughlin/ATP/).

Psalm 22 – Adapted from Cassiodorus, *Explanation of the Psalms*, trans. P. G. Walsh, ACW 51 (New York: Paulist, 1990), 230–31.

Psalm 23 – Gertrude, *Spiritual Exercises*, (Kalamazoo, MI: Cistercian Publications, 1989), 59, 111 (lines 59–65; 490–520).

Psalm 24 – Gertrude, *Spiritual Exercises* (Kalamazoo MI: Cistercian Publications, 1989), 60 (lines 75–83).

Psalm 25 – Adapted from Augustine, *Expositions on the Book of Psalms*, 25.2–5, 8–10 (*NPNF* 8:62–63).

Psalm 26 – Adapted from Augustine, *Expositions on the Book of Psalms*, 26. 2, 4–5, 9, 12 (*NPNF* 8:63–64).

Psalm 27 – Adapted from Augustine, *Expositions on the Book of Psalms*, 27.1, 4, 8–9 (*NPNF* 8:64–65).

Psalm 28 – Adapted from Theodoret of Cyrus, *Commentary on the Psalms: Psalms 1–72*, trans. Robert C. Hill, FC 101 (Washington, D.C.: Catholic University of America Press, 2000), 178–79.

Psalm 29 – Adapted from John Calvin, *Commentary on the Psalms*, trans. James Anderson, vol. 1 (Psalm 29) [ccel.org].

Psalm 30 – Adapted from Augustine, *Expositions on the Book of Psalms*, 30.2–4, 8, 12 (*NPNF* 8:67–68).

Psalm 31 – Adapted from Augustine, *Expositions on the Book of Psalms*, 30.10–13, 17, 20 (*NPNF* 8:69–70).

Psalm 32 – Adapted from John Calvin, *Commentary on the Book of Psalms*, trans. James Anderson, vol. 1 (Psalm 32) [ccel.org].

Psalm 33 – Adapted from Saint Basil, *Exegetic Homilies*, trans. Sister Agnes Clare Way, FC 46 (Washington, D.C.: Catholic University of America, 1963), 227–44.

Psalm 34 – Adapted from Augustine, *Expositions on the Book of Psalms*, 34.2, 8, 13–14, 21–22 (*NPNF* 8:73–78).

Psalm 35 – Adapted from Augustine, *Expositions on the Book of Psalms*, 35.2–3, 8–9 (NPNF 8:79–81, 85–86).

Psalm 36 – Adapted from Augustine, *Expositions on the Book of Psalms*, 36.1–2, 12 (NPNF 8:86–87, 89–90).

Psalm 37 – Adapted from Augustine, *Expositions on the Book of Psalms*, 37.2–4, 6 (NPNF 8:91–94, 102–103).

Psalm 38 – Adapted from Augustine, *Expositions on the Book of Psalms*, 38.20, 23 (NPNF 8:107–08, 109–10).

Psalm 39 – Adapted from Ambrose, *Commentary on Twelve Psalms*,. trans. Íde M. Ní Riain. (Dublin: Halcyon, 2000), 145–46, 149–50, 159.

Psalm 40 – Adapted from Augustine, *Expositions on the Book of Psalms*, 40.7, 25 (NPNF 8:121, 127).

Psalm 41 – Adapted from Saint Caesarius of Arles, *Sermons, Vol. 1*, trans. Sister Mary Magdeleine Mueller, FC 31 (Washington, D.C.: Catholic University of America Press, 1956), 293–95.

Psalm 42 – Adapted from Augustine, *Expositions on the Book of Psalms*, 42. 5, 6, 18 (NPNF 8:132–38).

Psalm 43 – Adapted from Augustine, *Expositions on the Book of Psalms*, 43.2–3 (NPNF 8:139–40).

Psalm 44 –Adapted from Augustine, *Expositions on the Book of Psalms*, 44.1, 8, 21 (NPNF 8:140–46).

Psalm 45 – Mary Sidney Herbert, *The Collected Works of Mary Sidney Herbert, Countess of Pembroke, Vol. 2: The Psalmes of David*, eds. Margaret P. Hannay, Noel J. Kinnamon, and Michael G. Brennan (Oxford: Clarendon Press, 1998), 38–40 (with updated spelling).

Psalm 46 – Gertrude, *Spiritual Exercises*, (Kalmazoo, MI: Cistercian Publications, 1989), 95–97 (lines 55–93).

Psalm 47 – Adapted from Augustine, *Expositions on the Book of Psalms*, 47.5, 10 (*NPNF* 8:179, 181).

Psalm 48 – Mary Sidney Herbert, *The Collected Works of Mary Sidney Herbert, Countess of Pembroke, Vol. 2: The Psalmes of David*, eds. Margaret P. Hannay, Noel J. Kinnamon, and Michael G. Brennan (Oxford: Clarendon Press, 1998), 43–44 (with updated spelling).

Psalm 49 – Adapted from Theodoret of Cyrus, *Commentary on the Psalms: Psalms 1–72*, trans. Robert C. Hill, FC 101 (Washington, D.C.: Catholic University of America Press, 2000), 283–86.

Psalm 50 – Adapted from Augustine, *Expositions on the Book of Psalms*, 50.7, 15, 22 (*NPNF* 8:178–81, 183–84, 186).

Psalm 51 – Katharina Schütz Zell, *Church Mother: The Writings of a Protestant Reformer in Sixteenth-Century Germany*, ed. and trans. Elsie McKee (Chicago: University of Chicago Press, 2006), 149–50.

Psalm 52 – Aquinas, *Commentary on the Psalms, Psalm 51* (a, d), trans. Gregory Sadler (accessed Aug 14, 2019: http://hosted.desales.edu/w4/philtheo/loughlin/ATP/Psalm_51.html).

Psalm 53 – Adapted from Augustine, *Expositions on the Book of Psalms*, 53.2, 8 (NPNF 8:202–205).

Psalm 54 – Adapted from Augustine, *Expositions on the Book of Psalms*, 53.1, 3 (NPNF 8:202–205).

Psalm 55 – Adapted from Augustine, *Expositions on the Book of Psalms*, 55.3, 9, 16 (NPNF 8:209–10, 212–13, 215).

Psalm 56 – Adapted from Augustine, *Expositions on the Book of Psalms*, 56.6, 9, 13, 15, 17–18 (NPNF 8:220–25).

Psalm 57 – Adapted from Athanasius, "The Ninth Letter, A.D. 339: The Wicked Dig a Pit for Themselves," in *The Resurrection Letters*, paraphrased by Jack N. Sparks, (Nashville: Thomas Nelson, 1979), 151–52, 155.

Psalm 58 – Adapted from Augustine, *Expositions on the Book of Psalms*, 58.1, 14 (NPNF 8:229–30, 234–35).

Psalm 59 – Adapted from John Calvin, *Commentary on the Book of Psalms*, trans. James Anderson, vol. 2 (Psalm 59) [ccel.org]; and adapted from Philip Melanchthon, *Comments on the Psalms* (MO 12:1144), in RCS, vol. VII, 422–23.

Psalm 60 – Adapted from John Calvin, *Commentary on the Book of Psalms*, trans. James Anderson, vol. 2 (Psalm 60) [ccel.org].

Psalm 61 – Mary Sidney Herbert, *The Collected Works of Mary Sidney Herbert, Countess of Pembroke, Vol. 2: The Psalmes of David*, eds. Margaret P. Hannay, Noel J. Kinnamon, and Michael G. Brennan (Oxford: Clarendon Press, 1998), 67–69 (with updated spelling).

Psalm 62 – Adapted from Augustine, *Expositions on the Book of Psalms*, 62.9–10, 14 (*NPNF* 8:255, 257–58).

Psalm 63 – Gertrude, *Spiritual Exercises*, (Kalamazoo, MI: Cistercian Publications, 1989), 73–74 (lines 10–29).

Psalm 64 – Adapted from Saint Basil, *Exegetic Homilies*, trans. Sister Agnes Clare Way, FC 46 (Washington, D.C.: Catholic University of America, 1963), 262–63.

Psalm 65 – Adapted from Augustine, *Expositions on the Book of Psalms*, 65.7–8 (*NPNF* 8:269–71).

Psalm 66 – Adapted from Augustine, *Expositions on the Book of Psalms*, 66.14, 18, 20 (*NPNF* 8:275, 278–79, 280–81).

Psalm 67 – Adapted from Augustine, *Expositions on the Book of Psalms*, 67.1, 4, 10 (*NPNF* 8:281–82, 284–85)

Psalm 68 – Adapted from Cassiodorus, *Explanation of the Psalms*, trans. P. G. Walsh, ACW 51 (New York: Paulist, 1990), 122–23, 140.

Psalm 69 – Adapted from John Calvin, *Commentary on the Book of Psalms*, trans. James Anderson, vol. 3 (Psalm 69) [ccel.org].

Psalm 70 – Adapted from John Cassian, *The Conferences*, trans. Boniface Ramsey, FC 57 (New York: Paulist, 1997), 10.2–5, pages 379–80, quoting Abba Isaac.

Psalm 71 – Adapted from Augustine, *Expositions on the Book of Psalms*, 71. 4–5, (*NPNF* 8:316–18, 322).

Psalm 72 – Adapted from Theodoret of Cyrus, *Commentary on the Psalms: Psalms 1–72*, trans. Robert C. Hill, FC 101 (Washington, D.C.: Catholic University of America Press, 2000), 417–20.

Psalm 73 – Adapted from Augustine, *Expositions on the Book of Psalms* 73.6–7, 9, 15, 24 (*NPNF* 8:335–36, 338, 341).

Psalm 74 – Adapted from Augustine, *Expositions on the Book of Psalms*, 74.21–22 (*NPNF* 8:349–50).

Psalm 75 – Adapted from Augustine, *Expositions on the Book of Psalms*, 75.8 (*NPNF* 8:350–53).

Psalm 76 – Adapted from Augustine, *Expositions on the Book of Psalms*, 76.3, 9, 13 (*NPNF* 8:356–60).

Psalm 77 – Adapted from Augustine, *Expositions on the Book of Psalms*, 77.2–3, 15 (*NPNF* 8:360–64).

Psalm 78 – Adapted from Augustine, *Expositions on the Book of Psalms*, 78.18–19, 29 (NPNF 8:373, 377).

Psalm 79 – Adapted from Augustine, *Expositions on the Book of Psalms*, 79.8, 12 (NPNF 8:382–84).

Psalm 80 – Adapted from Augustine, *Expositions on the Book of Psalms*, 80.4, 11 (NPNF 8:387–90).

Psalm 81 – Adapted from Augustine, *Expositions on the Book of Psalms*, 81.14–16, 20 (NPNF 8:393–95).

Psalm 82 – Gregory of Nazianzen, *On the Great Athanasius, Oration 21.17*, ACCS 8 (NPNF 27:274), 148.

Psalm 83 – Mary Sidney Herbert, *The Collected Works of Mary Sidney Herbert, Countess of Pembroke, Vol. 2: The Psalmes of David*, eds. Margaret P. Hannay, Noel J. Kinnamon, and Michael G. Brennan (Oxford: Clarendon Press, 1998), 120–21 (with updated spelling).

Psalm 84 – Adapted from Augustine, *Expositions on the Book of Psalms*, 84.3, 8, (NPNF 8:400–402, 404).

Psalm 85 – Adapted from Augustine, *Expositions on the Book of Psalms*, 85.6–7, 9, 12 (NPNF 8:406–409).

Psalm 86 – Gertrude, *Spiritual Exercises*, (Kalamazoo, MI: Cistercian Publishing, 1989), 105 (lines 319–45).

Psalm 87 – Adapted from Augustine, *Expositions on the Book of Psalms*, 87.8 (NPNF 8:423).

Psalm 88 – Adapted from Augustine, *Expositions on the
    Book of Psalms*, 88.2–3. 13 (*NPNF* 8:424–25,
    428–29).

Psalm 89 – Adapted from St. John Chrysostom, *On
    Repentance and Almsgiving*, trans. Gus George
    Christo, FC 96 (Washington, D.C.: Catholic
    University of America Press, 1998), Homily
    7.2.5, pages 89–90.

Psalm 90 – Adapted from Saint Basil, *Exegetic Homilies*,
    trans. Sister Agnes Clare Way, FC 46
    (Washington, D.C.: Catholic University of
    America, 1963), Homily 18.1–2, pages 298–99.

Psalm 91 – Gertrude, *Spiritual Exercises*, (Kalamazoo, MI:
    Cistercian Publishing, 1989), 60–61 (lines
    90–99).

Psalm 92 – Adapted from Augustine, *Expositions on the
    Book of Psalms*, 92.1–2, 6, 14 (*NPNF* 8:452–
    54, 456).

Psalm 93 – Adapted from Martin Luther, *First Lectures on
    the Psalms, Vol. 2: Psalms 76–126*, LW 11 (St.
    Louis: Concordia, 1976), 236.

Psalm 94 – Adapted from Augustine, *Expositions on the Book
    of Psalms*, 94. 3, 5, 8, 24 (*NPNF* 8:459–62,
    465, 467).

Psalm 95 – Adapted from Augustine, *Expositions on the Book
    of Psalms*, 95.2, 13 (*NPNF* 8:467–68, 470).

Psalm 96 – Adapted from Origen, *Against Celsus*, 7.69
    (*ANF* 4:638–39).

Psalm 97 – Adapted from John Calvin, *Commentary on the Book of Psalms*, trans. James Anderson, vol. 4 (Psalm 97) [ccel.org].

Psalm 98 – Adapted from Saint Peter Chrysologus, *Selected Sermons*, trans. George E. Ganss, FC 17 (Washington, D.C.: Catholic University of America Press, 1953), Sermon 6 (On Psalm 99:1–5), 52–53.

Psalm 99 – Adapted from John Calvin, *Commentary on the Book of Psalms*, trans. James Anderson, vol. 4 (Psalm 99) [ccel.org].

Psalm 100 – Adapted from Augustine, *Expositions on the Book* of Psalms, 100.3–6, 13 (*NPNF* 8:487–91).

Psalm 101 – Adapted from Cassiodorus, *Explanation of the Psalms, Vol. 2: Psalms 51–100*, trans. P. G. Walsh, ACW 52 (New York: Paulist, 1991), 447–48.

Psalm 102 – Adapted from Augustine, *Expositions on the Book of Psalms*, 102.3, 6, 10 (*NPNF* 8:494–500).

Psalm 103 – Gertrude of Helfta, *The Herald of Divine Love*, trans. Margaret Winkworth, Classics of Western Spirituality (New York: Paulist, 1993), 101 (updated to NIV).

Psalm 104 – Adapted from Saint Ambrose, *Letters*, trans. Sister Mary Celchior Beynka, FC 26 (Washington, D.C.: Catholic University of America, 1954) 274–75; and from Saint Ambrose, *Hexameron, Paradise, and Cain and Abel*, trans. John. J. Savage, FC 42

(Washington, D.C.: Catholic University of America Press, 1961) 16–17.

Psalm 105 – Adapted from Wolfgang Musculus, *Psalms of David*, RCS 8 (Psalterium, 1231), 180.

Psalm 106 – Adapted from Augustine, *Expositions on the Book of Psalms*, 106.3, 5–6, 11 (*NPNF* 8:520–22, 524).

Psalm 107 – Adapted from John Calvin, *Commentary on the Book of Psalms*, trans. James Anderson, vol. 4 (Psalm 107) [ccel.org].

Psalm 108 – Adapted from Cyril, *The Works of Saint Cyril of Jerusalem*, trans. Leo P. McCauley and Anthony A. Stephenson, vol. 1 (Washington D.C.: Catholic University of America Press, 1968), Catechesis 8.1–3, pages 180–81.

Psalm 109 – Adapted from John Calvin, *Commentary on the Book of Psalms*, trans. James Anderson, vol. 4 (Psalm 109) [ccel.org].

Psalm 110 – Adapted from John Calvin, *Commentary on the Book of Psalms*, trans. James Anderson, vol. 4 (Psalm 110) [ccel.org]; and from Philip Melanchthon, *Comments on the Psalms*, translated from (CR 13:1164) for RCS 8, 213.

Psalm 111 – Adapted from John Calvin, *Commentary on the Book of Psalms*, trans. James Anderson, vol. 4 (Psalm 111) [ccel.org].

Psalm 112 – Adapted from Augustine, *Expositions on the Book of Psalms*, 112.2–4 (*NPNF* 8:547–48).

Psalm 113 – Gertrude, *Spiritual Exercises*, (Kalamazoo, MI: Cistercian Publishing, 1989), 93–94 (lines 12–31).

Psalm 114 – Adapted from John Calvin, *Commentary on the Book of Psalms*, trans. James Anderson, vol. 4 (Psalm 114) [ccel.org].

Psalm 115 – Adapted from Augustine, *Expositions on the Book of Psalms*, 115.3–5, 8 (NPNF 8:551–53).

Psalm 116 – Adapted from Augustine, *Expositions on the Book of Psalms*, 116.1–2, 4 (NPNF 8:554–56).

Psalm 117 – Adapted from Cassiodorus, *Explanation of the Psalms*, Vol 3: Psalm 101–150, trans. P. G. Walsh, ACW 53 (New York: Paulist, 1991), 160–62.

Psalm 118 – Adapted from Augustine, *Expositions on the Book of Psalms*, 118.1, 4, 10, 12–13 (NPNF 8:557–59).

Psalm 119 – Gertrude, *Spiritual Exercises*, (Kalamazoo, MI: Cistercian Publishing, 1989), 67, 78, 118 (lines 280–86; 701–706; 114–51).

Psalm 120 – Adapted from Augustine, *Expositions on the Book of Psalms*, 120.5–6, 8 (NPNF 8:590–91).

Psalm 121 – Adapted from Augustine, *Expositions on the Book of Psalms*, 121.3, 8 (NPNF 8:591–93).

Psalm 122 – Adapted from John Calvin, *Commentary on the Book of Psalms*, trans. James Anderson, vol. 5 (Psalm 122) [ccel.org].

Psalm 123 – Adapted from Augustine, *Expositions on the Book of Psalms*, 123.5–8 (NPNF 8:597–98).

Psalm 124 – Adapted from Augustine, *Sermon 313B.I* (WSA 3 9:96), in ACCS, vol. VIII, 348.

Psalm 125 – Adapted from Augustine, *Expositions on the Book of Psalms*, 125.6–8 (NPNF 8:601–603).

Psalm 126 – Adapted from Augustine, *Expositions on the Book of Psalms*, 126.8–9 (NPNF 8:605).

Psalm 127 – Gertrude, *Spiritual Exercises*, (Kalamazoo, MI: Cistercian Publications, 1989), 89 (lines 442–63).

Psalm 128 – Adapted from Cassiodorus, *Explanation of the Psalms, Vol 3: Psalm 101–150*, trans. P. G. Walsh, ACW 53 (New York: Paulist, 1991), 302.

Psalm 129 – Adapted from Cassiodorus, *Explanation of the Psalms, Vol 3: Psalm 101–150*, trans. P. G. Walsh, ACW 53 (New York: Paulist, 1991), 308–309.

Psalm 130 – Katharina Schütz Zell, *Church Mother: The Writings of a Protestant Reformer in Sixteenth-Century Germany*, ed. and trans. Elsie McKee (Chicago: University of Chicago Press, 2006), 148–49.

Psalm 131 – Adapted from John Cassian, *The Institutes*, trans. Boniface Ramsey, ACW 58 (New York: Newman, 2000) 6.1–2; 7, pages 257–58; and adapted from Martin of Braga, *Iberian Fathers*, trans. Claude W. Barlow, vol. 1 (Washington, D.C.: Catholic University of America Press, 1969), "Exhortation to Humility 8," 57.

Psalm 132 – Adapted from Augustine, *Expositions on the Book of Psalms*, 132.2, 6, 17, 19 (*NPNF* 8:616–21).

Psalm 133 – Adapted from John Calvin, *Commentary on the Book of Psalms*, trans. James Anderson, vol. 5 (Psalm 133) [ccel.org].

Psalm 134 – Adapted from John Calvin, *Commentary on the Book of Psalms*, trans. James Anderson, vol. 5 (Psalm 134) [ccel.org].

Psalm 135 – Adapted from Augustine, *Expositions on the Book of Psalms*, 135.1, 3, 10 (*NPNF* 8:624–27).

Psalm 136 – Adapted from John Calvin, *Commentary on the Book of Psalms*, trans. James Anderson, vol. 5 (Psalm 136) [ccel.org].

Psalm 137 – Adapted from John Calvin, *Commentary on the Book of Psalms*, trans. James Anderson, vol. 5 (Psalm 137) [ccel.org].

Psalm 138 – Adapted from Augustine, *Expositions on the Book of Psalms*, 138.10–11, 13 (*NPNF* 8:633–35).

Psalm 139 – Adapted from Augustine, *Expositions on the Book of Psalms*, 139.7–8, 10 (*NPNF* 8:637).

Psalm 140 – Adapted from Augustine, *Expositions on the Book of Psalms*, 140.4, 6, 16 (*NPNF* 8:641–42, 644).

Psalm 141 – Adapted from Martin of Braga, *Iberian Fathers*, trans. Claude W. Barlow, vol. 1, FC 62 (Washington, D.C.: Catholic University of America Press, 1969), 52–53.

Psalm 142 – Adapted from Augustine, *Expositions on the Book of Psalms*, 142.6–8 (*NPNF* 8:650–51).

Psalm 143 – Adapted from Augustine, *Expositions on the Book of Psalms*, 143.2, 9, 12–13 (*NPNF* 8:651–54).

Psalm 144 – Mary Sidney Herbert, *The Collected Works of Mary Sidney Herbert, Countess of Pembroke, Vol. 2: The Psalmes of David*, eds. Margaret P. Hannay, Noel J. Kinnamon, and Michael G. Brennan (Oxford: Clarendon Press, 1998), 242–44 (with updated spelling).

Psalm 145 – Adapted from Augustine, *Expositions on the Book of Psalms*, 145.1–4, 10, 16 (*NPNF* 8:657–59, 661).

Psalm 146 – Adapted from Augustine, *Expositions on the Book of Psalms*, 146.1, 6 (*NPNF* 8:661–64).

Psalm 147 – Adapted from Augustine, *Expositions on the Book of Psalms*, 147.3, 9, 16 (*NPNF* 8:665–67, 669–71).

Psalm 148 – Adapted from Augustine, *Expositions on the Book of Psalms*, 148.1–2 (*NPNF* 8:673–77).

Psalm 149 – Adapted from Augustine, *Sermons 20–50*, trans. Edmund Hill, vol. 2, WSA 3 (Brooklyn: New City, 1990), Sermon 34.6, 168.

Psalm 150 – Mary Sidney Herbert, *The Collected Works of Mary Sidney Herbert, Countess of Pembroke, Vol. 2: The Psalmes of David*, eds. Margaret P. Hannay, Noel J. Kinnamon, and Michael G. Brennan (Oxford: Clarendon Press, 1998), 253 (with updated spelling).

Appendix – Adapted from Dhouda, *Handbook for her Warrior Son*, ed. and trans. Marcelle Thiebaux (Cambridge: Cambridge University Press, 1998), 233–37.

If you have enjoyed this taste of ancient writings and are hungry for more, here are some places to look:

Ancient Christian Writers Series. Westminster, MD: Newman; London: Paulist Press, 1946–. [ACW]

If you have library access, you can find many Christian classics translated to English in this seventy-five-volume series.

The Ante-Nicene Fathers. 10 vols. Grand Rapids: Eerdmans, 1973; Peabody, MS: Hendrickson, 1995. [ANF]

This series includes ten volumes of early Christian writers translated into English from before AD 325 (when the Council of Nicaea met). The contents are also available freely online at www.ccel.org.

Aquinas, Thomas. *Commentary on the Psalms*. The Aquinas Translation Project at DeSales University. http://hosted.desales.edu/w4/philtheo/loughlin/ATP/index.html

> English translations from Aquinas' original Latin are available for the first fifty-four psalms.

Augustine. *Expositions of the Psalms*. 6 vols. In *Works of Saint Augustine: A Translation for the 21st Century, Part III: Homilies*, vols. 15–20. Translated by Maria Boulding. Edited by John E. Rotelle. Hyde Park, NY: New City Press, 2000. [WSA]

> Selections from Augustine's commentary on the Psalms in this volume were adapted from A. Cleveland Coxe's translation and condensation of *Expositions on the Book of Psalms* for the Nicene and Post-Nicene Fathers (First Series, vol. 8), digitized on www.ccel.org. Maria Boulding's updated translation of the entire work (listed above) is part of the Works of Saint Augustine series.

Blaising, Craig A., and Carmen S. Hardin, eds. *Ancient Christian Commentary on Scripture: Old Testament, Vol. VII: Psalms 1–50*, Downers Grove, IL: IVP Academic, 2008. [ACCS]

> This volume includes excerpts on the first fifty psalms from a variety of interpreters in the first 600 years or so of the church.

Calvin, John. *Commentary on the Book of Psalms*. 5 vols. Original Latin, 1557. Translated by John Calvin into French, 1563. First translated into English by Arthur Goldling in 1571. New English translation by James Anderson, 1845. Digitized on www.ccel. org. Adapted and condensed for this project. [CC]

Calvin's Bible commentaries are freely available to read at ccel.org. If you browse by author, you will find the entire list of his digitized works.

Christian Classics Ethereal Library. www.ccel.org

Many dozens of early Christian writers are available here full-text in digital form, including the Ante-Nicene Fathers and the Nicene and Post-Nicene Fathers. Simply search for the ancient writer by name and browse the list of their available works.

Classics of Western Spirituality. 126 vols. London: Paulist Press. 1969–. [CWS]

The Pre-Reformation Spirituality Series includes 55 volumes dating to the first 15 centuries of the church. The Post-Reformation Christianity Series includes 44 more volumes of Christian Protestant and Catholic classics dating after the Protestant Reformation.

Drobner, Hubertus R. *The Fathers of the Church: A Comprehensive Introduction*. Translated by Siegfried S. Schatzmann. Grand Rapids: Baker Academic, 2007.

This is a more technical volume that does not include the writings themselves, but rather summaries of what they contain and full bibliographical information about where to find them.

Fathers of the Church Series. Washington, D.C.: Catholic University of America Press, 1946–. [FC]

If you have library access, you can find many Christian classics from the first five centuries of the church translated to English in this 127-volume series.

The Nicene and Post-Nicene Fathers: First Series. 14 vols. Grand Rapids: Eerdmans, 1956; Peabody, MA, 1995. [*NPNF1*]

This series of fourteen volumes preserves selected works from Augustine and Chrysostom in English. The contents are available freely online at www.ccel.org.

The Nicene and Post-Nicene Fathers: Second Series. 14 vols. Grand Rapids: Eerdmans, 1956; Peabody, MA, 1995. [*NPNF2*]

This second series of fourteen volumes preserves works from other early Christian writers in English translation after AD 325 including Ambrose, Athanasius, Gregory of Nyssa, Basil, and John Cassian, among others. The contents are available freely online at www.ccel.org.

Selderhuis, Herman J., ed. *Reformation Commentary on Scripture: Old Testament, Vol. VII: Psalms 1–72.* Downers Grove, IL: IVP Academic, 2015. [RCS]

This volume includes excerpts on the first seventy-two psalms from Protestant Reformers.

Selderhuis, Herman J., ed. *Reformation Commentary on Scripture: Old Testament, Vol. VIII: Psalms 73–150.* Downers Grove, IL: IVP Academic, 2018. [RCS]

This volume includes excerpts on the last seventy-eight psalms from Protestant Reformers.

Taylor, Marion Ann, editor. *Handbook of Women Biblical Interpreters: A Historical and Biographical Guide.* Grand Rapids: Baker, 2012.

This handy book helped me locate the women who "participated" in this project. It is a treasure-trove, including brief biographies of almost 200 female interpreters from the AD 300s until 2007 with a brief bibliography of books by and about each woman.

Wesselschmidt, Quentin F., ed. *Ancient Christian Commentary on Scripture: Old Testament, Vol. VIII: Psalms 51–150.* Downers Grove, IL: IVP Academic, 2007. [ACCS]

This volume includes excerpts on the last 100 psalms from a variety of interpreters in the first 600 years of the church.

Glossary

Church – many of these writers refer to the "church" while commenting on the Psalms. Sometimes they mean the people of Israel (a congregation of Jews), while other times they are thinking of the church in their own day. Technically, of course, the church does not begin until after the ascension of Christ. But the New Testament community of Jesus-followers connects in with the "congregation" of God's covenant people in the Old Testament. For this reason, psalms referring to the Old Testament faith community are often applied to the contemporary church.

LORD vs. Lord – When the word LORD appears in all capital letters in our English Bibles, it is translating the Hebrew divine name, Yahweh. Lord with lower case letters refers to God as master or sovereign.

LXX – the ancient Greek translation of the Hebrew Bible

Martyr – someone who is killed for their faith.

Psalms – refers to the entire book of Psalms or a list of multiple psalms.

Psalm – a single, poetic chapter of the book of Psalms, listed by number, or a psalm in general.

Psalmist – the writer of a psalm.

Psalter – another word for the book of Psalms.

Stanza – a section of a poem (similar to a paragraph).

Vice – immoral or wicked behavior.

Virtue – a quality considered morally good or desirable.

Map of Important Places:
Scholars of Note

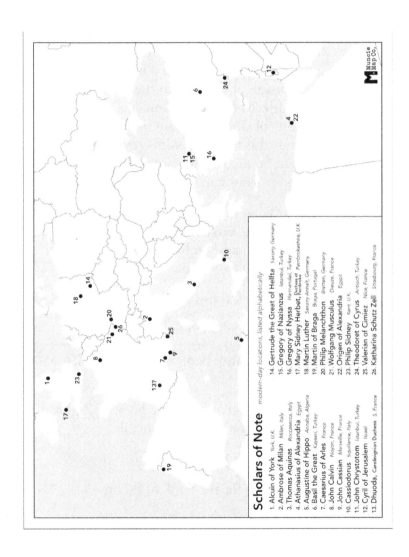

Scholars of Note *modern-day locations, listed alphabetically*

1. Alcuin of York *York, U.K.*
2. Ambrose of Milan *Milan, Italy*
3. Thomas Aquinas *Roccasecca, Italy*
4. Athanasius of Alexandria *Egypt*
5. Augustine of Hippo *Annaba, Algeria*
6. Basil the Great *Kayseri, Turkey*
7. Caesarius of Arles *France*
8. John Calvin *Noyon, France*
9. John Cassian *Marseille, France*
10. Cassiodorus *Squillance, Italy*
11. John Chrystotom *Istanbul, Turkey*
12. Cyril of Jerusalem *Israel*
13. Dhuoda, *Carolingnian Duchess S. France*
14. Gertrude the Great of Helfta *Saxony, Germany*
15. Gregory of Nazianzus *Istanbul, Turkey*
16. Gregory of Nyssa *Harmandali, Turkey*
17. Mary Sidney Herbet, *Duchess of Pembrokeshire, U.K.*
18. Martin Luther *Saxony Annalt, Germany*
19. Martin of Braga *Braga, Portugal*
20. Philip Melanchthon *Bretten, Germany*
21. Wolfgang Musculus *Dieuze, France*
22. Origen of Alexandria *Egypt*
23. Philip Sidney *Kent, U.K.*
24. Theodoret of Cyrus *Antioch, Turkey*
25. Valerian of Cimiez *Nice, France*
26. Katharina Schutz Zell *Strasbourg, France*

A Letter to God's Friends and Fellow Warriors On Why We Read the Sacred Roots Spiritual Classics Together

---

Scholars like big books; small books change the world.

~ Rev. Dr. Glen Scorgie

Dear Friends and Fellow Warriors,

Greetings in the strong name of Jesus! What a joy to know that Jesus calls us "Friend" (John 15). What an honor to stand with sisters and brothers from every century and culture to shout, "Worthy is the Lamb!" What a privilege to serve in the Lamb's army, not fighting flesh and blood, but God's *internal* (the flesh), *external* (the world) and *infernal* (the Devil) enemies. In light of this cosmic struggle, we put on a wartime (not peacetime) mindset as we follow Jesus. Moses stated that God is present and at work in every generation (Ps 90:1), and the *Sacred Roots Spiritual Classics* are for those who desire to be used within their sphere of influence like David was used by God in his generation (Ps 57:2; Acts 13:36).

Our Context: A Battle with God's Internal, External, and Infernal Enemies

Scripture teaches our daily need to choose a missional mindset (Matt 6:10). God's kingdom never advances in neutral territory. Every inch in creation, including each inch of our soul, is a contested battlefield. God's enemies are threefold. First, there is an *internal* enemy hiding within the heart of each redeemed child of God. God

loves us, even though we often battle a "Judas-heart"—
a tendency to betray our Lord (John 12:6). Scripture
names this brokenness the "flesh," the old "man" or the
"sin nature" (Rom 8; Gal 5–6). We work to kill ("mortify")
this sin lest it succeed in killing us (Rom 6:13).

Second, as followers of Jesus, we battle all *external*
enemies opposing the Lamb's kingdom. Sickened by sin,
polluted by greed, corrupted by self-centeredness,
idolatry and oppression; our world is not the way it is
supposed to be. What God created good has been twisted
and now often grieves the Holy Spirit. We choose to
stand with Shadrach, Meshach and Abednego in refusing
to bow to the principalities and powers of the age (Dan
3), or to accept the besetting sins of our ethnicities,
nations and generations. Scripture and our sacred roots
shine painful yet purifying light on our blind spots.

Finally, we are not ignorant of the Devil's schemes. We may
not know if a demon's name is "Screwtape" or "Legion,"
but we do know that an *infernal* enemy opposes God's
kingdom *shalom*. He is the Devil, Satan, the Father of
Lies, the Accuser, and one day soon he and his demons
will be completely crushed. In this time between the
times, the Lamb's followers resist and renounce the Devil
and all his ways with the sword of the Spirit which is the
Word of God.

Our Mission: To Be Faithful Stewards and Wise Servants in Our Generation

Scripture contains a number of "history" psalms (Pss 78,
105, 106, 136; Neh 9:6–38; cf. Heb 11). These songs
challenge us to reflect on women and men who chose to
serve God in their generation—Abraham and Sarah,

Moses, Phinehas, Rahab, David, Esther and many others. History psalms also warn of those who ignored or refused to participate in God's work (Pharaoh, Dathan, Abiram, Og). Leaders like Rahab the prostitute (Matt 1:5; Heb 11:35; James 2:25) and King David were far from perfect (Ps 51). Yet Scripture declares that leaders like David "served the purposes of God in his own generation" (Acts 13:36).

Do you want God to use you in your generation? Are you willing to be a David or Esther today? God is already at work in our communities, schools and workplaces. Sometimes the neighborhoods with the greatest challenges (those with giants like "Goliath" and armies of Philistine enemies) are the very places God finds servants and stewards he can use (1 Sam 17; 1 Cor 4:1).

Like King David, Prince Kaboo of the Kru people in Liberia chose to participate in God's work in his generation. As a child, Prince Kaboo (1873–1893) was taken hostage by a rival tribe and was about to be executed when he experienced a supernatural deliverance. After weeks of traveling through the jungle, Kaboo arrived a mission station near Monrovia, Liberia's capital. There, as a fourteen-year-old teenager, he wholeheartedly gave his life to Jesus Christ.

Prince Kaboo took on the name Samuel Kaboo Morris at his baptism, and he spent the next four years working and studying Scripture—especially Jesus' teaching about the Holy Spirit as recorded by his friend John (John 14–17). Kaboo was fascinated with the Holy Spirit, for he had personally experienced the Holy Spirit's powerful deliverance. Eventually, the missionaries told Kaboo they had taught him all they knew and that if he wanted to learn more about the Holy Spirit, he would need to travel to the United States. Kaboo felt the need for more training about the Holy Spirit before being ready to return to the Kru as an evangelist. With no shoes or money, Kaboo walked to Monrovia's harbor to find passage to New York—trusting his Father in Heaven to provide.

Kaboo's story is powerful. The ship that transported Kaboo experienced revival with the captain and many crew coming to Christ. Within a few hours of arriving in New York, Kaboo led seventeen men to Christ at an inner-city rescue mission. On his third day in the United States, the eighteen-year-old evangelist preached at a Sunday school meeting and revival broke out with a new missionary society organized that very day. God provided money for Kaboo's college tuition, housing, books and necessities. By the end of his first week in America, Kaboo had arrived in Fort Wayne, Indiana to begin studying at Taylor University—an evangelical college committed to raising up workers for the harvest fields who walk in the power of the Holy Spirit (Matt 9:36; Acts 1:8).

Prince Kaboo's arrival at Taylor University transformed not only Taylor University's campus, but also the whole city of Fort Wayne. On his first Sunday in town, Kaboo walked to the front of the church and asked for permission to pray. As he prayed, the power and presence of the Holy

Spirit descended on the congregation in a way none had ever experienced before. The pastor reported, "what I said and what Sammy said I do not remember, but I know my soul was on fire as never before. . . . No such visitation of the Holy Spirit had ever been witnessed" by our congregation.[1]

 Two years later, on May 12, 1893, at the age of twenty, Prince Samuel Kaboo Morris died from an illness contracted after traveling through a snowstorm to preach. Since his death, Kaboo's story has influenced thousands of students at Taylor University and elsewhere to participate with the Holy Spirit in mission and seek the Spirit's power in witness. John Wengatz was a student at Taylor in 1906, the year he first read Kaboo's story. Some fifty years later, after a lifetime invested as a missionary in Africa, Wengatz remarked "my tears never cease to flow as I read that unrepeatable story."[2] Although Kaboo died at twenty, he was used mightily by God in his generation. Will those who tell the story of your life say the same?

Our Vision: Toward Ten Thousand "Tozers"

If you are pursuing God with the same passion and hunger displayed by Samuel Kaboo Morris, than you will be glad to meet A. W. Tozer (1897–1963). Tozer grew up poor without the opportunity to complete high school. While working in a tire factory he heard the good news

---

1   Lindley Baldwin, *Samuel Morris: The African Boy God Sent to Prepare an American University for Its Mission to the World* (Minneapolis, MN: Bethany House, 1987), 59.

2   John Wengatz, *Sammy Morris: Spirit-Filled Life* (Upland, IN: Taylor University Press, 1954), Preface.

about Jesus, repented and believed. At nineteen, he began to preach, becoming one of the most influential pastors in his generation. His books *The Pursuit of God* and *The Knowledge of the Holy* have helped millions know and love the Triune God revealed in Scripture. When asked how he learned to read Scripture with such clarity and theological depth, Pastor Tozer would often point to his "friends" and "teachers." These teachers were a list of some thirty-five Christian spiritual classics read and reread throughout Tozer's life. *Sacred Roots Spiritual Classics* (*SRSC*) are for those with a hunger for the Holy Spirit like Prince Kaboo and a desire to be used like Pastor Tozer.

The Sacred Roots Project envisions ten thousand Christian leaders, serving in challenging ministry contexts across North America, engaging with spiritual classics in community by the year 2030. Will you join this growing community as we pursue God together by reading and discussing spiritual classics with gospel friends and kingdom co-workers (Matt 9:35)?

A larger dream also informs the Sacred Roots Project—a dream that imagines a million Christian workers equipped to serve among the global poor (Matt 9:36–38). The Center for the Study of Global Christianity reports that in the middle of 2020 there are approximately two and a half billion people living in urban poverty.[3] This number will increase to over four billion by the year 2050. Sacred Roots dreams of equipping one million Christian leaders among this great multitude—women and men like Prince Kaboo—with access to excellent editions of some of the greatest spiritual classics the Christian tradition has

---

3   For the most current statistics, see www.gordonconwell.edu/center-for-global-christianity/resources/status-of-global-christianity/.

produced. Ultimately, the goal is increased faithfulness as leaders mature in representing Christ in local churches that are centered on Scripture, grounded in Great Tradition truth (Nicene), and engaged in contextually relevant witness to Christ's love in thousands of diverse contexts.[4]

Our Strategy:
Scripture, Friendship and Spiritual Classics

Sacred Roots' strategy is simple. We believe fresh readings of Christian spiritual classics can lead Christian leaders into a deeper engagement with the God revealed in Scripture and into deeper friendships with one another.

Christian spiritual classics strengthen and deepen our roots in Scripture and help us produce the Spirit's fruit. One day Jesus asked a serious student of the Bible a simple question, "*How do you read it?*" (Luke 10:26). Of the more than three hundred questions asked by Jesus in the Gospels, few are more relevant today. Faithfulness in our generation demands that we learn to read Scripture in a way consistent with the foundational truths held by followers of Jesus in every culture since the first century. We read Christian spiritual classics to discover faithful and fruitful readings of Scripture. As Dr. Davis has noted, the church's "Great Tradition" perennially opens our eyes to new riches in Scripture's "Authoritative Tradition."[5]

A truth believed by all Christians, in all places, and at all times is that there is one God who exists as Father, Son, and Holy Spirit. From "before to beyond time," an eternal

---

4   Don Davis, *Sacred Roots: A Primer on Retrieving the Great Tradition* (Wichita, KS: The Urban Ministry Institute, 2010), 35–45.

5   Ibid.

friendship between the Trinity's three persons has existed at the center of reality. Spiritual friendship provides the start and heart of truth. Just as spiritual classics can reveal new riches from Scripture, so they help us grow in love for God and neighbors. They can provide practical help in deepening our friendships with the Father, the Son, the Holy Spirit and with other believers—both with believers in this generation and with those surrounding us in the great cloud of witnesses (Heb 12:1; 13:7). Why do Christian leaders desperately need to pursue strong friendships? Start with these three reasons.

1. First, each of us has eyes far too small to see what God wants to show us! No one can begin to grasp the great things God is doing across 100 billion galaxies and throughout the many generations since the universe's creation. Friends, standing in different places provides additional eyes to see from different perspectives what God is doing in the world and across history.

2. Second, each of us battles a sinful nature that distorts our perception of the truth. We need friends who speak truth to us, sharpening us like iron sharpening iron (Prov 27:17).

3. Third, all of us view creation through a particular culture's time and place. Each culture exists with a unique version of virtue and vice. Friends who speak to us from other cultures and centuries often affirm virtues in our culture, but they can also reflect ways our culture's vice habitually offends against kingdom *shalom*.

In sum, *Sacred Roots Spiritual Classics* help us grow in our friendship with God and neighbor (Matt 22:37–40). Neighbors include the living Christian leaders with whom we read and discuss this spiritual classic. However, "neighbor" also includes the author (or authors) of this spiritual classic. These women and men walked faithfully with God and neighbor. Their life and teachings produced good fruit in their generation and then continued to do so in the lives of other Christian leaders—often across many cultures and centuries. As an editorial team, we can personally testify to the fruitfulness of the time we have spent with our "friends," the "ancient witnesses" in the *Sacred Roots Spiritual Classics*. If you choose to invest in carefully conversation with these saints of old (Heb 13:7), we are confident you will not only experience practical fruit in the present, but you will also gain new friends for eternity.

Tactical Notes: Christian Leaders Are Christian Readers

Throughout church history, fruitful Christian leaders have been intentional readers. Augustine (d. 430), a pastor and bishop in Africa, was challenged to a new level of ministry by reading a spiritual biography about an Egyptian Christian leader named Anthony (d. 356).[6] Protestant leaders like Martin Luther, John Calvin, John Wesley, Elizabeth Fry, Phoebe Palmer and many others all published editions of spiritual classics for Christian leaders in their generation. Charles Harrison Mason (d. 1961), founder of the largest Pentecostal denomination in North America (Church of God in Christ), was called to ministry through a reading

---

6   Athanasius, *Renewal in Christ: Athanasius on the Christian Life*, ed. Jeremy Treat, *Sacred Roots Spiritual Classics 6* (Wichita, KS: The Urban Ministry Institute, 2022).

of the autobiography of missionary and evangelist Amanda Smith.[7] More recently, leaders like C. S. Lewis, A. W. Tozer, James Houston, and Rick Warren have encouraged Christian leaders to read wisely, especially choosing Christian spiritual classics.[8]

How to Read the Text

Plan **your reading.** Reading a spiritual classic is a bit like reading your Bible. You can read it anywhere or anytime, but there are times and places that will position you to better receive insight and truth. *SRSC* readers tend to read each spiritual classic several times, and many will "read" it in both a written version (print or electronic) and in an audible version (audio book). We read to hear what the original author of the text is saying and to understand what the Holy Spirit might be directing our attention to hear or reflect upon. On your day of rest (Sabbath) reserve some time to read or at least set aside some time to plan when you will read from your spiritual classic that week. If you have a daily commute, perhaps use some of the time to listen and reflect on an audible version of the *SRSC*.

Work **your reading plan.** Once you have planned to read your spiritual classic, begin with the **Introduction.** The introduction is written by a contemporary friend with significant ministry experience. This friend has spent much

---

7   Amanda Smith, *An Autobiography: The Story of the Lord's Dealings with Mrs. Amanda Smith, the Colored Evangelist; Containing an Account of Her Life Work of Faith, and Her Travels in America, England, Ireland, Scotland, India, and Africa, as an Independent Missionary* (Chicago: Meyer, 1893).

8   Explore the essays in Jamin Goggin and Kyle Strobel, eds., *Reading the Christian Spiritual Classics: A Guide for Evangelicals* (Downers Grove, IL: InterVarsity, 2013).

time reading and getting to know the spiritual classic and the author who wrote it. Often, the introduction is written by someone who has read the spiritual classic dozens, if not hundreds, of times. The introduction will help you get the most out of your first several readings of the text.

After reading the Introduction, notice that all *Sacred Roots Spiritual Classics* are divided into eight **Chapters.** These chapters are not always of equal length, but they all are weighty enough to engage your head, heart, and hands as well as your habitat and habits. Following the eight chapters, every *SRSC* includes a short section called **Continuing the Conversation.** If you enjoyed reading the spiritual classic, then Continuing the Conversation will help you discover more resources to engage the author(s) of the spiritual classic.

The *Sacred Roots Spiritual Classics* are divided into ten parts to make it easier to talk about the text with friends and co-workers. The table below provides four (of many) examples of how to read a *SRSC* with a group of friends. When friends commit to read and discuss a *SRSC* together, the group is called a **Sacred Roots Cohort.**

SRSC Section to Read	"Sunday School" Class	"Church-Based Seminary" Module	Monthly Pastor's Meeting	Quarterly Retreat Discussion Group
	Ten Weeks	*Eight Weeks*	*Monthly*	*Quarterly*
Introduction	*Week 1*	*Week 1*	*Month 1*	*Read text before retreat and then discuss*
Ch. 1	*Week 2*			
Ch. 2	*Week 3*	*Week 2*		
Ch. 3	*Week 4*	*Week 3*	*Month 2*	
Ch. 4	*Week 5*	*Week 4*		
Ch. 5	*Week 6*	*Week 5*		
Ch. 6	*Week 7*	*Week 6*		
Ch. 7	*Week 8*	*Week 7*	*Month 3*	
Ch. 8	*Week 9*	*Week 8*		
Continuing the Conversation	*Week 10*			

Review **your reading.** The best readers, like the best leaders, do more than make a plan and work it. They also pause to take time to review their work—or in this case—their reading.[9] Robert Clinton has noted that only around 25% of leaders in the Bible finished well.[10] If we hope to finish well in our generation we must learn to *attend* to our habitat, our head, our heart, our hands, and our habits. To *attend* means to pay attention, to apply our self, to prioritize and to value something enough to give it our time and our energy. Each chapter concludes with five types of questions aimed at helping you review your progress toward finishing well and hearing Jesus say, "Well done, good and faithful servant" (Matt 25:23).

Habitat? Habitat questions ask us to pause and look around at our environment, our culture, our generation, our nationality, and the things that make up the *Zeitgeist* (spirit of the times). Questions may ask about the author's habitat or our own. Since the *SRSC* were written across many centuries and cultures, they often help us notice aspects of our culture needing attention.

Head? Auguste Rodin's sculpture known as *The Thinker* sits before an 18-foot-tall sculpture called *The Gates of Hell*. The massive sculptural group reflects Rodin's engagement with a spiritual classic by Dante, *The Divine Comedy*. *Head questions* require serious intellectual

---

9   The PWR (Plan, Work, Review) process is explained further by Don Allsman, *The Heroic Venture: A Parable of Project Leadership* (Wichita, KS: The Urban Ministry Institute, 2006).

10   Robert Clinton, *The Making of a Leader: Recognizing the Lessons and Stages of Leadership Development*, Rev. ed. (Colorado Springs, CO: NavPress, 2012), 185–87.

engagement as you talk with friends about the author's ideas, claims, and proposals.

 Heart? In August of 1541 John Calvin wrote a letter to a friend with this promise: "When I remember that I am not my own, I offer up my heart presented as a sacrifice to God." Calvin's personal seal expressed this sincere desire. God not only owns our mind, but also our will and emotions. *Heart questions* will help you attend to the people and things to which you give your loves.

 Hands? Albrecht Dürer sketched a drawing called *Study of the Hands of an Apostle* in the year 1508. The apostles were men of action, yet Dürer portrays the apostle's hands in prayer. The action to which *SRSC* call us are often surprising. *Hands questions* will challenge you to evaluate carefully what action you are to take after a particular reading.

 Habits? Charlotte Mason (d. 1923) was a master teacher. She believed Christian formation must carefully attend to habit formation. Like laying railroad tracks, habit formation is hard work. But once laid, great work requires little effort just as railroad cars run smoothly on tracks. *Habit questions* challenge you to reflect on small daily or weekly actions that form your character and the character of those around you.

Reading with Friends

The *Sacred Roots Spiritual Classics* are not meant to be read alone; indeed, it is impossible to do so. Every time we open a *SRSC* we read a book that *has been read* by thousands of Christian leaders in previous generations, *is being read* by thousands of Christian leaders in our generation, and *will be read* (if the return of Christ tarries) by thousands of Christian leaders in generations after us. The readers before us have already finished their race. These thousands of Christian leaders read the text in hundreds of different cultures and across dozens of different generations. All these "friends" read this text with you now. As you read the *SRSC*, imagine yourself talking about *Benedict's Rule* (*SRSC 2*) with the reformer Martin Luther; or picture yourself discussing Madam Guyon's *A Short and Easy Method of Prayer* with the missionary Amy Carmichael. Remember you never read a *Sacred Roots Spiritual Classic* alone.

However, it is not just leaders who have gone before, it is also leaders in the present with whom you must imagine reading this *SRSC*. Whatever benefit you find in reading will be doubled when you share it with a friend. Whatever trouble or difficulty you find in reading the text will be halved when you share it with a friend. Resolve to never read a *Sacred Roots Spiritual Classic* alone.

Perhaps you have noticed that the word "generation" has already appeared in this preface more than fifteen times? The *SRSC* represent the work of many generations working together. Five generations of evangelicals have worked and prayed together on this project since its public commencement in 2018. But these five generations of living evangelicals represent only a small sample of the many generations who have tested the faithfulness and fruitfulness of the *SRSC*. Why does this matter? In part, it matters because these texts are treasures to use and then pass on to the next generation of leaders. Recognize the emerging leaders God has called you to serve and steward—share the *Sacred Roots Spiritual Classics* with them.

Careful readers of Scripture know that the most influential leaders among God's people have always worked in teams. King David's teams became legends—"the three," "the thirty." The list of Paul's missionary and ministry team members whose first name we know from the New Testament runs to nearly one hundred. Our Sacred Roots team of teams prays that this text will be a blessing and a reliable resource for you and your gospel friends as you pursue kingdom business together.

Grace and Peace,

Don, Uche, Greg, May, Ryan, Isaiah, and Hank

The Nicene Creed with Scriptural Support
The Urban Ministry Institute

We believe in one God,
>*Deut 6:4–5; Mark 12:29; 1 Cor 8:6*

the Father Almighty,
>*Gen 17:1; Dan 4:35; Matt 6:9; Eph 4:6; Rev 1:8*

Maker of heaven and earth
>*Gen 1:1; Isa 40:28; Rev 10:6*

and of all things visible and invisible.
>*Ps 148; Rom 11:36; Rev 4:11*

We believe in one Lord Jesus Christ, the only Begotten Son
of God, begotten of the Father before all ages, God
from God, Light from Light, True God from True God,
begotten not created, of the same essence as the Father,
>*John 1:1–2; 3:18; 8:58; 14:9–10; 20:28; Col 1:15, 17; Heb 1:3–6*

through whom all things were made.
>*John 1:3; Col 1:16*

Who for us men and for our salvation came down from
heaven and was incarnate by the Holy Spirit and the
Virgin Mary and became human.
>*Matt 1:20–23; Luke 19:10; John 1:14; 6:38*

Who for us too, was crucified under Pontius Pilate,
suffered and was buried.
>*Matt 27:1–2; Mark 15:24–39, 43–47; Acts 13:29; Rom 5:8;*
>*Heb 2:10; 13:12*

The third day he rose again according to the Scriptures,
Mark 16:5–7; Luke 24:6–8; Acts 1:3; Rom 6:9; 10:9; 2 Tim 2:8

ascended into heaven, and is seated at the right hand of
the Father.
Mark 16:19; Eph 1:19–20

He will come again in glory to judge the living and the
dead, and his Kingdom will have no end.
*Isa 9:7; Matt 24:30; John 5:22; Acts 1:11; 17:31; Rom 14:9; 2 Cor 5:10;
2 Tim 4:1*

We believe in the Holy Spirit, the Lord and life-giver,
*Gen 1:1–2; Job 33:4; Pss 104:30; 139:7–8; Luke 4:18–19; John 3:5–6;
Acts 1:1–2; 1 Cor 2:11; Rev 3:22*

who proceeds from the Father and the Son,
John 14:16–18, 26; 15:26; 20:22

who together with the Father and Son is worshiped and
glorified,
Isa 6:3; Matt 28:19; 2 Cor 13:14; Rev 4:8

who spoke by the prophets.
Num 11:29; Mic 3:8; Acts 2:17–18; 2 Pet 1:21

We believe in one holy, catholic, and apostolic Church.
Matt 16:18; 1 Cor 1:2; 10:17; Eph 5:25–28; 1 Tim 3:15; Rev 7:9

We acknowledge one baptism for the forgiveness of sin,
Acts 22:16; Eph 4:4–5; 1 Pet 3:21

And we look for the resurrection of the dead and the life
of the age to come.
Isa 11:6–10; Mic 4:1–7; Luke 18:29–30; Rev 21:1–5; 21:22–22:5

Amen.

Memory Verses

Below are suggested memory verses, one for each section of the Creed.

The Father

Rev 4:11 (ESV) — Worthy are you, our Lord and God, to receive glory and honor and power, for you created all things, and by your will they existed and were created.

The Son

John 1:1 (ESV) — In the beginning was the Word, and the Word was with God, and the Word was God.

The Son's Mission

1 Cor 15:3–5 (ESV) — For what I received I passed on to you as of first importance: that Christ died for our sins according to the Scriptures, that he was buried, that he was raised on the third day according to the Scriptures, and that he appeared to Peter, and then to the Twelve.

The Holy Spirit

Rom 8:11 (ESV) — If the Spirit of him who raised Jesus from the dead dwells in you, he who raised Christ Jesus from the dead will also give life to your mortal bodies through his Spirit who dwells in you.

The Church

1 Pet 2:9 (ESV) — But you are a chosen race, a royal priesthood, a holy nation, a people for his own possession, that you may proclaim the excellencies of him who called you out of darkness into his marvelous light.

Our Hope

1 Thess 4:16–17 (ESV) — For the Lord himself will descend from heaven with a cry of command, with the voice of an archangel, and with the sound of the trumpet of God. And the dead in Christ will rise first. Then we who are alive, who are left, will be caught up together with them in the clouds to meet the Lord in the air, and so we will always be with the Lord.

From Before to Beyond Time:
The Plan of God and Human History

Adapted from Suzanne de Dietrich. *God's Unfolding Purpose.*
Philadelphia: Westminster Press, 1976.

I. Before Time (Eternity Past)

1 Cor. 2:7 (ESV) – But we impart a secret and hidden wisdom of God, which God decreed before the ages for our glory (cf. Titus 1:2).

A. The Eternal Triune God
B. God's Eternal Purpose
C. The Mystery of Iniquity
D. The Principalities and Powers

II. Beginning of Time (Creation and Fall)

Gen. 1:1 (ESV) – In the beginning, God created the heavens and the earth.

A. Creative Word
B. Humanity
C. Fall
D. Reign of Death and First Signs of Grace

III. Unfolding of Time (God's Plan Revealed through Israel)

Gal. 3:8 (ESV) – And the Scripture, foreseeing that God would justify the Gentiles by faith, preached the Gospel beforehand to Abraham, saying, "In you shall all the nations be blessed" (cf. Rom. 9:4-5).

A. Promise (Patriarchs)
B. Exodus and Covenant at Sinai
C. Promised Land
D. The City, the Temple, and the Throne
    (Prophet, Priest, and King)
E. Exile
F. Remnant

IV. Fullness of Time (Incarnation of the Messiah)

Gal. 4:4-5 (ESV) – But when the fullness of time had come, God sent forth his Son, born of woman, born under the law, to redeem those who were under the law, so that we might receive adoption as sons.

A. The King Comes to His Kingdom
B. The Present Reality of His Reign
C. The Secret of the Kingdom: the Already and the Not Yet
D. The Crucified King
E. The Risen Lord

V. The Last Times (The Descent of the Holy Spirit)

Acts 2:16-18 (ESV) – But this is what was uttered through the prophet Joel: "'And in the last days it shall be,' God declares, 'that I will pour out my Spirit on all flesh, and your sons and your daughters shall prophesy, and your young men shall see visions, and your old men shall dream dreams; even on my male servants and female servants in those days I will pour out my Spirit, and they shall prophesy.'"

A. Between the Times: the Church as Foretaste of the Kingdom
B. The Church as Agent of the Kingdom
C. The Conflict Between the Kingdoms of Darkness and Light

VI. The Fulfillment of Time (The Second Coming)

Matt. 13:40-43 (ESV) – Just as the weeds are gathered and burned with fire, so will it be at the close of the age. The Son of Man will send his angels, and they will gather out of his Kingdom all causes of sin and all lawbreakers, and throw them into the fiery furnace. In that place there will be weeping and gnashing of teeth. Then the righteous will shine like the sun in the Kingdom of their Father. He who has ears, let him hear.

A. The Return of Christ
B. Judgment
C. The Consummation of His Kingdom

VII. Beyond Time (Eternity Future)

1 Cor. 15:24-28 (ESV) – Then comes the end, when he delivers the Kingdom to God the Father after destroying every rule and every authority and power. For he must reign until he has put all his enemies under his feet. The last enemy to be destroyed is death. For "God has put all things in subjection under his feet." But when it says, "all things are put in subjection," it is plain that he is excepted who put all things in subjection under him. When all things are subjected to him, then the Son himself will also be subjected to him who put all things in subjection under him, that God may be all in all.

A. Kingdom Handed Over to God the Father
B. God as All in All

About the Sacred Roots Project

The Sacred Roots Thriving in Ministry Project seeks to equip and empower under-resourced congregational leaders in urban, rural, and incarcerated communities. One avenue for accomplishing this goal is the *Sacred Roots Spiritual Classics*, a series of abridged Christian spiritual classics that equip congregational leaders to engage the wealth of the Great Tradition.

Other *Sacred Roots Spiritual Classics* include:

Becoming a Community of Disciples:
Guidelines from Abbot Benedict and Bishop Basil
Edited by Rev. Dr. Greg Peters

Spiritual Friendship:
Learning How to Be Friends with God and One Another
Edited by Rev. Dr. Hank Voss

Christian Mission and Poverty:
Wisdom from 2,000 Years of Church History
Edited by Rev. Dr. Andrew Draper

Books Jesus Read: Learning from the Apocrypha
Edited by Dr. Robert F. Lay

Renewal in Christ: Athanasius on the Christian Life
Edited by Rev. Dr. Jeremy Treat

Social Justice and Scripture: The Witness of Las Casas
Edited by Rev. Dr. Robert Chao Romero and
Rev. Marcos Canales

The Senior Editorial Team of the *Sacred Roots Spiritual Classics* includes:

Rev. Dr. Don Davis
Publisher
The Urban Ministry Institute

Rev. Dr. Hank Voss
Executive Editor
Taylor University

Dr. Uche Anizor
Senior Editor
Biola University, Talbot School of Theology

Rev. Dr. Greg Peters
Senior Editor
Biola University, Torrey Honors College

Dr. May Young
Senior Editor
Taylor University

Rev. Ryan Carter
Managing Editor
The Urban Ministry Institute

Isaiah Swain
Managing Editor
Taylor University

The Senior Editorial Team acknowledges and appreciates Dr. Gwenfair Adams (Gordon-Conwell Theological Seminary), Dr. Betsy Barber (Biola University), Rev. Dr. Nigel Black (Winslow Baptist Church), Dr. Jonathan

Calvillo (Boston University School of Divinity), Dr. Laura
Edwards (Taylor University), Rev. Nathan Esla (Lutheran
Bible Translators), Dr. Nancy Frazier (Dallas Theological
Seminary), Dr. Jeff Greenman (Regent College), Dr. Kevin
Hector (University of Chicago Divinity School), Rev. Dr.
Wil Hernandez (Centerquest), Dr. James Houston (Regent
College), Dr. Evan B. Howard (Spirituality Shoppe), Rev.
Susie Krehbiel (Missionary, Retired), Rev. Dr. Tim Larsen
(Wheaton College), Dr. Stephanie Lowery (Africa
International University), Dr. Daniel Owens (Hanoi Bible
College), Rev. Dr. Oscar Owens (West Angeles Church of
God), Dr. Bob Priest (Taylor University), Rev. Dr. Robert
Romero (University of California, Los Angeles), Rev. Dr.
Jerry Root (Wheaton College), Dr. Fred Sanders (Biola
University), Dr. Glen Scorgie (Bethel University), Dr. Kyle
Strobel (Biola University), Dr. Daniel Treier (Wheaton
College), and Dr. Kevin Vanhoozer (Trinity Evangelical
Divinity School) for their support and encouragement.
Illustrations throughout the *Sacred Roots* volumes are
done by Naomi Noyes.

The *Sacred Roots Spiritual Classics* are dedicated to all
Christian leaders who have loved the poor and have
recognized the importance of Christian spiritual classics
for nurturing the next generation. We especially
recognize these fourteen:

John Wesley (1703–1791)

Rebecca Protten (1718–1780)

Elizabeth Fry (1780–1845)

Phoebe Palmer (1807–1874)

Dora Yu (1873–1931)

A. W. Tozer (1897–1963)

Howard Thurman (1899–1981)

Watchman Nee (1903–1972)

James Houston (1922–)

J. I. Packer (1926–2020)

Tom Oden (1931–2016)

René Padilla (1932–)

Dallas Willard (1935–2013)

Bruce Demarest (1935–)

Remember your leaders,
those who spoke to you the word of God.
Consider the outcome of their way of life,
and imitate their faith.

~ Hebrews 13:7

Scripture Index